The Master Key System and Mental Chemistry
by Charles F. Haanel

©2007 Wilder Publications

Wilder Publications, LLC.
PO Box 3005
Radford VA 24143-3005

ISBN 10: 1-934451-27-4
ISBN 13: 978-1-934451-27-4

First Edition

10 9 8 7 6 5 4 3 2 1

The Master Key System

It is my privilege to enclose herewith Part One of The Master Key System. Would you bring into your life more power? Get the power consciousness. More health? Get the health consciousness. More happiness? Get the happiness consciousness. Live the spirit of these things until they become yours by right. It will then become impossible to keep them from you. The things of the world are fluid to a power within man by which he rules them.

You need not acquire this power. You already have it. But you want to understand it; you want to use it; you want to control it; you want to impregnate yourself with it, so that you can go forward and carry the world before you.

Day by day as you go on and on, as you gain momentum, as your inspiration deepens, as your plans crystallize, as you gain understanding, you will come to realize that this world is no dead pile of stones and timber, but that it is a living thing! It is made up of the beating hearts of humanity. It is a thing of life and beauty.

It is evident that it requires understanding to work with material of this description, but those who come into this understanding, are inspired by a new light, a new force, they gain confidence and greater power each day, they realize their hopes and their dreams come true, life has a deeper, fuller, clearer meaning than before.

And, now, Part One.

PART 1

1. That much gathers more is true on every plane of existence and that loss leads to greater loss is equally true.

2. Mind is creative, and conditions, environment and all experiences in life are the result of our habitual or predominant mental attitude.

3. The attitude of mind necessarily depends upon what we think. Therefore, the secret of all power, all achievement and all possession depends upon our method of thinking.

4. This is true because we must "be" before we can "do," and we can "do" only to the extent which we "are," and what we "are" depends upon what we "think."

5. We cannot express powers that we do not possess. The only way by which we may secure possession of power is to become conscious of power, and we can never become conscious of power until we learn that all power is from within.

6. There is a world within – a world of thought and feeling and power; of light and life and beauty and, although invisible, its forces are mighty.

7. The world within is governed by mind. When we discover this world we shall find the solution for every problem, the cause for every effect; and since the world within is subject to our control, all laws of power and possession are also within our control.

8. The world without is a reflection of the world within. What appears without is what has been found within. In the world within may be found infinite Wisdom, infinite Power, infinite Supply of all that is necessary, waiting for unfoldment, development and expression. If we recognize these potentialities in the world within they will take form in the world without.

9. Harmony in the world within will be reflected in the world without by harmonious conditions, agreeable surroundings, the best of everything. It is the foundation of health and a necessary essential to all greatness, all power, all attainment, all achievement and all success.

10. Harmony in the world within means the ability to control our thoughts, and to determine for ourselves how any experience is to affect us.

11. Harmony in the world within results in optimism and affluence; affluence within results in affluence without.

12. The world without reflects the circumstances and the conditions of the consciousness within.

13. If we find wisdom in the world within, we shall have the understanding to discern the marvelous possibilities that are latent in this world within, and we shall be given the power to make these possibilities manifest in the world without.

14. As we become conscious of the wisdom in the world within, we mentally take possession of this wisdom, and by taking mental possession we come into actual possession of the power and wisdom necessary to bring into manifestation the essentials necessary for our most complete and harmonious development.

15. The world within is the practical world in which the men and women of power generate courage, hope, enthusiasm, confidence, trust and faith, by which they are given the fine intelligence to see the vision and the practical skill to make the vision real.

16. Life is an unfoldment, not accretion. What comes to us in the world without is what we already possess in the world within.

17. All possession is based on consciousness. All gain is the result of an accumulative consciousness. All loss is the result of a scattering consciousness.

18. Mental efficiency is contingent upon harmony; discord means confusion; therefore, he who would acquire power must be in harmony with Natural Law.

19. We are related to the world without by the objective mind. The brain is the organ of this mind and the cerebro-spinal system of nerves puts us in conscious communication with every part of the body. This system of nerves responds to every sensation of light, heat, odor, sound and taste.

20. When this mind thinks correctly, when it understands the truth, when the thoughts sent through the cerebro-spinal nervous system to the body are constructive, these sensations are pleasant, harmonious.

21. The result is that we build strength, vitality and all constructive forces into our body, but it is through this same objective mind that all distress, sickness, lack, limitation and every form of discord and in harmony is admitted to our lives. It is therefore through the objective mind, by wrong thinking, that we are related to all destructive forces.

22. We are related to the world within by the subconscious mind. The solar plexus is the organ of this mind; the sympathetic system of nerves presides over all subjective sensations, such as joy, fear, love, emotion, respiration, imagination and all other subconscious phenomena. It is through the subconscious that we are connected with the Universal Mind and brought into relation with the Infinite constructive forces of the Universe.

23. It is the coordination of these two centers of our being, and the understanding of their functions, which is the great secret of life. With this knowledge we can bring the objective and subjective minds into conscious cooperation and thus coordinate the finite and the infinite. Our future is entirely within our own control. It is not at the mercy of any capricious or uncertain external power.

24. All agree that there is but one Principle or Consciousness pervading the entire Universe, occupying all space, and being essentially the same

in kind at every point of its presence. It is all powerful, all wisdom and always present. All thoughts and things are within Itself. It is all in all.

25. There is but one consciousness in the universe able to think; and when it thinks, its thoughts become objective things to it. As this Consciousness is omnipresent, it must be present within every individual; each individual must be a manifestation of that Omnipotent, Omniscient and Omnipresent Consciousness.

26. As there is only one Consciousness in the Universe that is able to think it necessarily follows that your consciousness is identical with the Universal Consciousness, or, in other words, all mind is one mind. There is no dodging this conclusion.

27. The consciousness that focuses in your brain cells is the same consciousness which focuses in the brain cells of every other individual. Each individual is but the individualization of the Universal, the Cosmic Mind.

28. The Universal Mind is static or potential energy; it simply is; it can manifest only through the individual, and the individual can manifest only through the Universal. They are one.

29. The ability of the individual to think is his ability to act on the Universal and bring it into manifestation. Human consciousness consists only in the ability of man to think. Mind in itself is believed to be a subtle form of static energy, from which arises the activities called 'thought,' which is the dynamic phase of mind. Mind is static energy, thought is dynamic energy - the two phases of the same thing. Thought is therefore the vibratory force formed by converting static mind into dynamic mind.

30. As the sum of all attributes are contained in the Universal Mind, which is Omnipotent, Omniscient and Omnipresent, these attributes must be present at all times in their potential form in every individual. Therefore, when the individual thinks, the thought is compelled by its nature to embody itself in an objectivity or condition which will correspond with its origin.

31. Every thought therefore is a cause and every condition an effect; for this reason it is absolutely essential that you control your thoughts so as to bring forth only desirable conditions.

32. All power is from within, and is absolutely under your control; it comes through exact knowledge and by the voluntary exercises of exact principles.

33. It should be plain that when you acquire a thorough understanding of this law, and are able to control your thought processes, you can apply it to any condition; in other words, you will have come into conscious cooperation with Omnipotent law which is the fundamental basis of all things.

34. The Universal Mind is the life principle of every atom which is in existence; every atom is continually striving to manifest more life; all are

intelligent, and all are seeking to carry out the purpose for which they were created.

35. A majority of mankind lives in the world without; few have found the world within, and yet it is the world within that makes the world without; it is therefore creative and everything which you find in your world without has been created by you in the world within.

36. This system will bring you into a realization of power which will be yours when you understand this relation between the world without and the world within. The world within is the cause, the world without the effect; to change the effect you must change the cause.

37. You will at once see that this is a radically new and different idea; most men try to change effects by working with effects. They fail to see that this is simply changing one form of distress for another. To remove discord, we must remove the cause, and this cause can be found only in the world within.

38. All growth is from within. This is evident in all nature. Every plant, every animal, every human is a living testimony to this great law, and the error of the ages is in looking for strength or power from without.

39. The world within is the Universal fountain of supply, and the world without is the outlet to the stream. Our ability to receive depends upon our recognition of this Universal Fountain, this Infinite Energy of which each individual is an outlet, and so is one with every other individual.

40. Recognition is a mental process, mental action is therefore the interaction of the individual upon the Universal Mind, and as the Universal Mind is the intelligence which pervades all space and animates all living things, this mental action and reaction is the law of causation, but the principle of causation does not obtain in the individual but in the Universal Mind. It is not an objective faculty but a subjective process, and the results are seen in an infinite variety of conditions and experiences.

41. In order to express life there must be mind; nothing can exist without mind. Everything which exists is some manifestation of this one basic substance from which and by which all things have been created and are continually being recreated.

42. We live in a fathomless sea of plastic mind substance. This substance is ever alive and active. It is sensitive to the highest degree. It takes form according to the mental demand. Thought forms the mold or matrix from which the substance expresses.

43. Remember that it is in the application alone that the value consists, and that a practical understanding of this law will substitute abundance for poverty, wisdom for ignorance, harmony for discord and freedom for tyranny, and certainly there can be no greater blessing than these from a material and social standpoint.

44. Now make the application: Select a room where you can be alone and undisturbed; sit erect, comfortably, but do not lounge; let your thoughts roam where they will but be perfectly still for from fifteen

minutes to half an hour; continue this for three or four days or for a week until you secure full control of your physical being.

45. Many will find this extremely difficult; others will conquer with ease, but it is absolutely essential to secure complete control of the body before you are ready to progress. Next week you will receive instructions for the next step; in the meantime you must have mastered this one.

PART 2

Our difficulties are largely due to confused ideas and ignorance of our true interests. The great task is to discover the laws of nature to which we are to adjust ourselves. Clear thinking and moral insight are, therefore, of incalculable value. All processes, even those of thought, rest on solid foundations.

The keener the sensibilities, the more acute the judgment, the more delicate the taste, the more refined the moral feelings, the more subtle the intelligence, the loftier the aspiration — the purer and more intense are the gratifications which existence yields. Hence it is that the study of the best that has been thought in the world gives supreme pleasure.

The powers, uses and possibilities of the mind under the new interpretations are incomparably more wonderful that the most extravagant accomplishment, or even dreams of material progress.

Thought is energy. Active thought is active energy; concentrated thought is a concentrated energy. Thought concentrated on a definite purpose becomes power. This is the power which is being used by those who do not believe in the virtue of poverty, or the beauty of self-denial. They perceive that this is the talk of weaklings.

The ability to receive and manifest this power depends upon the ability to recognize the Infinite Energy ever dwelling in man, constantly creating and recreating his body and mind, and ready at any moment to manifest through him in any needful manner. In exact proportion to the recognition of this truth will be the manifestation in the outer life of the individual.

Part Two explains the method by which this is accomplished.

1. The operations of the mind are produced by two parallel modes of activity, the one conscious, and the other subconscious. Professor Davidson says: "He who thinks to illuminate the whole range of mental action by the light of his own consciousness is not unlike the one who should go about to illuminate the universe with a rushlight."

2. The subconscious' logical processes are carried on with a certainty and regularity which would be impossible if there existed the possibility of error. Our mind is so designed that it prepares for us the most important foundations of cognition, whilst we have not the slightest apprehension of the modus operandi.

3. The subconscious soul, like a benevolent stranger, works and makes provision for our benefit, pouring only the mature fruit into our lap; thus ultimate analysis of thought processes shows that the subconscious is the theater of the most important mental phenomena.

4. It is through the subconscious that Shakespeare must have perceived, without effort, great truths which are hidden from the conscious mind of the student; that Phidias fashioned marble and bronze; that Raphael painted Madonnas and Beethoven composed symphonies.

5. Ease and perfection depend entirely upon the degree in which we cease to depend upon the consciousness; playing the piano, skating, operating the typewriter, the skilled trades, depend for their perfect execution on the process of the sub-conscious mind. The marvel of playing a brilliant piece on the piano, while at the same time conducting a vigorous conversation, shows the greatness of our subconscious powers.

6. We are all aware how dependent we are upon the subconscious, and the greater, the nobler, the more brilliant our thoughts are, the more it is obvious to ourselves that the origin lies beyond our ken. We find ourselves endowed with tact, instinct, sense of the beautiful in art, music, etc., or whose origin or dwelling place we are wholly unconscious.

7. The value of the subconscious is enormous; it inspires us; it warns us; it furnishes us with names, facts and scenes from the storehouse of memory. It directs our thoughts, tastes, and accomplishes tasks so intricate that no conscious mind, even if it had the power, has the capacity for.

8. We can walk at will; we can raise the arm whenever we choose to do so; we can give our attention through eye or ear to any subject at pleasure. On the other hand, we cannot stop our heartbeats nor the circulation of the blood, nor the growth of stature, nor the formation of nerve and muscle tissue, nor the building of the bones, nor many other important vital processes.

9. If we compare these two sets of action, the one decreed by the will of the moment, and the other proceeding in majestic, rhythmic course, subject to no vacillation, but constant at every moment, we stand in awe of the latter, and ask to have the mystery explained. We see at once that these are the vital processes of our physical life, and we can not avoid the inference that these all-important functions are designedly withdrawn from the domain of our outward will with its variations and transitions, and placed under the direction of a permanent and dependable power within us.

10. Of these two powers, the outward and changeable has been termed the "Conscious Mind," or the "Objective Mind" (dealing with outward objects). The interior power is called the "Subconscious Mind," or the "Subjective Mind," and besides its work on the mental plane it controls the regular functions which make physical life possible.

11. It is necessary to have a clear understanding of their respective functions on the mental plane, as well as of certain other basic principles. Perceiving and operating through the five physical senses, the conscious mind deals with the impressions and objects of the outward life.

12. It has the faculty of discrimination, carrying with it the responsibility of choice. It has the power of reasoning - whether inductive, deductive, analytical or syllogistic - and this power may be developed to a high degree. It is the seat of the will with all the energies that flow therefrom.

13. Not only can it impress other minds, but it can direct the subconscious mind. In this way the conscious mind becomes the responsible ruler and guardian of the subconscious mind. It is this high function which can completely reverse conditions in your life.

14. It is often true that conditions of fear, worry, poverty, disease, in harmony and evils of all kinds dominate us by reason of false suggestions accepted by the unguarded subconscious mind. All this the trained conscious mind can entirely prevent by its vigilant protective action. It may properly be called "the watchman at the gate" of the great subconscious domain.

15. One writer has expressed the chief distinction between the two phases of mind thus: "Conscious mind is reasoning will. Subconscious mind is instinctive desire, the result of past reasoning will."

16. The subconscious mind draws just and accurate inferences from premises furnished from outside sources. Where the premise is true, the subconscious mind reaches a faultless conclusion, but, where the premise or suggestion is an error, the whole structure falls. The subconscious mind does not engage in the process of proving. It relies upon the conscious mind, "the watchman at the gate," to guard it from mistaken impressions.

17. Receiving any suggestions as true, the subconscious mind at once proceeds to act thereon in the whole domain of its tremendous field of work. The conscious mind can suggest either truth or error. If the latter, it is at the cost of wide-reaching peril to the whole being.

18. The conscious mind ought to be on duty during every waking hour. When the "watchman" is "off guard," or when its calm judgment is suspended, under a variety of circumstances, then the subconscious mind is unguarded and left open to suggestion from all sources. During the wild excitement of panic, or during the height of anger, or the impulses of the irresponsible mob, or at any other time of unrestrained passion, the conditions are most dangerous. The subconscious mind is then open to the suggestion of fear, hatred, selfishness, greed, self-depreciation and other negative forces, derived from surrounding persons or circumstances. The result is usually unwholesome in the extreme, with effects that may endure to distress it for a long time. Hence, the great importance of guarding the subconscious mind from false impressions.

19. The subconscious mind perceives by intuition. Hence, its processes are rapid. It does not wait for the slow methods of conscious reasoning. In fact, it can not employ them.

20. The subconscious mind never sleeps, never rests, any more than does your heart, or your blood. It has been found that by plainly stating

to the subconscious mind certain specific things to be accomplished, forces are set in operation that lead to the result desired. Here, then, is a source of power which places us in touch with Omnipotence. Here in is a deep principle which is well worth our most earnest study.

21. The operation of this law is interesting. Those who put it into operation find that when they go out to meet the person with whom they anticipate a difficult interview, something has been there before them and dissolved the supposed differences; everything is changed; all is harmonious; they find that when some difficult business problem presents itself they can afford to make delay and something suggests the proper solution; everything is properly arranged; in fact, those who have learned to trust the subconscious find that they have infinite resources at their command.

22. The subconscious mind is the seat of our principles and our aspirations. It is the fount of our artistic and altruistic ideals. These instincts can only be overthrown by an elaborate and gradual process of undermining the innate principles.

23. The subconscious mind cannot argue controversially. Hence, if it has accepted wrong suggestions, the sure method of overcoming them is by the use of a strong counter suggestion, frequently repeated, which the mind must accept, thus eventually forming new and healthy habits of thought and life, for the subconscious mind is the seat of Habit. That which we do over and over becomes mechanical; it is no longer an act of judgment, but has worn its deep grooves in the subconscious mind. This is favorable for us if the habit be wholesome and right. If it be harmful, and wrong, the remedy is to recognize the omnipotence of the subconscious mind and suggest present actual freedom. The subconscious being creative and one with our divine source will at once create the freedom suggested.

24. To sum up: The normal functions of the subconscious on the physical side have to do with the regular and vital processes, with the preservation of life and the restoration of health; with the care of offspring, which includes an instinctive desire to preserve all life and improve conditions generally.

25. On the mental side, it is the storehouse of memory; it harbors the wonderful thought messengers, who work, unhampered by time or space; it is the fountain of the practical initiative and constructive forces of life: It is the seat of habit.

26. On the spiritual side, it is the source of ideals, of aspiration, of the imagination, and is the channel through which we recognize our Divine Source, and in proportion as we recognize this divinity do we come into an understanding of the source of power.

27. Some one may ask: "How can the subconscious change conditions?" The reply is, because the subconscious is a part of the Universal Mind and a part must be the same in kind and quality as the whole; the only

difference is one of degree. The whole, as we know, is creative, in fact, it is the only creator there is, consequently, we find that mind is creative, and as thought is the only activity which the mind possesses, thought must necessarily be creative also.

28. But we shall find that there is a vast difference between simply thinking, and directing our thought consciously, systematically and constructively; when we do this we place our mind in harmony with the Universal Mind, we come in tune with the Infinite, we set in operation the mightiest force in existence, the creative power of the Universal Mind. This, as everything else, is governed by natural law, and this law is the "Law of Attraction," which is that Mind is creative, and will automatically correlate with its object and bring it into manifestation.

29. Last week I gave you an exercise for the purpose of securing control of the physical body; if you have accomplished this you are ready to advance. This time you will begin to control your thought. Always take the same room, the same chair, and the same position, if possible. In some cases it is not convenient to take the same room, in this case simply make the best use of such conditions as may be available. Now be perfectly still as before, but inhibit all thought; this will give you control over all thoughts of care, worry and fear, and will enable you to entertain only the kind of thoughts you desire. Continue this exercise until you gain complete mastery.

30. You will not be able to do this for more that a few moments at a time, but the exercise is valuable, because it will be a very practical demonstration of the great number of thoughts which are constantly trying to gain access to your mental world.

31. Next week you will receive instructions for an exercise which may be a little more interesting, but it is necessary that you master this one first.

PART 3

You have found that the Individual may act on the Universal, and that the result of this action and interaction is cause and effect. Thought, therefore, is the cause, and the experiences with which you meet in life are the effect.

Eliminate, therefore, any possible tendency to complain of conditions as they have been, or as they are, because it rests with you to change them and make them what you would like them to be.

Direct your effort to a realization of the mental resources, always at your command, from which all real and lasting power comes.

Persist in this practice until you come to a realization of the fact that there can be no failure in the accomplishment of any proper object in life if you but understand your power and persist in your object, because the mind-forces are ever ready to lend themselves to a purposeful will, in the effort to crystallize thought and desire into actions, events and conditions.

Whereas in the beginning of each function of life and each action is the result of conscious thought, the habitual actions become automatic and the thought that controls them passes into the realm of the subconscious; yet it is just as intelligent as before. It is necessary that it become automatic, or subconscious, in order that the self-conscious mind may attend to other things. The new actions will, however, in their turn, be come habitual, then automatic, then subconscious in order that the mind again may be freed from this detail and advanced to still other activities.

When you realize this, you will have found a source of power which will enable you to take care of any situation in life which may develop.

1. The necessary interaction of the conscious and subconscious mind requires a similar interaction between the corresponding systems of nerves. Judge Troward indicates the very beautiful method in which this interaction is effected. He says: The cerebro-spinal system is the organ of the conscious mind and the sympathetic is the organ of the subconscious. The cerebro-spinal is the channel through which we receive conscious perception from the physical senses and exercise control over the movements of the body. This system of nerves has its center in the brain.

2. The Sympathetic System has its center in a ganglionic mass at the back of the stomach known as the Solar Plexus, and is the channel of that mental action which unconsciously supports the vital functions of the body.

3. The connection between the two systems is made by the vagus nerve which passes out of the cerebral region as a portion of the voluntary system to the thorax, sending out branches to the heart and lungs, and

finally passing through the diaphragm, it loses its outer coating and becomes identified with the nerves of the Sympathetic System, so forming a connecting link between the two and making man physically a "single entity."

4. We have seen that every thought is received by the brain, which is the organ of the conscious; it is here subjected to our power of reasoning. When the objective mind has been satisfied that the thought is true it is sent to the Solar Plexus, or the brain of the subjective mind, to be made into our flesh, to be brought forth into the world as reality. It is then no longer susceptible to any argument whatever. The subconscious mind cannot argue; it only acts. It accepts the conclusions of the objective mind as final.

5. The Solar Plexus has been likened to the sum of the body, because it is a central point of distribution for the energy which the body is constantly generating. This energy is very real energy, and this sun is a very real sun, and the energy is being distributed by very real nerves to all parts of the body, and is thrown off in an atmosphere which envelopes the body.

6. If this radiation is sufficiently strong the person is called magnetic; he is said to be filled with personal magnetism. Such a person may wield an immense power for good. His presence alone will often bring comfort to the troubled minds with which he comes in contact.

7. When the Solar Plexus is in active operation and is radiating life, energy and vitality to every part of the body, and to every one whom he meets, the sensations are pleasant, the body is filled with health and all with whom he comes in contact experience a pleasant sensation.

8. If there is any interruption of this radiation the sensations are unpleasant, the flow of life and energy to some part of the body is stopped, and this is the cause of every ill to the human race, physical, mental or environmental.

9. Physical because the sun of the body is no longer generating sufficient energy to vitalize some part of the body; mental because the conscious mind is dependent upon the subconscious mind for the vitality necessary to support its thought, and environmental, because the connection between the subconscious mind and the Universal mind, is being interrupted.

10. The Solar Plexus is the point at which the part meets with the whole, where the finite becomes Infinite, where the Uncreate becomes create, the Universal becomes individualized, the Invisible becomes visible. It is the point at which life appears and there is no limit to the amount of life an individual may generate from this Solar center.

11. This center of energy is Omnipotent because it is the point of contact with all life and all intelligence. It can therefore accomplish whatever it is directed to accomplish, and herein lies the power of the

conscious mind; the subconscious can and will carry out such plans and ideas as may be suggested to it by the conscious mind.

12. Conscious thought, then, is master of this sun center from which the life and energy of the entire body flows and the quality of the thought which we entertain determines the quality of the thought which this sun will radiate, and the character of the thought which our conscious mind entertains will determine the character of the thought which this sun will radiate, and the nature of the thought which our conscious mind entertains will determine the nature of thought which this sun will radiate, and consequently will determine the nature of the experience which will result.

13. It is evident, therefore, that all we have to do is let our light shine; the more energy we can radiate, the more rapidly shall we be enabled to transmute undesirable conditions into sources of pleasure and profit. The important question, then, is how to let this light shine; how to generate this energy.

14. Non-resistant thought expands the Solar Plexus; resistant thought contracts it. Pleasant thought expands it; unpleasant thought contracts it. Thoughts of courage, power, confidence and hope all produce a corresponding state, but the one arch enemy of the Solar Plexus which must be absolutely destroyed before there is any possibility of letting any light shine is fear. This enemy must be completely destroyed; he must be eliminated; he must be expelled forever; he is the cloud which hides the sun; which causes a perpetual gloom.

15. It is this personal devil which makes men fear the past, the present and the future; fear themselves, their friends and their enemies; fear everything and everybody. When fear is effectually and completely destroyed, your light will shine, the clouds will disperse and you will have found the source of power, energy and life.

16. When you find that you are really one with the Infinite power, and when you can consciously realize this power by a practical demonstration of your ability to overcome any adverse condition by the power of your thought, you will have nothing to fear; fear will have been destroyed and you will have come into possession of your birthright.

17. It is our attitude of mind toward life which determines the experiences with which we are to meet; if we expect nothing, we shall have nothing; if we demand much, we shall receive the greater portion. The world is harsh only as we fail to assert ourselves. The criticism of the world is bitter only to those who cannot compel room for their ideas. It is fear of this criticism that causes many ideas to fail to see the light of day.

18. But the man who knows that he has a Solar Plexus will not fear criticism or anything else; he will be too busy radiating courage, confidence, and power; he will anticipate success by his mental attitude; he will pound barriers to pieces, and leap over the chasm of doubt and hesitation which fear places in his path.

19. A knowledge of our ability to consciously radiate health, strength and harmony will bring us into a realization that there is nothing to fear because we are in touch with Infinite Strength.

20. This knowledge can be gained only by making practical application of this information. We learn by doing; through practice the athlete comes powerful.

21. As the following statement is of considerable importance, I will put it in several ways, so that you cannot fail to get the full significance of it. If you are religiously inclined, I would say, you can let your light shine. If your mind has a bias toward physical science, I would say you can wake the Solar Plexus; or, if you prefer the strictly scientific interpretation, I will say that you can impress your subconscious mind.

22. I have already told you what the result of this impression will be. It is the method in which you are now interested. You have already learned that the subconscious is intelligent and that it is creative, and responsive to the will of the conscious mind. What, then, is the most natural way of making the desired impression? Mentally concentrate on the object of your desire; when you are concentrating you are impressing the subconscious.

23. This is not the only way, but it is a simple and effective way, and the most direct way, and consequently the way in which the best results are secured. It is the method which is producing such extraordinary results that many think that miracles are being accomplished.

24. It is the method by which every great inventor, every great financier, every great statesman has been enabled to convert the subtle and invisible force of desire, faith and confidence into actual, tangible, concrete facts in the objective world.

25. The subconscious mind is a part of the Universal mind. The Universal is the creative principle of the Universe, a part must be the same in kind and quality as the whole. This means that this creative power is absolutely unlimited; it is not bound by precedent of any kind, and consequently has no prior existing pattern by which to apply its constructive principle.

26. We have found that the subconscious mind is responsive to our conscious will, which means that the unlimited creative power of the Universal Mind is within control of the conscious mind of the individual.

27. When making a practical application of this principle, in accordance with the exercises given in the subsequent lessons, it is well to remember that it is not necessary to outline the method by which the subconscious will produce the results you desire. The finite cannot inform the Infinite. You are simply to say what you desire, not how you are to obtain it.

28. You are the channel by which the undifferentiated is being differentiated, and this differentiation is being accomplished by appropriation. It only requires recognition to set causes in motion which will bring about results in accordance with your desire, and this is

accomplished because the Universal can act only through the individual, and the individual can act only through the Universal; they are one.

29. For your exercise this week, I will ask you to go one step further. I want you to not only be perfectly still, and inhibit all thought as far as possible, but relax, let go, let the muscles take their normal condition; this will remove all pressure from the nerves, and eliminate that tension which so frequently produces physical exhaustion.

30. Physical relaxation is a voluntary exercise of the will and the exercise will be found to be of great value, as it enables the blood to circulate freely to and from the brain and body.

31. Tensions leads to mental unrest and abnormal mental activity of the mind; it produces worry, care, fear and anxiety. Relaxation is therefore an absolute necessity in order to allow the mental faculties to exercise the greatest freedom.

32. Make this exercise as thorough and complete as possible, mentally determine that you will relax every muscle and nerve, until you feel quiet and restful and at peace with yourself and the world.

33. The Solar Plexus will then be ready to function and you will be surprised at the result.

PART 4

This part will show you why what you think, or do, or feel, is an indication of what you are.

Thought is energy and energy is power, and it is because all the religions, sciences and philosophies with which the world has heretofore been familiar have been based upon the manifestation of this energy instead of the energy itself, that the world has been limited to effects, while causes have been ignored or misunderstood.

For this reason we have God and the Devil in religion, positive and negative in science, and good and bad in philosophy.

The Master Key reverses the process; it is interested only in cause, and the letters received from students tell a marvelous story; they indicate conclusively that students are finding the cause whereby they may secure for themselves health, harmony, abundance, and whatever else may be necessary for their welfare and happiness.

Life is expressive and it is our business to express ourselves harmoniously and constructively. Sorrow, misery, unhappiness, disease and poverty are not necessities and we are constantly eliminating them.

But this process of eliminating consists in rising above and beyond limitation of any kind. He who has strengthened and purified his thought need not concern himself about microbes, and he who has come into an understanding of the law of abundance will go at once to the source of supply.

It is thus that fate, fortune, and destiny will be controlled as readily as a captain controls his ship, or an engineer, his train.

1. The "I" of you is not the physical body; that is simply an instrument which the "I" uses to carry out its purposes; the "I" cannot be the Mind, for the mind is simply another instrument which the "I" uses with which to think, reason, and plan.

2. The "I" must be something which controls and directs both the body and the mind; something which determines what they shall do and how they shall act. When you come into a realization of the true nature of this "I," you will enjoy a sense of power which you have never before known.

3. Your personality is made up of countless individual characteristics, peculiarities, habits, and traits of character; these are the result of your former method of thinking, but they have nothing to do with the real "I."

4. When you say "I think" the "I" tells the mind what it shall think; when you say "I go" the "I" tells the physical body where it shall go; the real nature of this "I" is spiritual, and is the source of the real power

which comes to men and women when they come into a realization of their true nature.

5. The greatest and most marvelous power which this "I" has been given is the power to think, but few people know how to think constructively, or correctly, consequently they achieve only indifferent results. Most people allow their thoughts to dwell on selfish purposes, the inevitable result of an infantile mind. When a mind becomes mature, it understands that the germ of defeat is in every selfish thought.

6. The trained mind knows that every transaction must benefit every person who is in any way connected with the transaction, and any attempt to profit by the weakness, ignorance or necessity of another will inevitably operate to his disadvantage.

7. This is because the individual is a part of the Universal. A part cannot antagonize any other part, but, on the contrary, the welfare of each part depends upon a recognition of the interest of the whole.

8. Those who recognize this principle have a great advantage in the affairs of life. They do not wear themselves out. They can eliminate vagrant thoughts with facility. They can readily concentrate to the highest possible degree on any subject. They do not waste time or money upon objects which can be of no possible benefit to them.

9. If you cannot do these things it is because you have thus far not made the necessary effort. Now is the time to make the effort. The result will be exactly in proportion to the effort expended. One of the strongest affirmations which you can use for the purpose of strengthening the will and realizing your power to accomplish, is, "I can be what I will to be."

10. Every time you repeat it realize who and what this "I" is; try to come into a thorough understanding of the true nature of the "I"; if you do, you will become invincible; that is, provided that your objects and purposes are constructive and are therefore in harmony with the creative principle of the Universe.

11. If you make use of this affirmation, use it continuously, night and morning, and as often during the day as you think of it, and continue to do so until it becomes a part of you; form the habit.

12. Unless you do this, you had better not start at all, because modern psychology tells us that when we start something and do not complete it, or make a resolution and do not keep it, we are forming the habit of failure; absolute, ignominious failure. If you do not intend to do a thing, do not start; if you do start, see it through even if the heavens fall; if you make up your mind to do something, do it; let nothing, no one, interfere; the "I" in you has determined, the thing is settled; the die is cast, there is no longer any argument.

13. If you carry out this idea, beginning with small things which you know you can control and gradually increase the effort, but never under any circumstances allowing your "I" to be overruled, you will find that you can eventually control yourself, and many men and women have found to

their sorrow that it is easier to control a kingdom than to control themselves.

14. But when you have learned to control yourself you will have found the "World Within" which controls the world without; you will have become irresistible; men and things will respond to your every wish without any apparent effort on your part.

15. This is not so strange or impossible as it may appear when you remember that the "World Within" is controlled by the "I" and that this "I" is a part or one with the Infinite "I" which is the Universal Energy or Spirit, usually called God.

16. This is not a mere statement or theory made for the purpose of confirming or establishing an idea, but it is a fact which has been accepted by the best religious thought as well as the best scientific thought.

17. Herbert Spender said: "Amid all the mysteries by which we are surrounded, nothing is more certain than that we are ever in the presence of an Infinite and Eternal Energy from which all things proceed."

18. Lyman Abbott, in an address delivered before the Alumni of Bangor Theological Seminary, said: "We are coming to think of God as dwelling in man rather than as operating on men from without."

19. Science goes a little way in its search and stops. Science finds the ever-present Eternal Energy, but Religion finds the Power behind this energy and locates it within man. But this is by no means a new discovery; the Bible says exactly the same thing, and the language is just as plain and convincing: "Know ye not that ye are the temple of the living God?" Here, then, is the secret of the wonderful creative power of the "World Within."

20. Here is the secret of power, of mastery. To overcome does not mean to go without things. Self-denial is not success. We cannot give unless we get; we cannot be helpful unless we are strong. The Infinite is not a bankrupt and we who are the representatives of Infinite power should not be bankrupts either, and if we wish to be of service to others we must have power and more power, but to get it we must give it; we must be of service.

21. The more we give the more we shall get; we must become a channel whereby the Universal can express activity. The Universal is constantly seeking to express itself, to be of service, and it seeks the channel whereby it can find the greatest activity, where it can do the most good, where it can be of greatest service to mankind.

22. The Universal cannot express through you as long as you are busy with your plans, your own purposes; quiet the senses, seek inspiration, focus the mental activity on the within, dwell in the consciousness of your unity with Omnipotence. "Still water runs deep;" contemplate the multitudinous opportunities to which you have spiritual access by the Omnipresence of power.

23. Visualize the events, circumstances and conditions which these spiritual connections may assist in manifesting. Realize the fact that the essence and soul of all things is spiritual and that the spiritual is the real, because it is the life of all there is; when the spirit is gone, the life is gone; it is dead; it has ceased to exist.

24. These mental activities pertain to the world within, to the world of cause; and conditions and circumstances which result are the effect. It is thus that you become a creator. This is important work, and the higher, loftier, grander and more noble ideals which you can conceive, the more important the work will become.

25. Over-work or over-play or over-bodily activity of any kind produces conditions of mental apathy and stagnation which makes it impossible to do the more important work which results in a realization of conscious power. We should, therefore, seek the Silence frequently. Power comes through repose; it is in the Silence that we can be still, and when we are still, we can think, and thought is the secret of all attainment.

26. Thought is a mode of motion and is carried by the law of vibration the same as light or electricity. It is given vitality by the emotions through the law of love; it takes form and expression by the law of growth; it is a product of the spiritual "I," hence its Divine, spiritual, and creative nature.

27. From this it is evident that in order to express power, abundance or any other constructive purpose, the emotions must be called upon to give feeling to the thought so that it will take form. How may this purpose be accomplished? This is the vital point; how may we develop the faith, the courage, the feeling, which will result in accomplishment?

28. The reply is, by exercise; mental strength is secured in exactly the same way that physical strength is secured, by exercise. We think something, perhaps with difficulty the first time; we think the same thing again, and it becomes easier this time; we think it again and again; it then becomes a mental habit. We continue to think the same thing; finally it becomes automatic; we can no longer help thinking this thing; we are now positive of what we think; there is no longer any doubt about it. We are sure; we know.

29. Last week I asked you to relax, to let go physically. This week, I am going to ask you to let go mentally. If you practiced the exercise given you last week fifteen or twenty minutes a day in accordance with the instructions, you can no doubt relax physically; and anyone who cannot consciously do this quickly and completely is not a master of himself. He has not obtained freedom; he is still a slave to conditions. But I shall assume that you have mastered the exercise and are ready to take the next step, which is mental freedom.

30. This week, after taking your usual position, remove all tension by completely relaxing, then mentally let go of all adverse conditions, such

as hatred, anger, worry, jealousy, envy, sorrow, trouble or disappointment of any kind.

31. You may say that you cannot "let go" of these things, but you can; you can do so by mentally determining to do so, by voluntary intention and persistence.

32. The reason that some cannot do this is because they allow themselves to be controlled by the emotions instead of by their intellect. But those who will be guided by the intellect will gain the victory. You will not succeed the first time you try, but practice makes perfect, in this as in everything else, and you must succeed in dismissing, eliminating and completely destroying these negative and destructive thoughts; because they are the seed which is constantly germinating into discordant conditions of every conceivable kind and description.

PART 5

After studying this part carefully, you will see that every conceivable force or object or fact is the result of mind in action.

Mind in action is thought, and thought is creative. Men are thinking now as they never thought before.

Therefore, this is a creative age, and the world is awarding its richest prizes to the thinkers. Matter is powerless, passive, inert. Mind is force, energy, power. Mind shapes and controls matter. Every form which matter takes is but the expression of some pre-existing thought.

But thought works no magic transformations; it obeys natural laws; it sets in motion natural forces; it releases natural energies; it manifests in your conduct and actions, and these in turn react upon your friends and acquaintances, and eventually upon the whole of your environment. You can originate thought, and, since thoughts are creative, you can create for yourself the things you desire.

1. At least ninety per cent of our mental life is subconscious, so that those who fail to make use of this mental power live within very narrow limits.

2. The subconscious can and will solve any problem for us if we know how to direct it. The subconscious processes are always at work; the only question is, are we to be simply passive recipients of this activity, or are we to consciously direct the work? Shall we have a vision of the destination to be reached, the dangers to be avoided, or shall we simply drift?

3. We have found that mind pervades every part of the physical body and is always capable of being directed or impressed by authority coming from the objective or the more dominant portion of the mind.

4. The mind, which pervades the body, is largely the result of heredity, which, in turn, is simply the result of all the environments of all past generations on the responsive and ever-moving life forces. An understanding of this fact will enable us to use our authority when we find some undesirable trait of character manifesting.

5. We can consciously use all the desirable characteristics with which we have been provided and we can repress and refuse to allow the undesirable ones to manifest.

6. Again, this mind which pervades our physical body is not only the result of hereditary tendencies, but is the result of home, business and social environment, where countless thousands of impressions, ideas, prejudices and similar thoughts have been received. Much of this has been received from others, the result of opinions, suggestions or statements;

much of it is the result of our own thinking, but nearly all of it has been accepted with little or no examination or consideration.

7. The idea seemed plausible, the conscious received it, passed it on to the subconscious, where it was taken up by the Sympathetic System and passed on to be built into our physical body. "The word has become flesh."

8. This, then, is the way we are consistently creating and recreating ourselves; we are today the result of our past thinking, and we shall be what we are thinking today, the Law of Attraction is bringing to us, not the things we should like, or the things we wish for, or the things some one else has, but it brings us "our own," the things which we have created by our thought processes, whether consciously or unconsciously. Unfortunately, many of us are creating these things unconsciously.

9. If either of us were building a home for ourselves, how careful we would be in regard to the plans; how we should study every detail; how we should watch the material and select only the best of everything; and yet how careless we are when it comes to building our Mental Home, which is infinitely more important than any physical home, as everything which can possibly enter into our lives depends upon the character of the material which enters into the construction of our Mental Home.

10. What is the character of this material? We have seen that it is the result of the impressions which we have accumulated in the past and stored away in our subconscious Mentality. If these impressions have been of fear, of worry, of care, of anxiety; if they have been despondent, negative, doubtful, then the texture of the material which we are weaving today will be of the same negative material. Instead of being of any value, it will be mildewed and rotten and will bring us only more toil and care and anxiety. We shall be forever busy trying to patch it up and make it appear at least genteel.

11. But if we have stored away nothing but courageous thought, if we have been optimistic, positive, and have immediately thrown any kind of negative thought on the scrap pile, have refused to have anything to do with it, have refused to associate with it or become identified with it in any way, what then is the result? Our mental material is now of the best kind; we can weave any kind of material we want; we can use any color we wish; we know that the texture is firm, that the material is solid, that it will not fade, and we have no fear, no anxiety concerning the future; there is nothing to cover, there are no patches to hide.

12. These are psychological facts; there is no theory or guesswork about these thinking processes; there is nothing secret about them; in fact, they are so plain that every one can understand them. The thing to do is to have a mental house-cleaning, and to have this house-cleaning every day, and keep the house clean. Mental, moral and physical cleanliness are absolutely indispensable if we are to make progress of any kind.

13. When this mental house-cleaning process has been completed, the material which is left will be suitable for the making of the kind of ideals or mental images which we desire to realize.

14. There is a fine estate awaiting a claimant. Its broad acres, with abundant crops, running water and fine timber, stretch away as far as the eye can see. There is a mansion, spacious and cheerful, with rare pictures, a well-stocked library, rich hangings, and every comfort and luxury. All the heir has to do is to assert his heirship, take possession, and use the property. He must use it; he must not let it decay; for use is the condition on which he holds it. To neglect it is to lose possession.

15. In the domain of mind and spirit, in the domain of practical power, such an estate is yours. You are the heir! You can assert your heirship and possess, and use this rich inheritance. Power over circumstances is one of its fruits, health, harmony and prosperity are assets upon its balance sheet. It offers you poise and peace. It costs you only the labor of studying and harvesting its great resources. It demands no sacrifice, except the loss of your limitations, your servitudes, your weakness. It clothes you with self-honor, and puts a scepter in your hands.

16. To gain this estate, three processes are necessary: You must earnestly desire it. You must assert your claim. You must take possession.

17. You admit that those are not burdensome conditions.

18. You are familiar with the subject of heredity. Darwin, Huxley, Haeckel, and other physical scientists have piled evidence mountain high that heredity is a law attending progressive creation. It is progressive heredity which gives man his erect attitude, his power of motion, the organs of digestions, blood circulation, nerve force, muscular force, bone structure and a host of other faculties on the physical side. There are even more impressive facts concerning heredity of mind force. All these constitute what may be called your human heredity.

19. But there is a heredity which the physical scientists have not compassed. It lies beneath and antecedent to all their researches. At a point where they throw up their hands in despair, saying they cannot account for what they see, this divine heredity is found in full sway.

20. It is the benignant force which decrees primal creation. It thrills down from the Divine, direct into every created being. It originates life, which the physical scientist has not done, nor ever can do. It stands out among all forces supreme, unapproachable. No human heredity can approach it. No human heredity measures up to it.

21. This Infinite Life flows through you; is you. Its doorways are but the faculties which comprise your consciousness. To keep open these doors is the Secret of Power. Is it not worthwhile to make the effort?

22. The great fact is, that the source of all life and all power is from within. Persons, circumstances and events may suggest need and opportunities, but the insight, strength and power to answer these needs will be found within.

23. Avoid counterfeits. Build firm foundations for your consciousness upon forces which flow direct from the Infinite source, the Universal Mind of which you are the image and likeness.

24. Those we have come into possession of this inheritance are never quite the same again. They have come into possession of a sense of power hitherto undreamed of. They can never again be timid, weak, vacillating, or fearful. They are indissolubly connected with Omnipotence. Something in them has been aroused; they have suddenly discovered that they possess a tremendous latent ability of which they were heretofore entirely unconscious.

25. This power is from within, but we cannot receive it unless we give it. Use is the condition upon which we hold this inheritance. We are each of us but the channel through which the Omnipotent power is being differentiated into form; unless we give, the channel is obstructed and we can receive no more. This is true on every plane of existence and in every field of endeavor and all walks of life. The more we give, the more we get. The athlete who wishes to get strong must make use of the strength he has, and the more he gives the more he will get. The financier who wishes to make money must make use of the money he has, for only by using it can he get more.

26. The merchant who does not keep his goods going out will soon have none coming in; the corporation which fails to give efficient service will soon lack customers; the attorney who fails to get results will soon lack clients, and so it goes everywhere; power is contingent upon a proper use of the power already in our possession; what is true in every field of endeavor, every experience in life, is true of the power from which every other power known among men is begotten — spiritual power. Take away the spirit and what is left? Nothing.

27. If then the spirit is all there is, upon the recognition of this fact must depend the ability to demonstrate all power, whether physical, mental or spiritual.

28. All possession is the result of the accumulative attitude of mind, or the money consciousness; this is the magic wand which will enable you to receive the idea, and it will formulate plans for you to execute, and you will find as much pleasure in the execution as in the satisfaction of attainment and achievement.

29. Now, go to your room, take the same seat, the same position as heretofore, and mentally select a place which has pleasant associations. Make a complete mental picture of it, see the buildings, the grounds, the trees, friends, associations, everything complete. At first, you will find yourself thinking of everything under the sun, except the ideal upon which you desire to concentrate. But do not let that discourage you. Persistence will win, but persistence requires that you practice these exercises every day without fail.

PART 6

This part will give you an excellent understanding of the most wonderful piece of mechanism which has ever been created. A mechanism whereby you may create for yourself Health, Strength, Success, Prosperity or any other condition which you desire.

Necessities are demands, and demands create action, and actions bring about results. The process of evolution is constantly building our tomorrows out of our todays. Individual development, like Universal development, must be gradual with an ever-increasing capacity and volume.

The knowledge that if we infringe upon the rights of others, we become moral thorns and find ourselves entangled at every turn of the road, should be an indication that success is contingent upon the highest moral ideal, which is "The greatest good to the greatest number." Aspiration, desire and harmonious relations constantly and persistently maintained will accomplish results. The greatest hindrance is erroneous and fixed ideas.

To be in tune with eternal truth we must possess poise and harmony within. In order to receive intelligence the receiver must be in tune with the transmitter.

Thought is a product of Mind and Mind is creative, but this does not mean that the Universal will change its modus operandi to suit us or our ideas, but it does mean that we can come into harmonious relationship with the Universal, and when we have accomplished this we may ask anything to which we are entitled, and the way will be made plain.

1. The Universal Mind is so wonderful that it is difficult to understand its utilitarian powers and possibilities and its unlimited producing effects.

2. We have found that this Mind is not only all intelligence but all substance. How, then, is it to be differentiated in form? How are we to secure the effect which we desire?

3. Ask any electrician what the effect of electricity will be and he will reply that "Electricity is a form of motion and its effect will depend upon the mechanism to which it is attached." Upon this mechanism will depend whether we shall have heat, light, power, music or any of the other marvelous demonstration of power to which this vital energy has been harnessed.

4. What effect can be produced by thought? The reply is that thought is mind in motion (just as wind is air in motion), and its effect will depend entirely on the "mechanism to which it is attached."

5. Here, then, is the secret of all mental power; it depends entirely on the mechanism which we attach.

6. What is this mechanism? You know something of the mechanism which has been invented by Edison, Bell, Marconi and other electrical wizards, by which place and space and time have become only figures of speech, but did you ever stop to think that the mechanism which has been given you for transforming the Universal, Omnipresent Potential Power was invented by a greater inventor than Edison?

7. We are accustomed to examining the mechanism of the implements which we use for tilling the soil, and we try to get an understanding of the mechanism of the automobile which we drive, but most of us are content to remain in absolute ignorance of the greatest piece of mechanism which as ever come into existence, the brain of man.

8. Let us examine the wonders of this mechanism; perhaps we shall thereby get a better understanding of the various effects of which it is the cause.

9. In the first place, there is the great mental world in which we live and move and have our being; this world is omnipotent, omniscient and omnipresent; it will respond to our desire in direct ratio to our purpose and faith; the purpose must be in accordance with the law of our being, that is, it must be creative or constructive; our faith must be strong enough to generate a current of sufficient strength to bring our purpose into manifestation. "As thy faith is, so be it unto thee," bears the stamp of scientific test.

10. The effects which are produced in the world without are the result of the action and reaction of the individual upon the universal; that is the process which we call thinking; the brain is the organ through which this process is accomplished; think of the wonder of it all! Do you love music, flowers, literature, or are you inspired by the thought of ancient or modern genius? Remember, every beauty to which you respond must have its corresponding outline in your brain before you can appreciate it.

11. There is not a single virtue or principle in the storehouse of nature which the brain cannot express. The brain is an embryonic world, ready to develop at any time as necessity may arise. If you can comprehend that this is a scientific truth and one of the wonderful laws of nature, it will be easier for you to get an understanding of the mechanism by which these extraordinary results are being accomplished.

12. The nervous system has been compared to an electric circuit with its battery of cells in which force is originated, and its white matter to insulated wires by which the current is conveyed; it is through these channels that every impulse or desire is carried through the mechanism.

13. The spinal cord is the great motor and sensory pathway by which messages are conveyed to and from the brain; then, there is the blood supply plunging through the veins and arteries, renewing our energy and strength, the perfectly arranged structure upon which the entire physical

body rests, and, finally, the delicate and beautiful skin, clothing the entire mechanism is a mantle of beauty.

14. This then is the "Temple of the living God" and the individual "I" is given control and upon his understanding of the mechanism which is within his control will the result depend.

15. Every thought sets the brain cells in action; at first the substance upon which the thought is directed fails to respond, but if the thought is sufficiently refined and concentrated, the substance finally yields and expresses perfectly.

16. This influence of the mind can be exerted upon any part of the body, causing the elimination of any undesirable effect.

17. A perfect conception and understanding of the laws governing in the mental world cannot fail to be of inestimable value in the transaction of business, as it develops the power of discernment and gives a clearer understanding and appreciation of facts.

18. The man who looks within instead of without cannot fail to make use of the mighty forces which will eventually determine his course in life and so bring him into vibration with all that is best, strongest and most desirable.

19. Attention or concentration is probably; the most important essential in the development of mind culture. The possibilities of attention when properly directed are so startling that they would hardly appear credible to the uninitiated. The cultivation of attention is the distinguishing characteristic of every successful man or woman, and is the very highest personal accomplishment which can be acquired.

20. The power of attention can be more readily understood by comparing it with a magnifying glass in which the rays of sunlight are focused; they possess no particular strength as long as the glass is moved about and the rays directed from one place to another; but let the glass be held perfectly still and let the rays be focused on one spot for any length of time, the effect will become immediately apparent.

21. So with the power of thought; let power be dissipated by scattering the thought from one object to another, and no result is apparent; but focus this power through attention or concentration on any single purpose for any length of time and nothing becomes impossible.

22. A very simple remedy for a very complex situation, some will say. All right, try it, you who have had no experience in concentrating the thought on a definite purpose or object. Choose any single object and concentrate your attention on it for a definite purpose for even ten minutes; you cannot do it; the mind will wander a dozen times and it will be necessary to bring it back to the original purpose, and each time the effect will have been lost and at the end of the ten minutes nothing will have been gained, because you have not been able to hold your thought steadily to the purpose.

23. It is, however, through attention that you will finally be able to overcome obstacles of any kind that appear in your path onward and upward, and the only way to acquire this wonderful power is by practice — practice makes perfect, in this as in anything else.

24. In order to cultivate the power of attention, bring a photograph with you to the same seat in the same room in the same position as heretofore. Examine it closely at least ten minutes, note the expression of the eyes, the form of the features, the clothing, the way the hair is arranged; in fact, note every detail shown on the photograph carefully. Now cover it and close your eyes and try to see it mentally; if you can see every detail perfectly and can form a good mental image of the photograph, you are to be congratulated; if not, repeat the process until you can.

25. This step is simply for the purpose of preparing the soil; next week we shall be ready to sow the seed.

26. It is by such exercises as these that you will finally be able to control your mental moods, your attitude, your consciousness.

27. Great financiers are learning to withdraw from the multitude more and more, that they may have more time for planning, thinking and generating the right mental moods.

28. Successful businessmen are constantly demonstrating the fact that it pays to keep in touch with the thought of other successful businessmen.

29. A single idea may be worth millions of dollars, and these ideas can only come to those who are receptive, who are prepared to receive them, who are in successful frame of mind.

30. Men are learning to place themselves in harmony with the Universal Mind; they are learning the unity of all things; they are learning the basic methods and principles of thinking, and this is changing conditions and multiplying results.

31. They are finding that circumstances and environment follow the trend of mental and spiritual progress; they find that growth follows knowledge; action follows inspiration; opportunity follows perception; always the spiritual first, then the transformation into the infinite and illimitable possibilities of achievement.

32. As the individual is but the channel for the differentiation of the Universal, these possibilities are necessarily inexhaustible.

33. Thought is the process by which we may absorb the Spirit of Power, and hold the result in our inner consciousness until it becomes a part of our ordinary consciousness. The method of accomplishing this result by the persistent practice of a few fundamental principles, as explained in this System, is the master key which unlocks the storehouse of Universal Truth.

34. The two great sources of human suffering at present are bodily disease and mental anxiety. These may be readily traced to the infringement of some Natural Law. This is, no doubt, owing to the fact that so far knowledge has largely remained partial, but the clouds of darkness which have accumulated through long ages are beginning to roll away and with them many of the miseries that attend imperfect information.

PART 7

Through all the ages man has believed in an invisible power, through which and by which all things have been created and are continually being re-created. We may personalize this power and call it God, or we may think of it as the essence or spirit, which permeates all things, but in either case the effect is the same.

So far as the individual is concerned, the objective, the physical, the visible, is the personal, that which can be cognized by the senses. It consists of body, brain and nerves. The subjective is the spiritual, the invisible, the impersonal.

The personal is conscious because it is a personal entity. The impersonal, being the same in kind and quality as all other Being, is not conscious of itself and has therefore been termed the subconscious.

The personal, or conscious, has the power of will and choice, and can therefore exercise discrimination in the selection of methods whereby to bring about the solution of difficulties.

The impersonal, or spiritual, being a part or one with the source, and origin of all power, can necessarily exercise no such choice, but, on the contrary, it has Infinite resources at its command. It can and does bring about results by methods concerning which the human or individual mind can have no possible conception.

You will therefore see that it is your privilege to depend upon the human will with all its limitations and misconceptions, or you may utilize the potentialities of Infinity by making use of the subconscious mind. Here, then, is the scientific explanation of the wonderful power which has been put within your control, if you but understand, appreciate and recognize it.

One method of consciously utilizing this omnipotent power is outlined in Part Seven.

1. Visualization is the process of making mental images, and the image is the mold or model which will serve as a pattern from which your future will emerge.

2. Make the pattern clear and make it beautiful; do not be afraid; make it grand; remember that no limitation can be placed upon you by any one but yourself; you are not limited as to cost or material; draw on the Infinite for your supply, construct it in your imagination; it will have to be there before it will ever appear anywhere else.

3. Make the image clear and clean-cut, hold it firmly in the mind and you will gradually and constantly bring the thing nearer to you. You can be what "you will to be."

4. This is another psychological fact which is well known, but unfortunately, reading about it will not bring about any result which you may have in mind; it will not even help you to form the mental image, much less bring it into manifestation. Work is necessary - labor, hard mental labor, the kind of effort which so few are willing to put forth.

5. The first step is idealization. It is likewise the most important step, because it is the plan on which you are going to build. It must be solid; it must be permanent. The architect, when he plans a 30-storey building, has every line and detail pictured in advance. The engineer, when he spans a chasm, first ascertains the strength requirements of a million separate parts.

6. They see the end before a single step is taken; so you are to picture in your mind what you want; you are sowing the seed, but before sowing any seed you want to know what the harvest is to be. This is Idealization. If you are not sure, return to the chair daily until the picture becomes plain; it will gradually unfold; first the general plan will be dim, but it will take shape, the outline will take form, then the details, and you will gradually develop the power by which you will be enabled to formulate plans which will eventually materialize in the objective world. You will come to know what the future holds for you.

7. Then comes the process of visualization. You must see the picture more and more complete, see the detail, and, as the details begin to unfold the ways and means for bringing it into manifestation will develop. One thing will lead to another. Thought will lead to action, action will develop methods, methods will develop friends, and friends will bring about circumstances, and, finally, the third step, or Materialization, will have been accomplished.

8. We all recognize the Universe must have been thought into shape before it ever could have become a material fact. And if we are willing to follow along the lines of the Great Architect of the Universe, we shall find our thoughts taking form, just as the universe took concrete form. It is the same mind operating through the individual. There is no difference in kind or quality, the only difference is one of degree.

9. The architect visualizes his building, he sees it as he wishes it to be. His thought becomes a plastic mold from which the building will eventually emerge, a high one or a low one, a beautiful one or a plain one, his vision takes form on paper and eventually the necessary material is utilized and the building stands complete.

10. The inventor visualizes his idea in exactly the same manner, for instance, Nikola Tesla, he with the giant intellect, one of the greatest inventors of all ages, the man who has brought forth the most amazing realities, always visualizes his inventions before attempting to work them out. He did not rush to embody them in form and then spend his time in correcting defects. Having first built up the idea in his imagination, he held it there as a mental picture, to be reconstructed and improved by his

thought. "In this way," he writes in the Electrical Experimenter. "I am enabled to rapidly develop and perfect a conception without touching anything. When I have gone so far as to embody in the invention every possible improvement I can think of, and see no fault anywhere, I put into concrete, the product of my brain. Invariably my devise works as I conceived it should; in twenty years there has not been a single exception."

11. If you can conscientiously follow these directions, you will develop Faith, the kind of Faith that is the "Substance of things hoped for, the evidence of things not seen"; you will develop confidence, the kind of confidence that leads to endurance and courage; you will develop the power of concentration which will enable you to exclude all thoughts except the ones which are associated with your purpose.

12. The law is that thought will manifest in form, and only one who knows how to be the divine thinker of his own thoughts can ever take a Master's place and speak with authority.

13. Clearness and accuracy are obtained only by repeatedly having the image in mind. Each repeated action renders the image more clear and accurate than the preceding, and in proportion to the clearness and accuracy of the image will the outward manifestation be. You must build it firmly and securely in your mental world, the world within, before it can take form in the world without, and you can build nothing of value, even in the mental world unless you have the proper material. When you have the material you can build anything you wish, but make sure of your material. You cannot make broadcloth from shoddy.

14. This material will be brought out by millions of silent mental workers and fashioned into the form of the image which you have in mind.

15. Think of it! You have over five million of these mental workers, ready and in active use; brain cells they are called. Besides this, there is another reserve force of at least an equal number, ready to be called into action at the slightest need. Your power to think, then, is almost unlimited, and this means that your power to create the kind of material which is necessary to build for yourself any kind of environment which you desire is practically unlimited.

16. In addition to these millions of mental workers, you have billions of mental workers in the body, every one of which is endowed with sufficient intelligence to understand and act upon any message or suggestion given. These cells are all busy creating and recreating the body, but, in addition to this, they are endowed with psychic activity whereby they can attract to themselves the substance necessary for perfect development.

17. They do this by the same law and in the same manner that every form of life attracts to itself the necessary material for growth. The oak, the rose, the lily, all require certain material for their most perfect expression and they secure it by silent demand, the Law of Attraction, the

most certain way for you to secure what you require for your most complete development.

18. Make the Mental Image; make it clear, distinct, perfect; hold it firmly; the ways and means will develop; supply will follow the demand; you will be led to do the right thing at the right time and in the right way. Earnest Desire will bring about Confident Expectation, and this in turn must be reinforced by Firm Demand. These three cannot fail to bring about Attainment, because the Earnest Desire is the feeling, the Confident Expectation is the thought, and the Firm Demand is the will, and, as we have seen, feeling gives vitality to thought and the will holds it steadily until the law of Growth brings it into manifestation.

19. Is it not wonderful that man has such tremendous power within himself, such transcendental faculties concerning which he had no conception? Is it not strange that we have always been taught to look for strength and power "without?" We have been taught to look everywhere but "within" and whenever this power manifested in our lives we were told that it was something supernatural.

20. There are many who have come to an understanding of this wonderful power, and who make serious and conscientious efforts to realize health, power and other conditions, and seem to fail. They do not seem able to bring the Law into operation. The difficulty in nearly every case is that they are dealing with externals. They want money, power, health and abundance, but they fail to realize that these are effects and can come only when the cause is found.

21. Those who will give no attention to the world without will seek only to ascertain the truth, will look only for wisdom, will find that this wisdom will unfold and disclose the source of all power, that it will manifest in thought and purpose which will create the external conditions desired. This truth will find expression in noble purpose and courageous action.

22. Create ideals only, give no thought to external conditions, make the world within beautiful and opulent and the world without will express and manifest the condition which you have within. You will come into a realization of your power to create ideals and these ideals will be projected into the world of effect.

23. For instance, a man is in debt. He will be continually thinking about the debt, concentrating on it, and as thoughts are causes the result is that he not only fastens the debt closer to him, but actually creates more debt. He is putting the great law of Attraction into operation with the usual and inevitable result — Loss leads to greater "Loss."

24. What, then, is the correct principle? Concentrate on the things you want, not on the things you do not want. Think of abundance; idealize the methods and plans for putting the Law of Abundance into operation. Visualize the condition which the Law of Abundance creates; this will result in manifestation.

25. If the law operates perfectly to bring about poverty, lack and every form of limitation for those who are continually entertaining thoughts of lack and fear, it will operate with the same certainty to bring about conditions of abundance and opulence for those who entertain thoughts of courage and power.

26. This is a difficult problem for many; we are too anxious; we manifest anxiety, fear, distress; we want to do something; we want to help; we are like a child who has just planted a seed and every fifteen minutes goes and stirs up the earth to see if it is growing. Of course, under such circumstances, the seed will never germinate, and yet this is exactly what many of us do in the mental world.

27. We must plant the seed and leave it undisturbed. This does not mean that we are to sit down and do nothing, by no means; we will do more and better work then we have ever done before, new channels will constantly be provided, new doors will open; all that is necessary is to have an open mind, be ready to act when the time comes.

28. Thought force is the most powerful means of obtaining knowledge, and if concentrated on any subject will solve the problem. Nothing is beyond the power of human comprehension, but in order to harness thought force and make it do your bidding, work is required.

29. Remember that thought is the fire that creates the steam that turns the wheel of fortune, upon which your experiences depend.

30. Ask yourself a few questions and then reverently await the response; do you not now and then feel the self with you? Do you assert this self or do you follow the majority? Remember that majorities are always led, they never lead. It was the majority that fought, tooth and nail, against the steam engine, the power loom and every other advance or improvement ever suggested.

31. For your exercise this week, visualize your friend, see him exactly as you last saw him, see the room, the furniture, recall the conversation, now see his face, see it distinctly, now talk to him about some subject of mutual interest; see his expression change, watch him smile. Can you do this? All right, you can; then arouse his interest, tell him a story of adventure, see his eyes light up with the spirit of fun or excitement. Can you do all of this? If so, your imagination is good, you are making excellent progress.

PART 8

In this Part you will find that you may freely choose what you think but the result of your thought is governed by an immutable law! Is not this a wonderful thought? Is it not wonderful to know that our lives are not subject to caprice or variability of any kind? That they are governed by law. This stability is our opportunity, because by complying with the law we can secure the desired effect with invariable precision.

It is the Law which makes the Universe one grand paean of Harmony. If it were not for law, the Universe would be a Chaos instead of a Cosmos.

Here, then, is the secret of the origin of both good and evil, this is all the good and evil there ever was or ever will be.

Let me illustrate. Thought results in action, if your thought is constructive and harmonious, the result will be good; if your thought is destructive or in harmonious, the result will be evil.

There is therefore but one law, one principle, on cause, one Source of Power, and good and evil are simply words which have been coined to indicate the result of our action, or our compliance or non-compliance with this law.

The importance of this is well illustrated in the lives of Emerson and Carlyle. Emerson loved the good and his life was a symphony of peace and harmony, Carlyle hated the bad, and his life was a record of perpetual discord and in harmony.

Here we have two grand men, each intent upon achieving the same ideal, but one makes use of constructive thought and is therefore in harmony with Natural Law, the other makes use of destructive thought and therefore brings upon himself discord of every kind and character.

It is evident therefore that we are to hate nothing, not even the "bad," because hatred is destructive, and we shall soon find that by entertaining destructive thought we are sowing the "wind" and in turn shall reap the "whirlwind."

PART EIGHT

1. Thought contains a vital principle, because it is the creative principle of the Universe and by its nature will combine with other similar thoughts.

2. As the one purpose of life is growth, all principles underlying existence must contribute to give it effect. Thought, therefore, takes form and the law of growth eventually brings it into manifestation.

3. You may freely choose what you think, but the result of your thought is governed by an immutable law. Any line of thought persisted in cannot fail to produce its result in the character, health and circumstances of the

individual. Methods whereby we can substitute habits of constructive thinking for those which we have found produce only undesirable effects are therefore of primary importance.

4. We all know that this is by no means easy. Mental habits are difficult to control, but it can be done and the way to do it is to begin at once to substitute constructive thought for destructive thought. Form the habit of analyzing every thought. If it is necessary, if its manifestation in the objective will be a benefit, not only to yourself, but to all whom it may affect in any way, keep it; treasure it; it is of value; it is in tune with the Infinite; it will grow and develop and produce fruit an hundred fold. On the other hand, it will be well for you to keep this quotation from George Matthews Adams, in mind, "Learn to keep the door shut, keep out of your mind, out of your office, and out of your world, every element that seeks admittance with no definite helpful end in view."

5. If your thought has been critical or destructive, and has resulted in any condition of discord or in harmony in your environment, it may be necessary for you to cultivate a mental attitude which will be conducive to constructive thought.

6. The imagination will be found to be a great assistance in this direction; the cultivation of the imagination leads to the development of the ideal out of which your future will emerge.

7. The imagination gathers up the material by which the Mind weaves the fabric in which your future is to be clothed.

8. Imagination is the light by which we can penetrate new worlds of thought and experience.

9. Imagination is the mighty instrument by which every discoverer, every inventor, opened the way from precedent to experience. Precedent said, "It cannot be done;" experience said, "It is done."

10. Imagination is a plastic power, molding the things of sense into new forms and ideals.

11. Imagination is the constructive form of thought which must precede every constructive form of action.

12. A builder cannot build a structure of any kind until he has first received the plans from the architect, and the architect must get them from his imagination.

13. The Captain of Industry cannot build a giant corporation which may coordinate hundreds of smaller corporations and thousands of employees, and utilize millions of dollars of capital until he has first created the entire work in his imagination. Objects in the material world are as clay in the potter's hand; it is in the Master Mind that the real things are created, and it is by the use of the imagination that the work is done. In order to cultivate the imagination it must be exercised. Exercise is necessary to cultivate mental muscle as well as physical muscle. It must be supplied with nourishment or it cannot grow.

14. Do not confuse Imagination with Fancy, or that form of daydreaming in which some people like to indulge. Daydreaming is a form of mental dissipation which may lead to mental disaster.

15. Constructive imagination means mental labor, by some considered to be the hardest kind of labor, but, if so, it yields the greatest returns, for all the great things in life have come to men and women who had the capacity to think, to imagine, and to make their dreams come true.

16. When you have become thoroughly conscious of the fact that Mind is the only creative principle, that it is Omnipotent, Omniscient and Omnipresent, and that you can consciously come into harmony with this Omnipotence through your power of thought, you will have taken a long step in the right direction.

17. The next step is to place yourself in position to receive this power. As it is Omnipresent, it must be within you. We know that this is so because we know that all power is from within, but it must be developed, unfolded, cultivated; in order to do this we must be receptive, and this receptivity is acquired just as physical strength is gained, by exercise.

18. The law of attraction will certainly and unerringly bring to you the conditions, environment, and experiences in life, corresponding with your habitual, characteristic, predominant mental attitude. Not what you think once in a while when you are in church, or have just read a good book, *but* your predominant mental attitude is what counts.

19. You can not entertain weak, harmful, negative thoughts ten hours a day and expect to bring about beautiful, strong and harmonious conditions by ten minutes of strong, positive, creative thought.

20. Real power comes from within. All power that anybody can possibly use is within man, only waiting to be brought into visibility by his first recognizing it, and then affirming it as his, working it into his consciousness until he becomes one with it.

21. People say that they desire abundant life, and so they do, but so many interpret this to mean that if they will exercise their muscles or breathe scientifically, eat certain foods in certain ways, drink so many glasses of water every day of just a certain temperature, keep out of drafts, they will attain the abundant life they seek. The result of such methods is but indifferent. However, when man awakens to the truth, and affirms his oneness with all Life, he finds that he takes on the clear eye, the elastic step, the vigor of youth; he finds that he has discovered the source of all power.

22. All mistakes are but the mistakes of ignorance. Knowledge gaining and consequent power is what determines growth and evolution. The recognition and demonstration of knowledge is what constitutes power, and this power is spiritual power, and this spiritual power is the power which lies at the heart of all things; it is the soul of the universe.

23. This knowledge is the result of man's ability to think; thought is therefore the germ of man's conscious evolution. When man ceases to

advance in his thoughts and ideals, his forces immediately begin to disintegrate and his countenance gradually registers these changing conditions.

24. Successful men make it their business to hold ideals of the conditions which they wish to realize. They constantly hold in mind the next step necessary to the ideal for which they are striving. Thoughts are the materials with which they build, and the imagination is their mental workshop. Mind is the ever-moving force with which they secure the persons and circumstance necessary to build their success structure, and imagination is the matrix in which all great things are fashioned.

25. If you have been faithful to your ideal, you will hear the call when circumstances are ready to materialize your plans and results will correspond in the exact ratio of your fidelity to your ideal. The ideal steadily held is what pre-determines and attracts the necessary conditions for its fulfillment.

26. It is thus that you may weave a garment of spirit and power into the web of your entire existence; it is thus that you may lead a charmed life and be forever protected from all harm; it is thus that you may become a positive force whereby conditions of opulence and harmony may be attracted to you.

27. This is the leaven which is gradually permeating the general consciousness and is largely responsible for the conditions of unrest which are everywhere evident.

28. In the last Part you created a mental image, you brought it from the invisible into the visible; this week I want you to take an object and follow it back to its origination, see of what it really consists. If you do this you will develop imagination, insight, perception, and sagacity. These come not by the superficial observation of the multitude, but by a keen analytical observation which sees below the surface.

29. It is the few who know that the things which they see are only effects, and understand the causes by which these effects were brought into existence.

30. Take the same position as heretofore and visualize a Battleship; see the grim monster floating on the surface of the water; there appears to be no life anywhere about; all is silence; you know that by far the largest part of the vessel is under water; out of sight; you know that the ship is as large and as heavy as a twenty-story skyscraper; you know that there are hundreds of men ready to spring to their appointed task instantly; you know that every department is in charge of able, trained, skilled officials who have proven themselves competent to take charge of this marvelous piece of mechanism; you know that although it lies apparently oblivious to everything else, it has eyes which see everything for miles around, and nothing is permitted to escape its watchful vision; you know that while it appears quiet, submissive and innocent, it is prepared to hurl a steel projectile weighing thousands of pounds at an enemy many miles away;

this and much more you can bring to mind with comparatively no effort whatever. But how did the battleship come to be where it is; how did it come into existence in the first place? All of this you want to know if you are a careful observer.

31. Follow the great steel plates through the foundries, see the thousands of men employed in their production; go still further back, and see the ore as it comes from the mine, see it loaded on barges or cars, see it melted and properly treated; go back still further and see the architect and engineers who planned the vessel; let the thought carry you back still further in order to determine why they planned the vessel; you will see that you are now so far back that the vessel is something intangible, it no longer exists, it is now only a thought existing in the brain of the architect; but from where did the order come to plan the vessel? Probably from the Secretary of Defense; but probably this vessel was planned long before the war was thought of, and that Congress had to pass a bill appropriating the money; possibly there was opposition, and speeches for or against the bill. Whom do these Congressmen represent? They represent you and me, so that our line of thought begins with the Battleship and ends with ourselves, and we find in the last analysis that our own thought is responsible for this and many other things, of which we seldom think, and a little further reflection will develop the most important fact of all and that is, if someone had not discovered the law by which this tremendous mass of steel and iron could be made to float upon the water, instead of immediately going to the bottom, the battleship could not have come into existence at all.

32. This law is that, "the specific gravity of any substance is the weight of any volume of it, compared with an equal volume of water." The discovery of this law revolutionized every kind of ocean travel, commerce and warfare, and made the existence of the battleship, aircraft carriers, and cruise ships possible.

33. You will find exercises of this kind invaluable. When the thought has been trained to look below the surface everything takes on a different appearance, the insignificant becomes significant, the uninteresting interesting; the things which we supposed to be of no importance are seen to be the only really vital things in existence.

In this Part you may learn to fashion the tools by which you may build for yourself any condition you desire. If you wish to change conditions you must change yourself. Your whims, your wishes, your fancies, your ambitions may be thwarted at every step, but your inmost thoughts will find expression just as certainly as the plant springs from the seed.

Suppose, then, we desire to change conditions, how are we to bring this about? The reply is simple: By the law of growth. Cause and effect are as absolute and undeviating in the hidden realm of thought as in the world of material things.

Hold in mind the condition desired; affirm it as an already existing fact. This indicates the value of a powerful affirmation. By constant repetition it becomes a part of ourselves. We are actually changing ourselves; are making ourselves what we want to be.

Character is not a thing of chance, but it is the result of continued effort. If you are timid, vacillating, self-conscious, or if you are over-anxious or harassed by thoughts of fear or impending danger, remember that is axiomatic that "two things cannot exist in the same place at the same time."

Exactly the same thing is true in the mental and spiritual world; so that your remedy is plainly to substitute thoughts of courage, power, self-reliance and confidence, for those of fear, lack and limitation.

The easiest and most natural way to do this is to select an affirmation which seems to fit your particular case.

The positive thought will destroy the negative as certainly as light destroys darkness, and the results will be just as effectual.

Act is the blossom of thought, and conditions are the result of action, so that you constantly have in your possession the tools by which you will certainly and inevitably make or unmake yourself, and joy or suffering will be the reward.

PART 9

1. There are only three things which can possibly be desired in the "world without" and each of them can be found in the "world within." The secret of finding them is simply to apply the proper "mechanism" of attachment to the omnipotent power to which each individual has access.

2. The three things which all mankind desires and which are necessary for his highest expression and complete development are Health, Wealth and Love. All will admit that Health is absolutely essential; no one can be happy if the physical body is in pain. All will not so readily admit that Wealth is necessary, but all must admit that a sufficient supply at least is necessary, and what would be considered sufficient for one, would be considered absolute and painful lack for another; and as Nature provides not only enough but abundantly, wastefully, lavishly, we realize that any lack or limitation is only the limitation which has been made by an artificial method of distribution.

3. All will probably admit that Love is the third, or maybe some will say the first essential necessary to the happiness of mankind; at any rate, those who possess all three, Health, Wealth, and Love, find nothing else which can be added to their cup of happiness.

4. We have found that the Universal substance is "All Health," "All Substance" and "All Love" and that the mechanism of attachment whereby we can consciously connect with this Infinite supply is in our method of thinking. To think correctly is therefore to enter into the "Secret Place of the Most High."

5. What shall we think? If we know this we shall have found the proper mechanism of attachment which will relate us to "Whatsoever things we desire." This mechanism may seem very simple when I give it to you, but read on; you will find that it is in reality the "Master Key," the "Aladdin's lamp," if you please; you will find that it is the foundation, the imperative condition, the absolute law of well-doing, which means, well-being.

6. To think correctly, accurately, we must know the "Truth." The truth then is the underlying principle in every business or social relation. It is a condition precedent to every right action. To know the truth, to be sure, to be confident, affords a satisfaction beside which no other is at all comparable; it is the only solid ground in a world of doubt, conflict and danger.

7. To know the Truth is to be in harmony with the Infinite and Omnipotent power. To know the truth is, therefore, to connect yourself with a power which is irresistible and which will sweep away every kind of discord, inharmony, doubt or error of any kind, because the "Truth is mighty and will prevail."

8. The humblest intellect can readily foretell the result of any action when he knows that it is based on truth, but the mightiest intellect, the most profound and penetrating mind loses its way hopelessly and can form no conception of the results which may ensue when his hopes are based on a premise which he knows to be false.

9. Every action which is not in harmony with Truth, whether through ignorance or design, will result in discord, and eventual loss in proportion to its extent and character.

10. How then are we to know the truth in order to attach this mechanism which will relate us to the Infinite?

11. We can make no mistake about this if we realize that truth is the vital principle of the Universal Mind and is Omnipresent. For instance, if you require health, a realization of the fact that the "I" in you is spiritual and that all spirit is one; that wherever a part is the whole must be, will bring about a condition of health, because every cell in the body must manifest the truth as you see it. If you see sickness; they will manifest sickness; if you see perfection they must manifest perfection. The affirmation, "I am whole, perfect, strong, powerful, loving, harmonious and happy," will bring about harmonious conditions. The reason for this is because the affirmation is in strict accordance with the Truth, and when truth appears every form of error or discord must necessarily disappear.

12. You have found that the "I" is spiritual, it must necessarily then always be no less than perfect, the affirmation. "I am whole, perfect, strong, powerful, loving, harmonious and happy" is therefore an exact scientific statement.

13. Thought is a spiritual activity and spirit is creative, therefore the result of holding this thought in mind, must necessarily bring about conditions in harmony with the thought.

14. If you require Wealth a realization of the fact that the "I" in you is one with the Universal mind which is all substance, and is Omnipotent, will assist you in bringing into operation the law of attraction which will bring you into vibration with those forces which make for success and bring about conditions of power and affluence in direct proportion with the character and purpose of your affirmation.

15. Visualization is the mechanism of the attachment which you require. Visualization is a very different process from seeing; seeing is physical, and is therefore related to the objective world, the "world without," but Visualization is a product of the imagination, and is therefore a product of the subjective mind, the "world within." It therefore possesses vitality; it will grow. The thing visualized will manifest itself in form. The mechanism is perfect; it was created by the Master Architect who "doeth all things well," but unfortunately sometimes the operator is inexperienced or inefficient, but practice and determination will overcome this defect.

16. If you require Love try to realize that the only way to get love is by giving it, that the more you give the more you will get, and the only way in which you can give it, is to fill yourself with it, until you become a magnet. The method was explained in another lesson.

17. He who has learned to bring the greatest spiritual truths into touch with the so-called lesser things of life has discovered the secret of the solution of his problem. One is always quickened, made more thoughtful, by his nearness of approach to great ideas, great events, great natural objects, and great men. Lincoln is said to have begotten in all who came near him the feeling awakened when one approaches a mountain, and this sense asserts itself most keenly when one comes to realize that he has laid hold upon things that are eternal, the power of Truth.

18. It is sometimes an inspiration to hear from someone who has actually put these principles to the test, someone who has demonstrated them in their own life. A letter from Frederick Andrews offers the following insight:

19. I was about thirteen years old when Dr. T. W. Marsee, since passed over, said to my mother: "There is no possible chance, Mrs. Andrews. I lost my little boy the same way, after doing everything for him that it was possible to do. I have made a special study of these cases, and I know there is no possible chance for him to get well."

20. She turned to him and said: "Doctor, what would you do if he were your boy?" and he answered, "I would fight, fight, as long as there is a breath of life to fight for."

21. That was the beginning of a long drawn-out battle, with many ups and downs, the doctors all agreeing that there was no chance for a cure, though they encouraged and cheered us the best they could.

22. But at last the victory came, and I have grown from a little, crooked, twisted, cripple, going about on my hands and knees, to a strong, straight, well formed man.

23. Now, I know you want the formula, and I will give it to you as briefly and quickly as I can.

24. I built up an affirmation for myself, taking the qualities I most needed, and affirming for myself over and over again, "I am whole, perfect, strong, powerful, loving, harmonious and happy." I kept up this affirmation, always the same, never varying, till I could wake up in the night and find myself repeating, "I am whole, perfect, strong, powerful, loving, harmonious and happy." It was the last thing on my lips at night and the first thing in the morning.

25. Not only did I affirm it for myself, but for others that I knew needed it. I want to emphasize this point. Whatever you desire for yourself, affirm it for others, and it will help you both. We reap what we sow. If we send out thoughts of love and health, they return to us like bread cast upon the waters; but if we send out thoughts of fear, worry, jealousy, anger, hate, etc., we will reap the results in our own lives.

26. It used to be said that man is completely built over every seven years, but some scientists now declare that we build ourselves over entirely every eleven months; so we are really only eleven months old. If we build the defects back into our bodies year after year, we have no one to blame but ourselves.

27. Man is the sum total of his own thoughts; so the question is, how are we going to entertain only the good thoughts and reject the evil ones? At first we can't keep the evil thoughts from coming, but we can keep from entertaining them. The only way to do this is to forget them — which means, get something for them. This is where the ready-made affirmation comes into play.

28. When a thought of anger, jealousy, fear or worry creeps in, just start your affirmation going. The way to fight darkness is with light — the way to fight cold is with heat — the way to overcome evils is with good. For myself, I never could find any help in denials. Affirm the good, and the bad will vanish. — Frederick Elias Andrews

29. If there is anything you require, it will be well for you to make use of this affirmation; it cannot be improved upon. Use it just as it is; take it into the silence with you, until it sinks into your subconsciousness, so that you can use it anywhere, in your car, in the office, at home; this is the advantage of spiritual methods; they are always available. Spirit is omnipresent, every ready; all that is required is a proper recognition of its omnipotence, and a willingness or desire to become the recipient of its beneficent effects.

30. If our predominant mental attitude is one of power, courage, kindliness and sympathy, we shall find that our environment will reject conditions in correspondence with these thoughts; if it is weak, critical, envious and destructive, we shall find our environment reflecting conditions corresponding to these thoughts.

31. Thoughts are causes and conditions are effects. Herein is the explanation of the origin of both good and evil. Thought is creative and will automatically correlate with its object. This is a Cosmological law (a universal law), the law of Attraction, the law of Cause and Effect; the recognition and application of this law will determine both beginning and end; it is the law by which in all ages and in all times the people were led to believe in the power of prayer. "As thy faith is, so be it unto thee," is simply another, shorter and a better way of stating it.

32. This week visualize a plant; take a flower, the one you most admire, bring it from the unseen into the seen, plant the tiny seed, water it, care for it, place it where it will get the direct rays of the morning sun, see the seed burst; it is now a living thing, something which is alive and beginning to search for the means of subsistence. See the roots penetrating the earth, watch them shoot out in all directions and remember that they are living cells dividing and subdividing, and that they will soon number millions, that each cell is intelligent, that it knows

what is wants and knows how to get it. See the stem shoot forward and upward, watch it burst through the surface of the earth, see it divide and form branches, see how perfect and symmetrical each branch is formed, see the leaves begin to form, and then the tiny stems, each one holding aloft a bud, and as you watch you see the bud begin to unfold and your favorite flower comes to view; and now if you will concentrate intently you will become conscious of a fragrance; it is the fragrance of the flower as the breeze gently sways the beautiful creation which you have visualized.

33. When you are enabled to make your vision clear and complete you will be enabled to enter into the spirit of a thing; it will become very real to you; you will be learning to concentrate and the process is the same, whether you are concentrating on health, a favorite flower, an ideal, a complicated business proposition or any other problem of life.

34. Every success has been accomplished by persistent concentration upon the object in view.

If you get a thorough understanding of the thought contained in Part Ten, you will have learned that nothing happens without a definite cause. You will be enabled to formulate your plans in accordance with exact knowledge. You will know how to control any situation by bringing adequate causes into play. When you win, as you will, you will know exactly why.

The ordinary man, who has no definite knowledge of cause and effect, is governed by his feelings or emotions.

He thinks chiefly to justify his action. If he fails as a businessman, he says that luck is against him. If he dislikes music, he says that music is an expensive luxury. If he is a poor office man, he says that he could succeed better at some outdoor work. If he lacks friends, he says his individuality is too fine to be appreciated.

He never thinks his problem through to the end. In short, he does not know that every effect is the result of a certain definite cause, but he seeks to console himself with explanations and excuses. He thinks only in self-defence.

On the contrary, the man who understands that there is no effect without an adequate cause thinks impersonally. He gets down to bedrock facts regardless of consequences. He is free to follow the trail of truth wherever it may lead. He sees the issue clear to the end, and he meets the requirements fully and fairly, and the result is that the world gives him all that it has to give, in friendship, honor, love and approval.

Part 10

1. Abundance is a natural law of the Universe. The evidence of this law is conclusive; we see it on every hand. Everywhere Nature is lavish, wasteful, extravagant. Nowhere is economy observed in any created thing. Profusion is manifested in everything. The millions and millions of trees and flowers and plants and animals and the vast scheme of reproduction where the process of creating and recreating is forever going on, all indicates the lavishness with which Nature has made provision for man. That there is an abundance for everyone is evident, but that many fail to participate in this abundance is also evident; they have not yet come into a realization of the Universality of all substance, and that mind is the active principle whereby we are related to the things we desire.

2. All wealth is the offspring of power; possessions are of value only as they confer power. Events are significant only as they affect power; all things represent certain forms and degrees of power.

3. Knowledge of cause and effect as shown by the laws governing electricity, chemical affinity and gravitation, enables man to plan courageously and execute fearlessly. These laws are called Natural Laws, because they govern in the physical world, but all power is not physical power; there is also mental power, and there is moral and spiritual power.

4. Spiritual power is superior because it exists on a higher plane. It has enabled man to discover the law by which these wonderful forces of Nature could be harnessed and made to do the work of hundreds and thousands of men. It has enabled man to discover laws whereby time and space have been annihilated and the law of gravitation to be overcome. The operation of this law is dependent upon spiritual contact, as Henry Drummond well says:

5. "In the physical world as we know it, there exists the organic and the inorganic. The inorganic of the mineral world is absolutely cut off from the plant or animal world; the passage is hermetically sealed. These barriers have never yet been crossed. No change of substance, no modification of environment, no chemistry, no electricity, no form of energy, no evolution of any kind can ever endow a single atom of the mineral world with the attribute of Life."

6. "Only by the bending down into this dead world of some living form can those dead atoms be gifted with the properties of vitality; without this contact with life they remain fixed in the inorganic sphere forever. Huxley says that the doctrine of Biogenesis (or life only from life) is victorious all along the line, and Tyndall is compelled to say: 'I affirm that no shred of trustworthy evidence exists to prove that life in our day has ever appeared independent of antecedent life.'

7. "Physical laws may explain the inorganic, Biology explains and accounts for the development of the organic, but of the point of contact Science is silent. A similar passage exists between the Natural world and the Spiritual world; this passage is hermetically sealed on the natural side. The door is closed; no man can open it, no organic change, no mental energy, no moral effort, no progress of any kind can enable any human being to enter the spiritual world."

8. But as the plant reaches down into the mineral world and touches it with the mystery of Life, so the Universal Mind reaches down into the human mind and endows it with new, strange, wonderful and even marvelous qualities. All men or women who have every accomplished anything in the world of industry, commerce or art have accomplished because of this process.

9. Thought is the connecting link between the Infinite and the finite, between the Universal and the individual. We have seen that there is an impassable barrier between the organic and the inorganic, and that the only way that matter can unfold is to be impregnated with life; as a seed reaches down into the mineral world and begins to unfold and reach out, the dead matter begins to live, a thousand invisible fingers begin to weave a suitable environment for the new arrival, and as the law of growth begins to take effect, we see the process continue until the Lily finally appears, and even "Solomon in all his glory was not arrayed like one of these."

10. Even so, a thought is dropped into the invisible substance of the Universal Mind, that substance from which all things are created, and as it takes root, the law of growth begins to take effect and we find that conditions and environment are but the objective form of our thought.

11. The law is that Thought is an active vital form of dynamic energy which has the power to correlate with its object and bring it out of the invisible substance from which all things are created into the visible or objective world. This is the law by which, and through which all things come into manifestation; it is the Master Key by which you are admitted into the Secret Place of the Most High and are "given dominion over all things." With an understanding of this law you may "decree a thing and it shall be established unto thee."

12. It could not be otherwise; if the soul of the Universe as we know it is the Universal Spirit, then the Universe is simply the condition which the Universal Spirit has made for itself. We are simply individualized spirit and are creating the conditions for our growth in exactly the same way.

13. This creative power depends upon our recognition of the potential power of spirit or mind and must not be confused with Evolution. Creation is the calling into existence of that which does not exist in the objective world. Evolution is simply the unfolding of potentialities involved in things which already exist.

14. In taking advantage of the wonderful possibilities opened up to us through the operation of this law, we must remember that we ourselves contribute nothing to its efficacy as the Great Teacher said: "It is not I that doeth the works, but the Father that dwelleth in me, He doeth the work." We must take exactly the same position; we can do nothing to assist in the manifestation, we simply comply with the law, and the All-originating Mind will bring about the result.

15. The great error of the present day is the idea that Man has to originate the intelligence whereby the Infinite can proceed to bring about a specific purpose or result. Nothing of this kind is necessary; the Universal Mind can be depended upon to find the ways and means for bringing about any necessary manifestation. We must, however, create the ideal, and this ideal should be perfect.

16. We know that the laws governing Electricity have been formulated in such a way that this invisible power can be controlled and used for our benefit and comfort in thousands of ways. We know that messages are carried around the world, that ponderous machinery does its bidding, that it now illuminates practically the whole world, but we know too that if we consciously or ignorantly violate its law by touching a live wire, when it is not properly insulated, the result will be unpleasant and possibly disastrous. A lack of understanding of the laws governing in the invisible world has the same result, and many are suffering the consequences all the time.

17. It has been explained that the law of causation depends upon polarity, a circuit must be formed; this circuit cannot be formed unless we operate in harmony with the law. How shall we operate in harmony with the law unless we know what the law is? How shall we know what the Law is? By study, by observation.

18. We see the law in operation everywhere; all nature testifies to the operation of the law by silently, constantly expressing itself in the law of growth. Where there is growth, there must be life; where there is life there must be harmony, so that everything that has life is constantly attracting to itself the conditions and the supply which is necessary for its most complete expression.

19. If your thought is in harmony with the creative Principle of Nature, it is in tune with the Infinite Mind, and it will form the circuit, it will not return to you void; but it is possible for you to think thoughts that are not in tune with the Infinite, and when there is no polarity, the circuit is not formed. What, then, is the result? What is the result when a dynamo is generating electricity, the circuit is cut off and there is no outlet? The dynamo stops.

20. It will be exactly the same with you, if you entertain thoughts which are not in accordance with the Infinite and cannot therefore be polarized; there is no circuit, you are isolated, the thoughts cling to you, harass you, worry you, and finally bring about disease and possibly death; the

physician may not diagnose the case exactly in this way, he may give it some fancy name which has been manufactured for the various ills which are the result of wrong thinking, but the cause is the same nevertheless.

21. Constructive thought must necessarily be creative, but creative thought must be harmonious, and this eliminates all destructive or competitive thought.

22. Wisdom, strength, courage and all harmonious conditions are the result of power and we have seen that all power is from within; likewise, every lack, limitation or adverse circumstance is the result of weakness, and weakness is simply absence of power; it comes from nowhere, it is nothing — the remedy then is simply to develop power, and this is accomplished in exactly the same manner that all power is developed, by exercise.

23. This exercise consists in making an application of your knowledge. Knowledge will not apply itself. You must make the application. Abundance will not come to you out of the sky, neither will it drop into your lap, but a conscious realization of the law of attraction and the intention to bring it into operation for a certain, definite and specific purpose, and the will to carry out this purpose will bring about the materialization of your desire by a natural law of transference. If you are in business, it will increase and develop along regular channels, possibly new or unusual channels of distribution will be opened and when the law becomes fully operative, you will find that the things you seek are seeking you.

24. This week select a blank space on the wall, or any other convenient spot, from where you usually sit, mentally draw a black horizontal line about six inches long, try to see the line as plainly as though it were painted on the wall; now mentally draw two vertical lines connecting with this horizontal line at either end; now draw another horizontal line connecting with the two vertical lines; now you have a square. Try to see the square perfectly; when you can do so draw a circle within the square; now place a point in the center of the circle; now draw the point toward you about 10 inches; now you have a cone on a square base; you will remember that your work was all in black; change it to white, to red, to yellow.

25. If you can do this, you are making excellent progress and will soon be enabled to concentrate on any problem you may have in mind.

PART 11

Your life is governed by law — by actual, immutable principles that never vary. Law is in operation at all times; in all places. Fixed laws underlie all human actions. For this reason, men who control giant industries are enabled to determine with absolute precision just what percentage of every hundred thousand people will respond to any given set of conditions.

It is well, however, to remember that while every effect is the result of a cause, the effect in turn becomes a cause, which creates other effects, which in turn create still other causes; so that when you put the law of attraction into operation you must remember that you are starting a train of causation for good or otherwise which may have endless possibilities.

We frequently hear it said, "A very distressing situation came into my life, which could not have been the result of my thought, as I certainly never entertained any thought which could have such a result." We fail to remember that like attracts like in the mental world, and that the thought which we entertain brings to us certain friendships, companionships of a particular kind, and these in turn bring about conditions and environment, which in turn are responsible for the conditions of which we complain.

1. Inductive reasoning is the process of the objective mind by which we compare a number of separate instances with one another until we see the common factor that gives rise to them all.

2. Induction proceeds by comparison of facts; it is this method of studying nature which has resulted in the discovery of a reign of law which has marked an epoch in human progress.

3. It is the dividing line between superstition and intelligence; it has eliminated the elements of uncertainty and caprice from men's lives and substituted law, reason, and certitude.

4. It is the "Watchman at the Gate" mentioned in a former lesson.

5. When, by virtue of this principle, the world to which the senses were accustomed had been revolutionized; when the sun had been arrested in his course, the apparently flat earth had been shaped into a ball and set whirling around him; when the inert matter had been resolved into active elements, and the universe presented itself wherever we directed the telescope and microscope, full of force, motion and life; we are constrained to ask by what possible means the delicate forms of organization in the midst of it are kept in order and repair.

6. Like poles and like forces repel themselves or remain impenetrable to each other, and this cause seems in general sufficient to assign a proper

place and distance to stars, men and forces. As men of different virtues enter into partnership, so do opposite poles attract each other, elements that have no property in common like acids and gases cling to each other in preference and a general exchange is kept up between the surplus and the demand.

7. As the eye seeks and receives satisfaction from colors complementary to those which are given, so does need, want and desire, in the largest sense, induce, guide and determine action.

8. It is our privilege to become conscious of the principle and act in accordance with it. Cuvier sees a tooth belonging to an extinct race of animals. This tooth wants a body for the performance of its function, and it defines the peculiar body it stands in need of with such precision that Cuvier is able to reconstruct the frame of this animal.

9. Perturbations are observed in the motion of Uranus. Leverrier needs another star at a certain place to keep the solar system in order, and Neptune appears in the place and hour appointed.

10. The instinctive wants of the animal and the intellectual wants of Cuvier, the wants of nature and of the mind of Leverrier were alike, and thus the results; here the thoughts of an existence, there an existence. A well-defined lawful want, therefore, furnishes the reason for the more complex operations of nature.

11. Having recorded correctly the answers furnished by nature and stretched our senses with the growing science over her surface; having joined hands with the levers that move the earth; we become conscious of such a close, varied and deep contact with the world without, that our wants and purposes become no less identified with the harmonious operations of this vast organization, than the life, liberty, and happiness of the citizen is identified with the existence of his government.

12. As the interests of the individual are protected by the arms of the country, added to his own; and his needs may depend upon certain supply in the degree that they are felt more universally and steadily; in the same manner does conscious citizenship in the Republic of nature secure us from the annoyances of subordinate agents by alliance with superior powers; and by appeal to the fundamental laws of resistance or inducement offered to mechanical or chemical agents, distribute the labor to be performed between them and man to the best advantage of the inventor.

13. If Plato could have witnessed the pictures executed by the sun with the assistance of the photographer, or a hundred similar illustrations of what man does by induction, he would perhaps have been reminded of the intellectual midwifery of his master and, in his own mind might have arisen the vision of a land where all manual, mechanical labor and repetition is assigned to the power of nature, where our wants are satisfied by purely mental operations set in motion by the will, and where the supply is created by the demand.

14. However distant that land may appear, induction has taught men to make strides toward it and has surrounded him with benefits which are, at the same time, rewards for past fidelity and incentives for more assiduous devotion.

15. It is also an aid in concentrating and strengthening our faculties for the remaining part, giving unerring solution for individual as well as universal problems, by the mere operations of mind in the purest form.

16. Here we find a method, the spirit of which is, to believe that what is sought has been accomplished, in order to accomplish it: a method, bequeathed upon us by the same Plato who, outside of this sphere, could never find how the ideas became realities.

17. This conception is also elaborated by Swedenborg in his doctrine of correspondences; and a still greater teacher has said, "What things soever ye desire, when ye pray, believe that ye receive them, and ye shall have them." (Mark 11:24) The difference of the tenses in this passage is remarkable.

18. We are first to believe that our desire has already been fulfilled, its accomplishment will then follow. This is a concise direction for making use of the creative power of thought by impressing on the Universal subjective mind, the particular thing which we desire as an already existing fact.

19. We are thus thinking on the plane of the absolute and eliminating all consideration of conditions or limitation and are planting a seed which, if left undisturbed, will finally germinate into external fruition.

20. To review: Inductive reasoning is the process of the objective mind, by which we compare a number of separate instances with one another until we see the common factor that gives rise to them all. We see people in every civilized country on the globe, securing results by some process which they do not seem to understand themselves, and to which they usually attach more or less mystery. Our reason is given to us for the purpose of ascertaining the law by which these results are accomplished.

21. The operation of this thought process is seen in those fortunate natures that possess everything that others must acquire by toil, who never have a struggle with conscience because they always act correctly, and can never conduct themselves otherwise than with tact, learn everything easily, complete everything they begin with a happy knack, live in eternal harmony with themselves, without ever reflecting much what they do, or ever experiencing difficulty or toil.

22. The fruit of this thought is, as it were, a gift of the gods, but a gift which few as yet realize, appreciate, or understand. The recognition of the marvelous power which is possessed by the mind under proper conditions and the fact that this power can be utilized, directed, and made available for the solution of every human problem is of transcendental importance.

23. All truth is the same, whether stated in modern scientific terms or in the language of apostolic times. There are timid souls who fail to realize

that the very completeness of truth requires various statements — that no one human formula will show every side of it.

24. Changing, emphasis, new language, novel interpretations, unfamiliar perspectives, are not, as some suppose, signs of departure from truth but on the contrary, they are evidence that the truth is being apprehended in new relations to human needs, and is becoming more generally understood.

25. The truth must be told to each generation and to every people in new and different terms, so that when the Great Teacher said — "Believe that ye receive and ye shall receive" or, when Paul said — "Faith is the substance of things hoped for, the evidence of things not seen" or, when modern science says — "The law of attraction is the law by which thought correlates with its object," each statement when subjected to analysis, is found to contain exactly the same truth. The only difference being in the form of presentation.

26. We are standing on the threshold of a new era. The time has arrived when man has learned the secrets of mastery and the way is being prepared for a new social order, more wonderful than anything every heretofore dreamed of. The conflict of modern science with theology, the study of comparative religions, the tremendous power of new social movements, all of these are but clearing the way for the new order. They may have destroyed traditional forms which have become antiquated and impotent, but nothing of value has been lost.

27. A new faith has been born, a faith which demands a new form of expression, and this faith is taking form in a deep consciousness of power which is being manifested, in the present spiritual activity found on every hand.

28. The spirit which sleeps in the mineral, breathes in the vegetable, moves in the animal and reaches its highest development in man is the Universal Mind, and it behooves us to span the gulf between being and doing, theory and practice, by demonstrating our understanding of the dominion which we have been given.

29. By far the greatest discovery of all the centuries is the power of thought. The importance of this discovery has been a little slow in reaching the general consciousness, but it has arrived, and already in every field of research the importance of this greatest of all great discoveries is being demonstrated.

30. You ask in what does the creative power of thought consist? It consists in creating ideas, and these in turn objectify themselves by appropriating, inventing, observing, discerning, discovering, analyzing, ruling, governing, combining, and applying matter and force. It can do this because it is an intelligent creative power.

31. Thought reaches its loftiest activity when plunged into its own mysterious depth; when it breaks through the narrow compass of self and

passes from truth to truth to the region of eternal light, where all which is, was or ever will be, melt into one grand harmony.

32. From this process of self contemplation comes inspiration which is creative intelligence, and which is undeniably superior to every element, force or law of nature, because it can understand, modify, govern and apply them to its own ends and purposes and therefore possess them.

33. Wisdom begins with the dawn of reason, and reason is but an understanding of the knowledge and principles whereby we may know the true meaning of things. Wisdom, then, is illuminated reason, and this wisdom leads to humility, for humility is a large part of Wisdom.

34. We all know many who have achieved the seemingly impossible, who have realized life-long dreams, who have changed everything including themselves. We have sometimes marveled at the demonstration of an apparently irresistible power, which seemed to be ever available just when it was most needed, but it is all clear now. All that is required is an understanding of certain definite fundamental principles and their proper application.

35. For your exercise this week, concentrate on the quotation taken from the Bible, "Whatsoever things ye desire, when ye pray, believe that ye receive them and ye shall have them"; notice that there is no limitation, "Whatsoever things" is very definite and implies that the only limitation which is placed upon us in our ability to think, to be equal to the occasion, to rise to the emergency, to remember that Faith is not a shadow, but a substance, "the substance of things hoped for, the evidence of things not seen."

Death is but the natural process whereby all material forms are thrown into the crucible for reproduction in fresh diversity.

PART 12

In the fourth paragraph you will find the following statement: "You must first have the knowledge of your power; second, the courage to dare; third, the faith to do." If you concentrate upon the thoughts given, if you give them your entire attention, you will find a world of meaning in each sentence, and will attract to yourself other thoughts in harmony with them, and you will soon grasp the full significance of the vital knowledge upon which you are concentrating.

Knowledge does not apply itself; we as individuals must make the application, and the application consists in fertilizing the thought with a living purpose.

The time and thought which most persons waste in aimless effort would accomplish wonders if properly directed with some special object in view. In order to do this, it is necessary to center your mental force upon a specific thought and hold it there, to the exclusion of all other thoughts. If you have ever looked through the viewfinder of a camera, you found that when the object was not in focus, the impression was indistinct and possibly blurred, but when the proper focus was obtained the picture was clear and distinct. This illustrates the power of concentration. Unless you can concentrate upon the object which you have in view, you will have but a hazy, indifferent, vague, indistinct and blurred outline of your ideal and the results will be in accordance with your mental picture.

1. There is no purpose in life that cannot be best accomplished through a scientific understanding of the creative power of thought.

2. This power to think is common to all. Man is, because he thinks. Man's power to think is infinite, consequently his creative power is unlimited.

3. We know that thought is building for us the thing we think of and actually bringing it nearer, yet we find it difficult to banish fear, anxiety or discouragement, all of which are powerful thought forces, and which continually send the things we desire further away, so that it is often one step forward and two steps backward.

4. The only way to keep from going backward is to keep going forward. Eternal vigilance is the price of success. There are three steps, and each one is absolutely essential. You must first have the knowledge of your power; second, the courage to dare; third, the faith to do.

5. With this as a basis you can construct an ideal business, an ideal home, ideal friends, and an ideal environment. You are not restricted as to material or cost. Thought is omnipotent and has the power to draw on

the Infinite bank of primary substance for all that it requires. Infinite resources are therefore at your command.

6. But your ideal must be sharp, clear-cut, definite; to have one ideal today, another tomorrow, and a third next week, means to scatter your forces and accomplish nothing; your result will be a meaningless and chaotic combination of wasted material.

7. Unfortunately this is the result which many are securing, and the cause is self evident. If a sculptor started out with a piece of marble and a chisel and changed his ideal every fifteen minutes, what result could he expect? And why should you expect any different result in molding the greatest and most plastic of all substances, the only real substance?

8. The result of this indecision and negative thought is often found in the loss of material wealth. Supposed independence which required many years of toil and effort suddenly disappears. It is often found then that money and property are not independence at all. On the contrary, the only independence is found to be a practical working knowledge of the creative power of thought.

9. This practical working method cannot come to you until you learn that the only real power which you can have is the power to adjust yourself to Divine and unchangeable principles. You cannot change the Infinite, but you can come into an understanding of Natural laws. The reward of this understanding is a conscious realization of your ability to adjust your thought faculties with the Universal Thought which is Omnipresent. Your ability to cooperate with this Omnipotence will indicate the degree of success with which you meet.

10. The power of thought has many counterfeits which are more or less fascinating, but the results are harmful instead of helpful.

11. Of course, worry, fear, and all negative thoughts produce a crop after their kind; those who harbor thoughts of this kind must inevitably reap what they have sown.

12. Again, there are the Phenomena seekers who gormandize on the so-called proofs and demonstration obtained at materializing séances. They throw open their mental doors and soak themselves in the most poisonous currents which can be found in the psychic world. They do not seem to understand that it is the ability to become negative, receptive and passive, and thus drain themselves of all their vital force, which enables them to bring about these vibratory thought forms.

13. There are also the Hindu worshippers, who see in the materializing phenomena which are performed by the so-called adepts, a source of power, forgetting, or never seeming to realize that as soon as the will is withdrawn the forms wither, and the vibratory forces of which they are composed vanish.

14. Telepathy, or thought transference, has received considerable attention, but as it requires a negative mental state on the part of the receiver, the practice is harmful. A thought may be sent with the

intention of hearing or seeing, but it will bring the penalty attached to the inversion of the principle involved.

15. In many instances, hypnotism is positively dangerous to the subject as well as the operator. No one familiar with the laws governing in the mental world would think of attempting to dominate the will of another, for by so doing, he will gradually (but surely) divest himself of his own power.

16. All of these perversions have their temporary satisfaction and for some a keen fascination, but there is an infinitely greater fascination in a true understanding of the world of power within, a power which increases with use; is permanent instead of fleeing; which not only is potent as a remedial agency to bring about the remedy for past error or results of wrong thinking, but is a prophylactic agency protecting us from all manner and form of danger, and finally is an actual creative force with which we can build new conditions and new environment.

17. The law is that thought will correlate with its object and bring forth in the material world the correspondence of the thing thought or produced in the mental world. We then discern the absolute necessity of seeing that every thought has the inherent germ of truth in order that the law of growth will bring into manifestation good, for good alone can confer any permanent power.

18. The principle which gives the thought the dynamic power to correlate with its object, and therefore to master every adverse human experience, is the law of attraction, which is another name for love. This is an eternal and fundamental principle, inherent in all things, in every system of Philosophy, in every Religion, and in every Science. There is no getting away from the law of love. It is feeling that imparts vitality to thought. Feeling is desire, and desire is love. Thought impregnated with love becomes invincible.

19. We find this truth emphasized wherever the power of thought is understood, The Universal Mind is not only Intelligence, but it is substance, and this substance is the attractive force which brings electrons together by the law of attraction so that they form atoms; the atoms in turn are brought together by the same law and form molecules; molecules take objective forms; and so we find that the law of love is the creative force behind every manifestation, not only of atoms, but of worlds, of the Universe, of everything of which the imagination can form any conception.

20. It is the operation of this marvelous law of attraction which has caused men in all ages and all times to believe that there must be some personal being who responded to their petitions and desires, and manipulated events in order to comply with their requirements.

21. It is the combination of Thought and Love which forms the irresistible force, called the law of attraction. All natural laws are irresistible, the law of Gravitation, or Electricity, or any other law

operates with mathematical exactitude. There is no variation; it is only the channel of distribution which may be imperfect. If a bridge falls, we do not attribute the collapse to any variation of the law of gravitation. If a light fails us, we do not conclude that the laws governing electricity cannot be depended upon, and if the law of attraction seems to be imperfectly demonstrated by an inexperienced or uninformed person, we are not to conclude that the greatest and most infallible law upon which the entire system of creation depends has been suspended. We should rather conclude that a little more understanding of the law is required, for the same reason that a correct solution of a difficult problem in Mathematics is not always readily and easily obtained.

22. Things are created in the mental or spiritual world be fore they appear in the outward act or event. by the simple process of governing our thought forces today, we help create the events which will come into our lives in the future, perhaps even tomorrow. Educated desire is the most potent means of bringing into action the law of attraction.

23. Man is so constituted that he must first create the tools, or implements by which he gains the power to think. The mind cannot comprehend an entirely new idea until a corresponding vibratory brain cell has been prepared to receive it. This explains why it is so difficult for us to receive or appreciate an entirely new idea; we have no brain cell capable of receiving it; we are therefore incredulous; we do not believe it.

24. If, therefore, you have not been familiar with the Omnipotence of the law of attraction, and the scientific method by which it can be put into operation, or if you have not been familiar with the unlimited possibilities which it opens to those who are enabled to take advantage of the resources it offers, begin now and create the necessary brain cells which will enable you to comprehend the unlimited powers which may be yours by cooperating with Natural Law. This is done by concentration or attention.

25. The intention governs the attention. Power comes through repose. It is by concentration that deep thoughts, wise speech, and all forces of high potentiality are accomplished.

26. It is in the Silence that you get into touch with the Omnipotent power of the subconscious mind from which all power is evolved.

27. He who desires wisdom, power, or permanent success of any kind will find it only within; it is an unfoldment. The unthinking may conclude that the silence is very simple and easily attained, but it should be remembered that only in absolute silence may one come into contact with Divinity itself; may learn of the unchangeable law and open for himself the channels by which persistent practice and concentration lead to perfection.

28. This week go to the same room, take the same chair, the same position as previously; be sure to relax, let go, both mentally and physically; always do this; never try to do any mental work under

pressure; see that there are no tense muscles or nerves, that you are entirely comfortable. Now realize your unity with omnipotence; get into touch with this power, come into a deep and vital understanding, appreciation, and realization of the fact that your ability to think is your ability to act upon the Universal Mind, and bring it into manifestation, realize that it will meet any and every requirement; that you have exactly the same potential ability which any individual ever did have or ever will have, because each is but an expression or manifestation of the One, all are parts of the whole, there is no difference in kind or quality, the only difference being one of degree.

PART 13

Physical science is responsible for the marvelous age of invention in which we are now living, but spiritual science is now setting out on a career whose possibilities no one can foretell.

Spiritual science has previously been the football of the uneducated, the superstitious, the mystical, but men are now interested in definite methods and demonstrated facts only.

We have come to know that thinking is a spiritual process, that vision and imagination preceded action and event, that the day of the dreamer has come.

The following lines by Mr. Herbert Kaufman are interesting in this connection.

"They are the architects of greatness, their vision lies within their souls, they peer beyond the veils and mists of doubt and pierce the walls of unborn Time. The belted wheel, the trail of steel, the churning screw, are shuttles in the loom on which they weave their magic tapestries. Makers of Empire, they have fought for bigger things than crowns and higher seats than thrones. Your homes are set upon the land a dreamer found. The pictures on its walls are visions from a dreamer's soul. They are the chose few — the blazers of the way. Walls crumble and Empires fall, the tidal wave sweeps from the sea and tears a fortress from its rocks. The rotting nations drop off from Time's bough, and only things the dreamer's make live on."

Part Thirteen which follows tells why the dreams of the dreamer come true. It explains the law of causation by which dreamers, inventors, authors, financiers, bring about the realization of their desires. It explains the law by which the thing pictured upon our mind eventually becomes our own.

1. It has been the tendency, and, as might be proved, a necessity for science to seek the explanation of everyday facts by a generalization of those others which are less frequent and form the exception. Thus does the eruption of the volcano manifest the heat which is continually at work in the interior of the earth and to which the latter owes much of her configuration.

2. Thus does the lightning reveal a subtle power constantly busy to produce changes in the inorganic world, and, as dead languages now seldom heard were once ruling among the nations, so does a giant tooth in Siberia, or a fossil in the depth of the earth, not only bear record of the evolution of past ages, but thereby explains to us the origin of the hills and valleys which we inhabit today.

3. In this way a generalization of facts which are rare, strange, or form the exception, has been the magnetic needle guiding to all the discoveries of inductive science.

4. This method is founded upon reason and experience and thereby destroyed superstition, precedent and conventionality.

5. It is almost three-hundred years since Lord Bacon recommended this method of study, to which the civilized nations owe the greater part of their prosperity and the more valuable part of their knowledge; purging the mind from narrow prejudices, denominated theories, more effectually than by the keenest irony; calling the attention of men from heaven to earth more successfully by surprising experiments than by the most forcible demonstration of their ignorance; educating the inventive faculties more powerfully by the near prospect of useful discoveries thrown open to all, than by talk of bringing to light the innate laws of our mind.

6. The method of Bacon has seized the spirit and aim of the great philosophers of Greece and carried them into effect by the new means of observation which another age offered; thus gradually revealing a wondrous field of knowledge in the infinite space of astronomy, in the microscopic egg of embryology, and the dim age of geology; disclosing an order of the pulse which the logic of Aristotle could never have unveiled, and analyzing into formerly unknown elements the material combinations which no dialectic of the scholastics could force apart.

7. It has lengthened life; it has mitigated pain; it has extinguished diseases; it has increased the fertility of the soil; it has given new securities to the mariner; it has spanned great rivers with bridges of form unknown to our fathers; it has guided the thunderbolt from heaven to earth; it has lighted up night with the splendor of day; it has extended the range of human vision; it has multiplied the power of the human muscles; it has accelerated motion; it has annihilated distance; it has facilitated intercourse, correspondence, all friendly offices, all dispatch of business; it has enabled men to descend into the depths of the sea, to soar into the air, to penetrate securely into the noxious recesses of the earth.

8. This then is the true nature and scope of induction. But the greater the success which men have achieved in the inductive science, the more does the whole tenor of their teachings and example impress us with the necessity of observing carefully, patiently, accurately, with all the instruments and resources at our command the individual facts before venturing upon a statement of general laws.

9. To ascertain the bearing of the spark drawn from the electric machine under every variety of circumstances, that we thus may be emboldened with Franklin to address, in the form of a kite, the question to the cloud about the nature of the lightning. To assure ourselves of the manner in which bodies fall with the exactness of a Galileo, that with

Newton we may dare to ask the moon about the force that fastens it to the earth.

10. In short, by the value we set upon truth, by our hope in a steady and universal progress, not to permit a tyrannical prejudice to neglect or mutilate unwelcome facts, but to rear the superstructure of science upon the broad and unchangeable basis, of full attention paid to the most isolated as well as the most frequent phenomena.

11. An ever-increasing material may be collected by observation, but the accumulated facts are of very different value for the explanation of nature, and as we esteem most highly those useful qualities of men which are of the rarest occurrence, so does natural philosophy sift the facts and attach a pre-eminent importance to that striking class which cannot be accounted for by the usual and daily observation of life.

12. If then, we find that certain persons seem to possess unusual power, what are we to conclude? First, we may say, it is not so, which is simply an acknowledgment of our lack of information because every honest investigator admits that there are many strange and previously unaccountable phenomena constantly taking place. Those, however, who become acquainted with the creative power of thought, will no longer consider them unaccountable.

13. Second, we may say that they are the result of supernatural interference, but a scientific understanding of Natural Laws will convince us that there is nothing supernatural. Every phenomenon is the result of an accurate definite cause, and the cause is an immutable law or principle, which operates with invariable precision, whether the law is put into operation consciously or unconsciously.

14. Third, we may say that we are on "forbidden ground," that there are some things which we should not know. This objection was used against every advance in human knowledge. Every individual who ever advanced a new idea, whether a Columbus, a Darwin, a Galileo, a Fulton or an Emerson, was subjected to ridicule or persecution; so that this objection should receive no serious consideration; but, on the contrary, we should carefully consider every fact which is brought to our attention; by doing this we will more readily ascertain the law upon which it is based.

15. It will be found that the creative power of thought will explain every possible condition or experience, whether physical, mental or spiritual.

16. Thought will bring about conditions in correspondence with the predominant mental attitude. Therefore, if we fear disaster, as fear is a powerful form of thought, disaster will be the certain result of our thinking. It is this form of thought which frequently sweeps away the result of many years of toil and effort.

17. If we think of some form of material wealth we may secure it. By concentrated thought the required conditions will be brought about, and the proper effort put forth, which will result in bringing about the circumstances necessary to realize our desires; but we often find that

when we secure the things we thought we wanted, they do not have the effect we expected. That is, the satisfaction is only temporary, or possibly is the reverse of what we expected.

18. What, then, is the proper method of procedure? What are we to think in order to secure what we really desire? What you and I desire, what we all desire, what every one is seeking, is Happiness and Harmony. If we can be truly happy we shall have everything the world can give. If we are happy ourselves we can make others happy.

19. But we cannot be happy unless we have, health, strength, congenial friends, pleasant environment, sufficient supply, not only to take care of our necessities but to provide for those comforts and luxuries to which we are entitled.

20. The old orthodox way of thinking was to be "a worm," to be satisfied with our portion whatever it is; but the modern idea is to know that we are entitled to the best of everything, that the "Father and I are one" and that the "Father" is the Universal Mind, the Creator, the Original Substance from which all things proceed.

21. Now admitting that this is all true in theory, and it has been taught for two thousand years, and is the essence of every system of Philosophy or Religion, how are we to make it practical in our lives? How are we to get the actual, tangible results here and now?

22. In the first place, we must put our knowledge into practice. Nothing can be accomplished in any other way. The athlete may read books and lessons on physical training all his life, but unless he begins to give out strength by actual work he will never receive any strength; he will eventually get exactly what he gives; but he will have to give it first. It is exactly the same with us; we will get exactly what we give, but we shall have to give it first. It will then return to us many fold, and the giving is simply a mental process, because thoughts are causes and conditions are effects; therefore in giving thoughts of courage, inspiration, health or help of any kind we are setting causes in motion which will bring about their effect.

23. Thought is a spiritual activity and is therefore creative, but make no mistake, thought will create nothing unless it is consciously, systematically, and constructively directed; and herein is the difference between idle thinking, which is simply a dissipation of effort, and constructive thinking, which means practically unlimited achievement.

24. We have found that everything we get comes to us by the Law of Attraction. A happy thought cannot exist in an unhappy consciousness; therefore the consciousness must change, and, as the consciousness changes, all conditions necessary to meet the changed consciousness must gradually change, in order to meet the requirements of the new situation.

25. In creating a Mental Image or an Ideal, we are projecting a thought into the Universal Substance from which all things are created. This Universal Substance is Omnipresent, Omnipotent and Omniscient. Are

we to inform the Omniscient as to the proper channel to be used to materialize our demand? Can the finite advise the Infinite? This is the cause of failure; of every failure. We recognize the Omnipresence of the Universal Substance, but we fail to appreciate the fact that this substance is not only Omnipresent, but is Omnipotent and Omniscient, and consequently will set causes in motion concerning which we may be entirely ignorant.

26. We can best conserve our interests by recognizing the Infinite Power and Infinite Wisdom of the Universal Mind, and in this way become a channel whereby the Infinite can bring about the realization of our desire. This means that recognition brings about realization, therefore for your exercise this week make use of the principle, recognize the fact that you are a part of the whole, and that a part must be the same in kind and quality as the whole; the only difference there can possibly by, is in degree.

27. When this tremendous fact begins to permeate your consciousness, when you really come into a realization of the fact that you (not your body, but the Ego), the "I," the spirit which thinks is an integral part of the great whole, that it is the same in substance, in quality, in kind, that the Creator could create nothing different from Himself, you will also be able to say, "The Father and I are one" and you will come into an understanding of the beauty, the grandeur, the transcendental opportunities which have been placed at your disposal.

PART 14

You have found from your study thus far that thought is a spiritual activity and is therefore endowed with creative power. This does not mean that some thought is creative, but that all thought is creative. This same principle can be brought into operation in a negative way, through the process of denial.

The conscious and subconscious are but two phases of action in connection with one mind. The relation of the subconscious to the conscious is quite analogous to that existing between a weather vane and the atmosphere.

Just as the least pressure of the atmosphere causes an action on the part of the weather vane, so does the least thought entertained by the conscious mind produce within your subconscious mind action in exact proportion to the depth of feeling characterizing the thought and the intensity with which the thought is indulged.

It follows that if you deny unsatisfactory conditions, you are withdrawing the creative power of your thought from these conditions. You are cutting them away at the root. You are sapping their vitality.

Remember that the law of growth necessarily governs every manifestation in the objective, so that a denial of unsatisfactory conditions will not bring about instant change. A plant will remain visible for some time after its roots have been cut, but it will gradually fade away and eventually disappear, so the withdrawal of your thought from the contemplation of unsatisfactory conditions will gradually, but surely, terminate these conditions.

You will see that this is an exactly opposite course from the one which we would naturally be inclined to adopt.

It will therefore have an exactly opposite effect to the one usually secured. Most persons concentrate intently upon unsatisfactory conditions, thereby giving the condition that measure of energy and vitality which is necessary in order to supply a vigorous growth.

1. The Universal Energy in which all motion, light, heat, and color have their origin, does not partake of the limitation of the many effects of which it is the cause, but it is supreme over them all. This Universal Substance is the source of all Power, Wisdom and Intelligence.

2. To recognize this Intelligence is to acquaint yourself with the knowing quality of Mind and through it to move upon the Universal Substance, and bring it into harmonious relations in your affairs.

3. This is something that the most learned physical science teacher has not attempted — a field of discovery upon which he has not yet launched;

in fact, but few of the materialistic schools have ever caught the first ray of this light. It does not seem to have dawned upon them that wisdom is just as much present everywhere as are force and substance.

4. Some will say, if these principles are true, why are we not demonstrating them? As the fundamental principle is obviously correct, why do we not get proper results? We do. We get results in exact accordance with our understanding of the law and our ability to make the proper application. We secured no results from the laws governing electricity until someone formulated the law and showed us how to apply it.

5. This puts us in an entirely new relation to our environment, opening up possibilities previously undreamed of, and this by an orderly sequence of law which is naturally involved in our new mental attitude.

6. Mind is creative and the principle upon which this law is based is sound and legitimate and is inherent in the nature of things; but this creative power does not originate in the individual, but in the Universal, which is the source and fountain of all energy and substance, the individual is simply the channel for the distribution of this energy. The individual is the means by which the Universal produces the various combinations which result in the formation of phenomena.

7. We know that scientists have resolved matter into an immense number of molecules; these molecules have been resolved into atoms, and the atoms into electrons. The discovery of electrons in high vacuum glass tubes containing fused terminals of hard metal, indicates conclusively that these electrons fill all space; that they exist everywhere, that they are omnipresent. They fill all material bodies and occupy the whole of what we call empty space. This, then, is the Universal Substance from which all things proceed.

8. Electrons would forever remain electrons unless directed where to go to be assembled into atoms and molecules, and this director is Mind. A number of electrons revolving around a center of force constitutes an atom; atoms unite in absolutely regular mathematical ratios and form molecules, and these unite with each other to form a multitude of compounds which unite to build the Universe.

9. The lightest known atom is hydrogen and this is 1,700 times heavier than an electron. An atom of mercury is 300,000 times heavier than an electron. Electrons are pure negative electricity, and as they have the same potential velocity as all other cosmic energy, such as heat, light, electricity and thought, neither time nor space require consideration. The manner in which the velocity of light was ascertained is interesting.

10. The velocity of light was obtained by the Danish astronomer Roemer in 1676, by observing the eclipses of Jupiter's moons. When the earth was nearest to Jupiter, the eclipse appeared about eight and one-half minutes too soon for the calculations, and when the earth was most remote from Jupiter, they were about eight and one-half minutes too late. Roemer

concluded the reason to be that it required 17 minutes for light from the planet to traverse the diameter of the earth's orbit, which measured the difference of the distances of the earth from Jupiter. This calculation has since been verified, and proves that light travels about 186,000 miles a second.

11. Electrons manifest in the body as cells, and possess mind and intelligence sufficient for them to perform their functions in the human physical anatomy. Every part of the body is composed of cells, some of which operate independently; others in communities. Some are busy building tissue, while others are engaged in forming the various secretions necessary for the body. Some act as carriers of material; others are the surgeons whose work it is to repair damage; others are scavengers, carrying off waste; others are constantly ready to repel invaders or other undesirable intruders of the germ family.

12. All these cells are moving for a common purpose and each one is not only a living organism, but has sufficient intelligence to enable it to perform its necessary duties. It is also endowed with sufficient intelligence to conserve the energies and perpetuate its own life. It must, therefore, secure sufficient nourishment and it has been found that it exercises choice in the selection of such nourishment.

13. Each cell is born, reproduces itself, dies and is absorbed. The maintenance of health and life itself depends upon the constant regeneration of these cells.

14. It is therefore apparent that there is mind in every atom of the body; this mind is negative mind, and the power of the individual to think makes him positive, so that he can control this negative mind. This is the scientific explanation for metaphysical healing, and will enable anyone to understand the principle upon which this remarkable phenomenon rests.

15. This negative mind, which is contained in every cell of the body, has been called the subconscious mind, because it acts without our conscious knowledge. We have found that this subconscious mind is responsive to the will of the conscious mind.

16. All things have their origin in mind, and appearances are the result of thought. So that we see that things in themselves have no origin, permanency, or reality. Since they are produced by thought, they can be erased by thought.

17. In mental, as in natural science, experiments are being made and each discovery lifts man one step higher toward his possible goal. We find that every man is the reflection of the thought he has entertained during his lifetime. This is stamped on his face, his form, his character, his environment.

18. Back of every effect there is a cause, and if we follow the trail to its starting point, we shall find the creative principle out of which it grew. Proofs of this are now so complete that this truth is generally accepted.

19. The objective world is controlled by an unseen and, heretofore, unexplainable power. We have, heretofore, personalized this power and called it God. We have now, however, learned to look upon it as the permeating essence or Principle of all that exists — the Infinite or Universal Mind.

20. The Universal Mind, being infinite and omnipotent, has unlimited resources at its command, and when we remember that it is also omnipresent, we cannot escape the conclusion that we must be an expression or manifestation of that Mind.

21. A recognition and understanding of the resources of the subconscious mind will indicate that the only difference between the subconscious and the Universal is one of degree. They differ only as a drop of water differs from the ocean. They are the same in kind and quality, the difference is one of degree only.

22. Do you, can you, appreciate the value of this all-important fact; do you realize that a recognition of this tremendous fact places you in touch with Omnipotence? The subconscious mind being the connecting link between the Universal Mind and the conscious mind, is it not evident that the conscious mind can consciously suggest thoughts which the subconscious mind will put into action, and as the subconscious is one with the Universal, is it not evident that no limit can be placed upon its activities?

23. A scientific understanding of this principle will explain the wonderful results which are secured through the power of prayer. The results which are secured in this way are not brought about by any special dispensations of providence, but on the contrary, they are the result of the operation of a perfectly natural law. There is, therefore, nothing either religious or mysterious about it.

24. Yet there are many who are not ready to enter into the discipline necessary to think correctly, even though it is evident that wrong thinking has brought failure.

25. Thought is the only reality; conditions are but the outward manifestations; as the thought changes, all outward or material conditions must change in order to be in harmony with their creator, which is thought.

26. But the thought must be clear cut, steady, fixed, definite, unchangeable; you cannot take one step forward and two steps backward, neither can you spend twenty or thirty years of your life building up negative conditions as the result of negative thoughts, and then expect to see them all melt away as the result of fifteen or twenty minutes of right thinking.

27. If you enter into the discipline necessary to bring about a radical change in your life, you must do so deliberately, after giving the matter careful thought and full consideration, and then you must allow nothing to interfere with your decision.

28. This discipline, this change of thought, this mental attitude will not only bring you the material things which are necessary for your highest and best welfare, but will bring health and harmonious conditions generally.

29. If you wish harmonious conditions in your life, you must develop an harmonious mental attitude.

30. Your world without will be a reflection of your world within.

31. For your exercise this week, concentrate on Harmony, and when I say concentrate, I mean all that the word implies; concentrate so deeply, so earnestly, that you will be conscious of nothing but harmony. Remember, we learn by doing. Reading these lessons will get you nowhere. It is in the practical application that the value consists.

PART 15

Experiments with parasites found on plants indicate that even the lowest order of life is enabled to take advantage of natural law. This experiment was made by Jacques Loch, M.D., Ph. D., a member of the Rockefeller Institute.

"In order to obtain the material, potted rose bushes are brought into a room and placed in front of a closed window. If the plants are allowed to dry out, the aphids (parasites), previously wingless, change to winged insects. After the metamorphosis, the animals leave the plants, fly to the window and then creep upward on the glass."

It is evident that these tiny insects found that the plants on which they had been thriving were dead, and that they could therefore secure nothing more to eat and drink from this source. The only method by which they could save themselves from starvation was to grow temporary wings and fly, which they did.

Experiments such as these indicate that Omniscience as well as Omnipotence is omnipresent and that the tiniest living thing can take advantage of it in an emergency.

Part Fifteen will tell you more about the law under which we live. It will explain that these laws operate to our advantage; that all conditions and experiences that come to us are for our benefit; that we gain strength in proportion to the effort expended, and that our happiness is best attained through a conscious cooperation with natural laws.

1. The laws under which we live are designed solely for our advantage. These laws are immutable and we cannot escape from their operation.

2. All the great eternal forces act in solemn silence, but it is in our power to place ourselves in harmony with them and thus express a life of comparative peace and happiness.

3. Difficulties, inharmonies, and obstacles, indicate that we are either refusing to give out what we no longer need, or refusing to accept what we require.

4. Growth is attained through an exchange of the old for the new, of the good for the better; it is a conditional or reciprocal action, for each of us is a complete thought entity and this completeness makes it possible for us to receive only as we give.

5. We cannot obtain what we lack if we tenaciously cling to what we have. We are able to consciously control our conditions as we come to sense the purpose of what we attract, and are able to extract from each experience only what we require for our further growth. Our ability to do this determines the degree of harmony or happiness we attain.

6. The ability to appropriate what we require for our growth, continually increases as we reach higher planes and broader visions, and the greater our abilities to know what we require, the more certain we shall be to discern its presence, to attract it and to absorb it. Nothing may reach us except what is necessary for our growth.

7. All conditions and experiences that come to us do so for our benefit. Difficulties and obstacles will continue to come until we absorb their wisdom and gather from them the essentials of further growth.

8. That we reap what we sow is mathematically exact. We gain permanent strength exactly to the extent of the effort required to overcome difficulties.

9. The inexorable requirements of growth demand that we exert the greatest degree of attraction for what is perfectly in accord with us. Our highest happiness will be best attained through our understanding of, and conscious cooperation with natural laws.

10. In order to possess vitality thought must be impregnated with love. Love is a product of the emotions. It is therefore essential that the emotions be controlled and guided by the intellect and reason.

11. It is love which imparts vitality to thought and thus enables it to germinate. The law of attraction, or the law of love, for they are one and the same, will bring to it the necessary material for its growth and maturity.

12. The first form which thought will find is language, or words; this determines the importance of words; they are the first manifestation of thought — the vessels in which thought is carried. They take hold of the ether and by setting it in motion reproduce the thought to others in the form of sound.

13. Thought may lead to action of any kind, but whatever the action, it is simply the thought attempting to express itself in visible form. It is evident, therefore, that if we wish desirable conditions, we can afford to entertain only desirable thoughts.

14. This leads to the inevitable conclusion that if we wish to express abundance in our lives, we can afford to think abundance only, and as words are only thoughts taking form, we must be especially careful to use nothing but constructive and harmonious language, which when finally crystallized into objective forms, will prove to our advantage.

15. We cannot escape from the pictures we incessantly photograph on the mind, and this photography of erroneous conceptions is exactly what is being done by the use of words, when we use any form of language which is not identified with our welfare.

16. We manifest more and more life as our thought becomes clarified and takes higher planes. This is obtained with greater facility as we use word pictures that are clearly defined, and relieved of the conceptions attached to them on lower planes of thought.

17. It is with words that we must express our thoughts, and if we are to make use of higher forms of truth, we may use only such material as has been carefully and intelligently selected with this purpose in view.

18. This wonderful power of clothing thoughts in the form of words is what differentiates man from the rest of the animal kingdom; by the use of the written word he has been enabled to look back over the centuries and see the stirring scenes by which he has come into his present inheritance.

19. He has been enabled to come into communion with the greatest writers and thinkers of all time, and the combined record which we possess today is therefore the expression of Universal Thought as it has been seeking to take form in the mind of Man.

20. We know that the Universal Thought has for its goal the creation of form, and we know that the individual thought is likewise forever attempting to express itself in form, and we know that the word is a thought form, and a sentence is a combination of thought forms, therefore, if we wish our ideal to be beautiful or strong, we must see that the words out of which this temple will eventually be created are exact, that they are put together carefully, because accuracy in building words and sentences is the highest form of architecture in civilization and is a passport to success.

21. Words are thoughts and are therefore an invisible and invincible power which will finally objectify themselves in the form they are given.

22. Words may become mental places that will live forever, or they may become shacks which the first breeze will carry away. They may delight the eye as well as the ear; they may contain all knowledge; in them we find the history of the past as well as the hope of the future; they are living messengers from which every human and superhuman activity is born.

23. The beauty of the word consists in the beauty of the thought; the power of the word consists in the power of the thought, and the power of the thought consists in its vitality. How shall we identify a vital thought? What are its distinguishing characteristics? It must have principle. How shall we identify principle?

24. There is a principle of Mathematics, but none of error; there is a principle of health, but none of disease; there is a principle of truth, but none of dishonesty; there is a principle of light, but none of darkness, and there is a principle of abundance, but none of poverty.

25. How shall we know that this is true? Because if we apply the principle of Mathematics correctly we shall be certain of our results. Where there is health there will be no disease. If we know the Truth we cannot be deceived by error. If we let in light there can be no darkness, and where there is abundance there can be no poverty.

26. These are self-evident facts, but the all-important truth that a thought containing principle is vital and therefore contains life and

consequently takes root, and eventually but surely and certainly displaces the negative thoughts, which by their very nature can contain no vitality, is one which seems to have been overlooked.

27. But this is a fact which will enable you to destroy every manner of discord, lack and limitation.

28. There can be no question but that he who "is wise enough to understand" will readily recognize that the creative power of thought places an invincible weapon in his hands and makes him a master of destiny.

29. In the physical world there is a law of compensation which is that "the appearance of a given amount of energy anywhere means the disappearance of the same amount somewhere else," and so we find that we can get only what we give; if we pledge ourselves to a certain action we must be prepared to assume the responsibility for the development of that action. The subconscious cannot reason. It takes us at our word; we have asked for something; we are now to receive it; we have made our bed, we are now to lie in it; the die has been cast; the threads will carry out the pattern we have made.

30. For this reason Insight must be exercised so that the thought which we entertain contains no mental, moral or physical germ which we do not wish objectified in our lives.

31. Insight is a faculty of the mind whereby we are enabled to examine facts and conditions at long range, a kind of human telescope; it enables us to understand the difficulties, as well as the possibilities, in any undertaking.

32. Insight enables us to be prepared for the obstacles which we shall meet; we can therefore overcome them before they have any opportunity of causing difficulty.

33. Insight enables us to plan to advantage and turn our thought and attention in the right direction, instead of into channels which can yield no possible return.

34. Insight is therefore absolutely essential for the development of any great achievement, but with it we may enter, explore and possess any mental field.

35. Insight is a product of the world within and is developed in the Silence, by concentration.

36. For your exercise this week, concentrate on Insight; take your accustomed position and focus the thought on the fact that to have a knowledge of the creative power of thought does not mean to possess the art of thinking. Let the thought dwell on the fact that knowledge does not apply itself. That our actions are not governed by knowledge, but by custom, precedent and habit. That the only way we can get ourselves to apply knowledge is by a determined conscious effort. Call to mind the fact that knowledge unused passes from the mind, that the value of the information is in the application of the principle; continue this line of thought until you gain sufficient insight to formulate a definite program for applying this principle to your own particular problem.

PART 16

The vibratory activities of the planetary Universe are governed by a law of periodicity. Everything that lives has periods of birth, growth, fruitage, and decline. These periods are governed by the Septimal Law.

The Law of Sevens governs the days of the week, the phases of the moon, the harmonies of sound, light, heat, electricity, magnetism, atomic structure. It governs the life of individuals and of nations, and it dominates the activities of the commercial world.

Life is growth, and growth is change, each seven years period takes us into a new cycle. The first seven years is the period of infancy. The next seven the period of childhood, representing the beginning of individual responsibility. The next seven represents the period of adolescence. The fourth period marks the attainment of full growth. The fifth period is the constructive period, when men begin to acquire property, possessions, a home and family. The next from 35 to 42, is a period of reactions and changes, and this in turn is followed by a period of reconstruction, adjustment and recuperation, so as to be ready for a new cycle of sevens, beginning with the fiftieth year.

There are many who think that the world is just bout to pass out of the sixth period; that it will soon enter into the seventh period, the period of readjustment, reconstruction and harmony; the period which is frequently referred to as the Millennium.

Those familiar with these cycles will not be disturbed when things seem to go wrong, but can apply the principle outlined in these lessons with the full assurance that a higher law will invariably control all other laws, and that through an understanding and conscious operation of spiritual laws, we can convert every seeming difficulty into a blessing.

1. Wealth is a product of labor. Capital is an effect, not a cause; a servant, not a master; a means, not an end.

2. The most commonly accepted definition of wealth is that it consists of all useful and agreeable things which possess exchange value. It is this exchange value which is the predominant characteristic of wealth.

3. When we consider the small addition made by wealth to the happiness of the possessor, we find that the true value consists not in its utility but in its exchange.

4. This exchange value makes it a medium for securing the things of real value whereby our ideals may be realized.

5. Wealth should then never be desired as an end, but simply as a means of accomplishing an end. Success is contingent upon a higher ideal

than the mere accumulation of riches, and he who aspires to such success must formulate an ideal for which he is willing to strive.

6. With such an ideal in mind, the ways and means can and will be provided, but the mistake must not be made of substituting the means for the end. There must be a definite fixed purpose, an ideal.

7. Prentice Mulford said: "The man of success is the man possessed of the greatest spiritual understanding and every great fortune comes of superior and truly spiritual power." Unfortunately, there are those who fail to recognize this power; they forget that Andrew Carnegie's mother had to help support the family when they came to America, that Harriman's father was a poor clergyman with a salary of only $200 a year, that Sir Thomas Lipton started with only 25 cents. These men had no other power to depend upon, but it did not fail them.

8. The power to create depends entirely upon spiritual power; there are three steps, idealization, visualization and materialization. Every captain of industry depends upon this power exclusively. In an article in Everybody's Magazine, Henry M. Flagler, the Standard Oil multi-millionaire, admitted that the secret of his success was his power to see a thing in its completeness. The following conversation with the reporter shows his power of idealization, concentration and visualization, all spiritual powers:

9. "Did you actually vision to yourself the whole thing? I mean, did you, or could you, really close your eyes and see the tracks? And the trains running? And hear the whistles blowing? Did you go as far as that?" "Yes." "How clearly?" "Very clearly."

10. Here we have a vision of the law, we see "cause and effect," we see that thought necessarily precedes and determines action. If we are wise, we shall come into a realization of the tremendous fact that no arbitrary condition can exist for a moment, and that human experience is the result of an orderly and harmonious sequence.

11. The successful businessman is more often than not an idealist and is every striving for higher and higher standards. The subtle forces of thought as they crystallize in our daily moods is what constitutes life.

12. Thought is the plastic material with which we build images of our growing conception of life. Use determines its existence. As in all other things our ability to recognize it and use it properly is the necessary condition for attainment.

13. Premature wealth is but the forerunner of humiliation and disaster, because we cannot permanently retain anything which we do not merit or which we have not earned.

14. The conditions with which we meet in the world without, correspond to the conditions which we find in the world within. This is brought about by the law of attraction. How then shall we determine what is to enter into the world within?

15. Whatever enters the mind through the senses or the objective mind will impress the mind and result in a mental image which will become a pattern for the creative energies. These experiences are largely the result of environment, chance, past thinking and other forms of negative thought, and must be subjected to careful analysis before being entertained. On the other hand, we can form our own mental images, through our own interior processes of thought regardless of the thoughts of others, regardless of exterior conditions, regardless of environment of every kind, and it is by the exercise of this power that we can control our own destiny, body, mind and soul.

16. It is by the exercise of this power that we take our fate out of the hands of chance, and consciously make for ourselves the experiences which we desire, because when we consciously realize a condition, that condition will eventually manifest in our lives; it is therefore evident that in the last analysis thinking is the one great cause in life.

17. Therefore, to control thought is to control circumstances, conditions, environment, and destiny.

18. How then are we to control thought; what is the process? To think is to create a thought, but the result of the thought will depend upon its form, its quality and its vitality.

19. The form will depend upon the mental images from which it emanates; this will depend upon the depth of the impression, the predominance of the idea, the clarity of the vision, the boldness of the image.

20. The quality depends upon its substance, and this depends upon the material of which the mind is composed; if this material has been woven from thoughts of vigor, strength, courage, determination, the thought will possess these qualities.

21. And finally, the vitality depends upon the feeling with which the thought is impregnated. If the thought is constructive, it will possess vitality; it will have life, it will grow, develop, expand, it will be creative; it will attract to itself everything necessary for its complete development.

22. If the thought is destructive, it will have within itself the germ of its own dissolution; it will die, but in the process of dying, it will bring sickness, disease, and every other form of discord.

23. This we call evil, and when we bring it upon ourselves, some of us are disposed to attribute our difficulties to a Supreme Being, but this supreme being is simply Mind in equilibrium.

24. It is neither good nor bad, it simply is.

25. Our ability to differentiate it into form is our ability to manifest good or evil.

26. Good and evil therefore are not entities, they are simply words which we use to indicate the result of our actions, and these actions are in turn predetermined by the character of our thought.

27. If our thought is constructive and harmonious we manifest good; if it is destructive and discordant we manifest evil.

28. If you desire to visualize a different environment, the process is simply to hold the ideal in mind, until your vision has been made real; give no thought to persons, places or things; these have no place in the absolute; the environment you desire will contain everything necessary; the right persons, and the right things will come at the right time and in the right place.

29. It is sometimes not plain how character, ability, attainment, achievement, environment and destiny can be controlled through the power of visualization, but this is an exact scientific fact.

30. You will readily see that what we think determines the quality of mind, and that the quality of mind in turn determines our ability and mental capacity, and you can readily understand that the improvement in our ability will naturally be followed by increase in attainment and a greater control of circumstances.

31. It will thus be seen that Natural laws work in a perfectly natural and harmonious manner; everything seems to "just happen." If you want any evidence of this fact simply compare results of your efforts in your own life, when your actions were prompted by high ideals and when you had selfish or ulterior motives in mind. You will need no further evidence.

32. If you wish to bring about the realization of any desire, form a mental picture of success in your mind, by consciously visualizing your desire; in this way you will be compelling success, you will be externalizing it in your life by scientific methods.

33. We can only see what already exists in the objective world, but what we visualize, already exists in the spiritual world, and this visualization is a substantial token of what will one day appear in the objective world, if we are faithful to our ideal. The reason for this is not difficult; visualization is a form of imagination; this process of thinking forms impressions on the mind, and these impressions in turn form concepts and ideals, and they in turn are the plans from which the Master architect will weave the future.

34. The psychologists have come to the conclusion that there is but one sense, the sense of feeling, and that all other senses are but modifications of this one sense; this being true, we know why feeling is the very fountain head of power, why the emotions so easily overcome the intellect, and why we must put feeling into our thought, if we wish results. Thought and feeling is the irresistible combination.

35. Visualization must, of course, be directed by the will; we are to visualize exactly what we want; we must be careful not to let the imagination run riot. Imagination is a good servant but a poor master, and unless it is controlled it may easily lead us into all kinds of speculations and conclusions which have no basis or foundation of fact

whatever. Every kind of plausible opinion is liable to be accepted without any analytical examination and the inevitable result is mental chaos.

36. We must therefore construct only such mental images as are known to be scientifically true. Subject every idea to a searching analysis and accept nothing which is not scientifically exact. When you do this you will attempt nothing but what you know you can carry out and success will crown your efforts; this is what businessmen call far-sightedness; it is much the same as insight, and is one of the great secrets of success in all important undertakings.

37. For your exercise this week, try to bring yourself to a realization of the important fact that harmony and happiness are states of consciousness and do not depend upon the possession of things. That things are effects and come as a consequence of correct mental states. So that if we desire material possession of any kind our chief concern should be to acquire the mental attitude which will bring about the result desired. This mental attitude is brought about by a realization of our spiritual nature and our unity with the Universal Mind which is the substance of all things. This realization will bring about everything which is necessary for our complete enjoyment. This is scientific or correct thinking. When we succeed in bringing about this mental attitude it is comparatively easy to realize our desire as an already accomplished fact; when we can do this we shall have found the "Truth" which makes us "free" from every lack or limitation of any kind.

PART 17

The kind of Deity which a man, consciously or unconsciously, worships, indicates the intellectual status of the worshiper.

Ask the Indian of God, and he will describe to you a powerful chieftain of a glorious tribe. Ask the Pagan of God, and he will tell you of a God of fire, a God of water, a god of this, that, and the other.

Ask the Israelite of God, and he will tell you of the God of Moses, who conceived it expedient to rule by coercive measures; hence, the Ten Commandments. Or of Joshua, who led the Israelites into battle, confiscated property, murdered the prisoners, and laid waste to cities.

The so-called heathen made "graven images" of their Gods, whom they were accustomed to worship, but among the most intelligent, at least, these images were but the visible fulcrums with which they were enabled to mentally concentrate on the qualities which they desired to externalize in their lives.

We of the twentieth century worship a God of Love in theory, but in practice we make for ourselves "graven images" of "Wealth," "Power," "Fashion," "Custom" and "Conventionality." We "fall down" before them and worship them. We concentrate on them and they are thereby externalized in our lives.

The student who masters the contents of Part Seventeen will not mistake the symbols for the reality; he will be interested in causes, rather than effects. He will concentrate on the realities of life, and will then not be disappointed in the results.

1. We are told that Man has "dominion over all things"; this dominion is established through Mind. Thought is the activity which controls every principle beneath it. The highest principle by reason of its superior essence and qualities necessarily determines the circumstances, aspects and relation of everything with which it comes in contact.

2. The vibrations of mental forces are the finest and consequently the most powerful in existence. To those who perceive the nature and transcendency of mental force, all physical power sinks into insignificance.

3. We are accustomed to look upon the Universe with a lens of five senses, and from these experiences our anthropomorphic conceptions originate, but true conceptions are only secured by spiritual insight. This insight requires a quickening of the vibrations of the Mind, and is only secured when the mind is continuously concentrated in a given direction.

4. Continuous concentration means an even, unbroken flow of thought and is the result of patient, persistent, persevering and well-regulated system.

5. Great discoveries are the result of long-continued investigation. The science of mathematics requires years of concentrated effort to master it, and the greatest science — that of the Mind — is revealed only through concentrated effort.

6. Concentration is much misunderstood; there seems to be an idea of effort or activity associated with it, when just the contrary is necessary. The greatness of an actor lies in the fact that he forgets himself in the portrayal of his character, becoming so identified with it, that the audience is swayed by the realism of the performance. This will give you a good idea of true concentration; you should be so interested in your thought, so engrossed in your subject, as to be conscious of nothing else. Such concentration leads to intuitive perception and immediate insight into the nature of the object concentrated upon.

7. All knowledge is the result of concentration of this kind; it is thus that the secrets of Heaven and Earth have been wrested; it is thus that the mind becomes a magnet and the desire to know draws the knowledge, irresistibly attracts it, makes it your own.

8. Desire is largely subconscious; conscious desire rarely realizes its object when the latter is out of immediate reach. Subconscious desire arouses the latent faculties of the mind, and difficult problems seem to solve themselves.

9. The subconscious mind may be aroused and brought into action in any direction and made to serve us for any purpose, by concentration. The practice of concentration requires the control of the physical, mental, and physical being; all modes of consciousness whether physical, mental, or physical, must be under control.

10. Spiritual Truth is therefore the controlling factor; it is this which will enable you to grow out of limited attainment and reach a point where you will be able to translate modes of thought into character and consciousness.

11. Concentration does not mean mere thinking of thoughts, but the transmutation of these thoughts into practical values; the average person has no conception of the meaning of concentration. There is always the cry "to have" but never the cry "to be"; they fail to understand that they cannot have one without the other, that they must first find the "kingdom" before they can have the "things added." Momentary enthusiasm is of no value; it is only with unbounded self-confidence that the goal is reached.

12. The mind may place the ideal a little too high and fall short of the mark; it may attempt to soar on untrained wings and instead of flying, fall to earth; but that is no reason for not making another attempt.

13. Weakness is the only barrier to mental attainment; attribute your weakness to physical limitations or mental uncertainties and try again; ease and perfection are gained by repetition.

14. The astronomer centers his mind on the stars and they give forth their secrets; the geologists centers his mind on the construction of the earth and we have geology; so with all things. Men center their minds on the problems of life, and the result is apparent in the vast and complex social order of the day.

15. All mental discovery and attainment are the result of desire plus concentration; desire is the strongest mode of action; the more persistent the desire, the more authoritative the revelation. Desire added to concentration will wrench any secret from nature.

16. In realizing great thoughts, in experiencing great emotions that correspond with great thoughts, the mind is in a state where it appreciates the value of higher things.

17. The intensity of one moment's earnest concentration and the intense longing to become and to attain may take you further than years of slow normal and forced effort; it will unfasten the prison bars of unbelief, weakness, impotence and self-belittlement, and you will come into a realization of the joy of overcoming.

18. The spirit of initiative and originality is developed through persistence and continuity of mental effort. Business teaches the value of concentration and encourages decision of character; it develops practical insight and quickness of conclusion. The mental element in every commercial pursuit is dominant as the controlling factor, and desire is the predominating force; all commercial relations are the externalization of desire.

19. Many of the sturdy and substantial virtues are developed in commercial employment; the mind is steadied and directed; it becomes efficient. The principal necessity is the strengthening of the mind so that it rises superior to the distractions and wayward impulses of instinctive life and thus successfully overcomes in the conflict between the higher and lower self.

20. All of us are dynamos, but the dynamo of itself is nothing; the mind must work the dynamo; then it is useful and its energy can be definitely concentrated. The mind is an engine whose power is undreamed; thought is an omni-working power. It is the ruler and creator of all form and all events occurring in form. Physical energy is nothing in comparison with the omnipotence of thought, because thought enables man to harness all other natural power.

21. Vibration is the action of thought; it is vibration which reaches out and attracts the material necessary to construct and build. There is nothing mysterious concerning the power of thought; concentration simply implies that consciousness can be focalized to the point where it becomes identified with the object of its attention. As food absorbed is the essence of the body, so the mind absorbs the object of its attention, gives it life and being.

22. If you concentrate on some matter of importance, the intuitive power will be set in operation, and help will come in the nature of information which will lead to success.

23. Intuition arrives at conclusions without the aid of experience or memory. Intuition often solves problems that are beyond the grasp of the reasoning power. Intuition often comes with a suddenness that is startling; it reveals the truth for which we are searching, so directly that it seems to come from a higher power. Intuition can be cultivated and developed; in order to do this it must be recognized and appreciated; if the intuitive visitor is given a royal welcome when he comes, he will come again; the more cordial the welcome the more frequent his visits will become, but if he is ignored or neglected he will make his visits few and far apart.

24. Intuition usually comes in the Silence; great minds seek solitude frequently; it is here that all the larger problems of life are worked out. For this reason every businessman who can afford it has a private office, where he will not be disturbed; if you cannot afford a private office you can at least find somewhere, where you can be alone a few minutes each day, to train the thought along lines which will enable you to develop that invincible power which is necessary to achieve.

25. Remember that fundamentally the subconscious is omnipotent; there is no limit to the things that can be done when it is given the power to act. Your degree of success is determined by the nature of your desire. If the nature of your desire is in harmony with Natural Law or the Universal Mind, it will gradually emancipate the mind and give you invincible courage.

26. Every obstacle conquered, every victory gained, will give you more faith in your power, and you will have greater ability to win. Your strength is determined by your mental attitude; if this attitude is one of success, and is permanently held with an unswerving purpose, you will attract to you from the invisible domain the things you silently demand.

27. By keeping the thought in mind, it will gradually take tangible form. A definite purpose sets causes in motion which go out in the invisible world and find the material necessary to serve your purpose.

28. You may be pursuing the symbols of power, instead of power itself. You may be pursuing fame instead of honor, riches instead of wealth, position instead of servitude; in either event you will find that they turn to ashes just as you overtake them.

29. Premature wealth or position cannot be retained because it has not been earned; we get only what we give, and those who try to get without giving always find that the law of compensation is relentlessly bringing about an exact equilibrium.

30. The race has usually been for money and other mere symbols of power, but with an understanding of the true source of power, we can afford to ignore the symbols. The man with a large bank account finds it

unnecessary to load his pockets down with gold; so with the man who has found the true source of power; he is no longer interested in its shams or pretensions.

31. Thought ordinarily leads outwardly in evolutionary directions, but it can be turned within where it will take hold of the basic principles of things, the heart of things, the spirit of things. When you get to the heart of things it is comparatively easy to understand and command them.

32. This is because the Spirit of a thing is the thing itself, the vital part of it, the real substance. The form is simply the outward manifestation of the spiritual activity within.

33. For your exercise this week concentrate as nearly as possible in accordance with the method outlined in this lesson; let there be no conscious effort or activity associated with your purpose. Relax completely, avoid any thought of anxiety as to results. Remember that power comes through repose. Let the thought dwell upon your object, until it is completely identified with it, until you are conscious of nothing else.

34. If you wish to eliminate fear, concentrate on courage.

35. If you wish to eliminate lack, concentrate on abundance.

36. If you wish to eliminate disease, concentrate on health.

37. Always concentrate on the ideal as an already existing fact; this is the germ cell, the life principle which goes forth and sets in motion those causes which guide, direct and bring about the necessary relation, which eventually manifest in form.

PART 18

In order to grow we must obtain what is necessary for our growth. This is brought about through the law of attraction. This principle is the sole means by which the individual is differentiated from the Universal.

Think for a moment, what would a man be if he were not a husband, father, or brother, if he were not interested in the social, economical, political or religious world. He would be nothing but an abstract theoretical ego. He exists, therefore, only in his relation to the whole, in his relation to other men, in his relation to society. This relation constitutes his environment and in no other way.

It is evident, therefore, that the individual is simply the differentiation of the one Universal Mind "which lighteth every man that cometh into the world," and his so-called individuality or personality consists of nothing but the manner in which he relates with the whole.

This we call his environment and is brought about by the law of attraction. Part Eighteen, which follows, has something more to say concerning this important law.

1. There is a change in the thought of the world. This change is silently transpiring in our midst, and is more important than any which the world has undergone since the downfall of Paganism.

2. These present revolution in the opinions of all classes of men, the highest and most cultured of men as well as those of the laboring class, stands unparalleled in the history of the world.

3. Science has of late made such vast discoveries, has revealed such an infinity of resources, has unveiled such enormous possibilities and such unsuspected forces, that scientific men more and more hesitate to affirm certain theories as established and beyond doubt or to deny other theories as absurd or impossible.

4. A new civilization is being born; customs, creeds, and precedent are passing; vision, faith and service are taking their place. The fetters of tradition are being melted off from humanity, and as the impurities of materialism are being consumed, thought is being liberated and truth is rising full robed before an astonished multitude.

5. The whole world is on the eve of a new consciousness, a new power, and a new realization within the self.

6. Physical Science has resolved matter into molecules, molecules into atoms, atoms into energy, and it has remained for Mr. J. A. Fleming, in an address before the Royal Institution, to resolve this energy into mind. He says, "In its ultimate essence, energy may be incomprehensible by us

except as an exhibition of the direct operation of that which we call Mind or Will."

7. And this mind is the indwelling and ultimate. It is imminent in matter as in spirit. It is the sustaining, energizing, all pervading Spirit of the universe.

8. Every living thing must be sustained by this omnipotent Intelligence, and we find the difference in individual lives to be largely measured by the degree of this intelligence, which they manifest. It is greater intelligence that places the animal in a higher scale of being than the plant, the man higher than the animal, and we find that this increased intelligence is again indicated by the power of the individual to control modes of action and thus to consciously adjust himself to his environment.

9. It is this adjustment that occupies the attention of the greatest minds, and this adjustment consists in nothing else than the recognition of an existing order in the universal mind, for it is well known that this mind will obey us precisely in proportion as we first obey it.

10. It is the recognition of Natural Laws that has enabled us to annihilate time and space, to soar in the air and to make iron float, and the greater the degree of intelligence the greater will be our recognition of these Natural Laws and the greater will be the power we can possess.

11. It is the recognition of the self as an individualization of this Universal Intelligence that enables the individual to control those forms of intelligence which have not yet reached this level of self-recognition; they do not know that this Universal Intelligence permeates all things ready to be called into action; they do not know that it is responsive to every demand, and they are therefore in bondage to the law of their own being.

12. Thought is creative and the principle on which the law is based is sound and legitimate and is inherent in the nature of things; but this creative power does not originate in the individual, but in the universal, which is the source and foundation of all energy and substance; the individual is simply the channel for the distribution of this energy.

13. The individual is simply the means by which the universal produces the various combinations which result in the formation of phenomena, which depends upon the law of vibration, whereby various rates of rapidity of motion in the primary substance form new substances only in certain exact numerical ratios.

14. Thought is the invisible link by which the individual comes into communication with the Universal, the finite with the Infinite, the seen with the Unseen. Thought is the magic by which the human is transformed into a being who thinks and knows and feels and acts.

15. As the proper apparatus has enabled the eye to discover worlds without number millions of miles away, so, with the proper understanding, man has been enabled to communicate with the Universal Mind, the source of all power.

16. The Understanding which is usually developed is nothing more than a "belief," which means nothing at all. The savages of the Cannibal Islands believe something; but that proves nothing.

17. The only belief which is of any value to anyone is a belief that has been put to a test and demonstrated to be a fact; it is then no longer a belief, but has become a living Faith or Truth.

18. And this Truth has been put to the test by hundreds of thousands of people and has been found to be the Truth exactly in proportion to the usefulness of the apparatus which they used.

19. A man would not expect to locate stars hundreds of millions of miles away without a sufficiently strong telescope, and for this reason Science is continually engaged in building larger and more powerful telescopes and is continually rewarded by additional knowledge of the heavenly bodies.

20. So with understanding; men are continually making progress in the methods which they use to come into communication with the Universal Mind and its infinite possibilities.

21. The Universal Mind manifests itself in the objective, through the principle of attraction that each atom has for every other atom, in infinite degrees of intensity.

22. It is by this principle of combining and attracting that things are brought together. This principle is of universal application and is the sole means whereby the purpose of existence is carried into effect.

23. The expression of growth is met in a most beautiful manner through the instrumentality of this Universal Principle.

24. In order to grow we must obtain what is essential for our growth, but as we are at all times a complete thought entity, this completeness makes it possible for us to receive only as we give; growth is therefore conditioned on reciprocal action, and we find that on the mental plane like attracts like, that mental vibrations respond only to the extent of their vibratory harmony.

25. It is clear, therefore, that thoughts of abundance will respond only to similar thoughts; the wealth of the individual is seen to be what he inherently is. Affluence within is found to be the secret of attraction for affluence without. The ability to produce is found to be the real source of wealth of the individual. It is for this reason that he who has his heart in his work is certain to meet with unbounded success. He will give and continually give; and the more he gives, the more he will receive.

26. What do the great financiers of Wall Street, the captains of industry, the statesmen, the great corporation attorneys, the inventors, the physicians, the authors — what do each of these contribute to the sum of human happiness but the power of their thought?

27. Thought is the energy which the law of attraction is brought into operation, which eventually manifests in abundance.

28. The Universal Mind is static Mind or Substance in equilibrium. It is differentiated into form by our power to think. Thought is the dynamic phase of mind.

29. Power depends upon consciousness of power; unless we use it, we shall lose it, and unless we are conscious of it, we cannot use it.

30. The use of this power depends upon attention; the degree of attention determines our capacity for the acquirement of knowledge which is another name for power.

31. Attention has been held to be the distinguishing mark of genius. The cultivation of attention depends upon practice.

32. The incentive of attention is interest; the greater the interest, the greater the attention; the greater the attention, the greater the interest, action and reaction; begin by paying attention; before long you will have aroused interest; this interest will attract more attention, and this attention will produce more interest, and so on. This practice will enable you to cultivate the power of attention.

33. This week concentrate upon your power to create; seek insight, perception; try to find a logical basis for the faith which is in you. Let the thought dwell on the fact that the physical man lives and moves and has his being in the sustainer of all organic life air, that he must breathe to live. Then let the thought rest on the fact that the spiritual man also lives and moves and has his being in a similar but subtler energy upon which he must depend for life, and that as in the physical world no life assumes form until after a seed is sown, and no higher fruit than that of the parent stock can be produced; so in the spiritual world no effect can be produced until the seed is sown and the fruit will depend upon the nature of the seed, so that the results which you secure depend upon your perception of law in the mighty domain of causation, the highest evolution of human consciousness.

Part 19

Fear is a powerful form of thought. It paralyzes the nerve centers, thus affecting the circulation of the blood.

This, in turn, paralyzes the muscular system, so that fear affects the entire being, body, brain and nerve, physical, mental, and muscular.

Of course the way to overcome fear is to become conscious of power. What is this mysterious vital force which we call power? We do not know, but then, neither do we know what electricity is.

But we do know that by conforming to the requirements of the law by which electricity is governed, it will be our obedient servant; that it will light our homes, our cities, run our machinery, and serve us in many useful capacities.

And so it is with vital force. Although we do not know what it is, and possibly may never know, we do know that it is a primary force which manifests through living bodies, and that by complying with the laws and principles by which it is governed, we can open ourselves to a more abundant inflow of this vital energy, and thus express the highest possible degree of mental, moral, and spiritual efficiency.

This part tells of a very simple way of developing this vital force. If you put into practice the information outlined in this lesson you will soon develop the sense of power which has ever been the distinguishing mark of genius.

1. The search for truth is no longer a haphazard adventure, but it is a systematic process, and is logical in its operation. Every kind of experience is given a voice in shaping its decision.

2. In seeking the truth we are seeking ultimate cause; we know that every human experience is an effect; then if we may ascertain the cause, and if we shall find that this cause is one which we can consciously control, the effect or the experience will be within our control also.

3. Human experience will then no longer be the football of fate; a man will not be the child of fortune, but destiny. Fate and fortune will be controlled as readily as a captain controls his ship, or an engineer his train.

4. All things are finally resolvable into the same element and as they are thus translatable, one into the other, they must ever be in relation and may never be in opposition to one another.

5. In the physical world there are innumerable contrasts, and these may for convenience sake, be designated by distinctive names. There are sizes, colors, shades or ends to all things. There is a North Pole, and a

South Pole, an inside and an outside, a seen and an unseen, but these expressions merely serve to place extremes in contrast.

6. They are names given to two different parts of one quantity. The two extremes are relative; they are not separate entities, but are two parts or aspects of the whole.

7. In the mental world we find the same law; we speak of knowledge and ignorance, but ignorance is but a lack of knowledge and is therefore found to be simply a word to express the absence of knowledge; it has no principle in itself.

8. In the Moral World we again find the same law; we speak of good and evil, but Good is a reality, something tangible, while Evil is found to be simply a negative condition, the absence of Good. Evil is sometimes thought to be a very real condition, but it has no principle, no vitality, no life; we know this because it can always be destroyed by Good; just as Truth destroys Error and light destroys darkness, so Evil vanishes when Good appears; there is therefore but one principle in the Moral World.

9. We find exactly the same law obtaining in the Spiritual world; we speak of Mind and Matter as two separate entities, but clearer insight makes it evident that there is but one operative principle and that is Mind.

10. Mind is the real and the eternal. Matter is forever changing; we know that in the eons of time a hundred years is but as a day. If we stand in any large city and let the eye rest on the innumerable large and magnificent buildings, the vast array of conveniences of modern civilization, we may remember that not one of them was there just over a century ago, and if we could stand on the same spot in a hundred years from now, in all probability we should find that but few of them remained.

11. In the animal kingdom we find the same law of change. The millions and millions of animals come and go, a few years constituting their span of life. In the plant world the change is still more rapid. Many plants and nearly all grasses come and go in a single year. When we pass to the inorganic, we expect to find something more substantial, but as we gaze on the apparently solid continent, we are told that it arose from the ocean; we see the giant mountain and are told that the place where it now stands was once a lake; and as we stand in awe before the great cliffs in the Yosemite Valley we can easily trace the path of the glaciers which carried all before them.

12. We are in the presence of continual change, and we know that this change is but the evolution of the Universal Mind, the grand process whereby all things are continually being created anew, and we come to know that matter is but a form which Mind takes and is therefore simply a condition. Matter has no principle; Mind is the only principle.

13. We have then come to know that Mind is the only principle which is operative in the physical, mental, moral and spiritual world.

14. We also know that this mind is static, mind at rest, we also know that the ability of the individual to think is his ability to act upon the Universal Mind and convert it into dynamic mind, or mind in motion.

15. In order to do this fuel must be applied in the form of food, for man cannot think without eating, and so we find that even a spiritual activity such as thinking cannot be converted into sources of pleasure and profit except by making use of material means.

16. It requires energy of some kind to collect electricity and convert it into a dynamic power, it requires the rays of the sun to give the necessary energy to sustain plant life, so it also requires energy in the form of food to enable the individual to think and thereby act upon the Universal Mind.

17. You may know that thought constantly, eternally is taking form, is forever seeking expression, or you may not, but the fact remains that if your thought is powerful, constructive, and positive, this will be plainly evident in the state of your health, your business and your environment; if your thought is weak, critical, destructive and negative generally, it will manifest in your body as fear, worry and nervousness, in your finance as lack and limitation, and in discordant conditions in your environment.

18. All wealth is the offspring of power; possessions are of value only as they confer power. Events are significant only as they affect power; all things represent certain forms and degrees of power.

19. A knowledge of cause and effect as shown by the laws governing steam, electricity, chemical affinity and gravitation enables men to plan courageously and to execute fearlessly. These laws are called Natural Laws, because they govern the physical world, but all power is not physical power; there is also mental power, and there is moral and spiritual power.

20. What are our schools, our universities, but mental powerhouses, places where mental power is being developed?

21. As there are many mighty powerhouses for the application of power to ponderous machinery, whereby raw material is collected and converted into the necessities and comforts of life, so the mental powerhouses collect the raw material and cultivate and develop it into a power which is infinitely superior to all the forces of nature, marvelous though they may be.

22. What is this raw material which is being collected in these thousands of mental powerhouses all over the world and developed into a power which is evidently controlling every other power? In its static form it is Mind — in its dynamic form, it is Thought.

23. This power is superior because it exists on a higher plane, because it has enabled man to discover the law by which these wonderful forces of Nature could be harnessed and made to do the work of hundreds and thousands of men. It has enabled man to discover laws whereby time and space have been annihilated, and the law of gravitation overcome.

24. Thought is the vital force or energy which is being developed and which has produced such startling results in the last half century as to bring about a world which would be absolutely inconceivable to a man existing only 50 or 25 years ago. If such results have been secured by organizing these mental powerhouses in 50 years, what may not be expected in another 50 years?

25. The substance from which all things are created is infinite in quantity; we know that light travels at the rate of 186,000 miles per second, and we know that there are stars so remote that it takes light 2,000 years to reach us, and we know that such stars exist in all parts of the heaven; we know, too, that this light comes in waves, so that if the ether on which these waves travel was not continuous the light would fail to reach us; we can then only come to the conclusion that this substance, or ether, or raw material, is universally present.

26. How, then, does it manifest in form? In electrical science a battery is formed by connecting the opposite poles of zinc and copper, which causes a current to flow from one to the other and so provides energy. This same process is repeated in respect to every polarity, and as all form simply depends upon the rate of vibration and consequent relations of atoms to each other, if we wish to change the form of manifestation we must change the polarity. This is the principle of causation.

27. For your exercise this week, concentrate, and when I use the word concentrate, I mean all that the word implies; become so absorbed in the object of your thought that you are conscious of nothing else, and do this a few minutes every day. You take the necessary time to eat in order that the body may be nourished, why not take the time to assimilate your mental food?

28. Let the thought rest on the fact that appearances are deceptive. The earth is not flat, neither is it stationary; the sky is not a dome, the sun does not move, the stars are not small specks of light, and matter which was once supposed to be fixed has been found to be in a state of perpetual flux.

29. Try to realize that the day is fast approaching — its dawn is now at hand — when modes of thought and action must be adjusted to rapidly increasing knowledge of the operation of eternal principles.

PART 20

For many years there has been an endless discussion as to the origin of evil. Theologians have told us that God is Love, and that God is Omnipresent. If this be true, there is no place where God is not. Where, then, is Evil, Satan and Hell?

Let us see:

God is Spirit.

Spirit is the Creative Principle of the Universe.

Man is made in the image and likeness of God.

Man is therefore a spiritual being.

The only activity which spirit possesses is the power to think.

Thinking is therefore a creative process.

All form is therefore the result of the thinking process.

The destruction of form must also be a result of the thinking process.

Fictitious representations of form are the result of the creative power of thought, as in Hypnotism.

Apparent representation of form are the result of the creative power of thought, as in Spiritualism.

Invention, organization and constructive work of all kinds are the result of the creative power of thought, as in concentration.

When the creative power of thought is manifested for the benefit of humanity, we call the result good.

When the creative power of thought is manifested in a destructive or evil manner, we call the result evil.

This indicates the origin of both good and evil; they are simply words which have been coined in order to indicate the nature of the result of the thinking or creative process. Thought necessarily precedes and predetermines action; action precedes and predetermines condition.

Part Twenty will throw more light upon this important subject.

1. The spirit of a thing is that thing; it is necessarily fixed, changeless and eternal. The spirit of you is — you; without the spirit you would be nothing. It becomes active through your recognition of it and its possibilities.

2. You may have all the wealth in Christendom, but unless you recognize it and make use of it, it will have no value; so with your spiritual wealth: unless you recognize it and use it, it will have no value. The one and only condition of spiritual power is use or recognition.

3. All great things come through recognition; the scepter of power is consciousness, and thought is its messenger, and this messenger is

constantly molding the realities of the invisible world into the conditions and environments of your objective world.

4. Thinking is the true business of life, power is the result. You are at all times dealing with the magical power of thought and consciousness. What results can you expect so long as you remain oblivious to the power which has been placed within your control?

5. So long as you do this you limit yourself to superficial conditions, and make of yourself a beast of burden for those who think; those who recognize their power; those who know that unless we are willing to think we shall have to work, and the less we think the more we shall have to work, and the less we shall get for our work.

6. The secret of power is a perfect understanding of the principles, forces, methods and combinations of Mind, and a perfect understanding of our relationship to the Universal Mind. It is well to remember that this principle is unchangeable; if this were not so, it would not be reliable; all principles are changeless.

7. This stability is your opportunity; you are its active attribute, the channel for its activity; the Universal can act only through the individual.

8. When you begin to perceive that the essence of the Universal is within yourself — is you — you begin to do things; you begin to feel your power; it is the fuel which fires the imagination; which lights the torch of inspiration; which gives vitality to thought; which enables you to connect with all the invisible forces of the Universe. It is this power which will enable you to plan fearlessly, to execute masterfully.

9. But perception will come only in the Silence; this seems to be the condition required for all great purposes. You are a visualizing entity. Imagination is your workshop. It is here that your ideal is to be visualized.

10. As a perfect understanding of the nature of this power is a primary condition for its manifestation, visualize the entire method over and over again, so that you may use it whenever occasion requires. The infinity of wisdom is to follow the method whereby we may have the inspiration of the omnipotent Universal Mind on demand at any time.

11. We can fail to recognize this world within, and so exclude it from our consciousness, but it will still be the basic fact of all existence; and when we learn to recognize it, not only in ourselves, but in all persons, events, things and circumstances we shall have found the "Kingdom of heaven" which we are told is "within" us.

12. Our failures are a result of the operation of exactly the same principle; the principle is unchangeable; its operation is exact, there is no deviation; if we think lack, limitation, discord, we shall find their fruits on every hand; if we think poverty, unhappiness or disease, the thought messengers will carry the summons as readily as any other kind of thought and the result will be just as certain. If we fear a coming calamity, we shall be able to say with Job, "the thing I feared has come

upon me"; if we think unkindly or ignorantly we shall thus attract to ourselves the results of our ignorance.

13. This power of thought, if understood and correctly used, is the greatest labor-saving device ever dreamed of, but if not understood or improperly used, the result will in all probability be disastrous, as we have already seen; by the help of this power you can confidently undertake things that are seemingly impossible, because this power is the secret of all inspiration, all genius.

14. To become inspired means to get out of the beaten path, out of the rut, because extraordinary results require extraordinary means. When we come into a recognition of the Unity of all things and that the source of all power is within, we tap the source of inspiration.

15. Inspiration is the art of imbibing, the art of self-realization; the art of adjusting the individual mind to that of the Universal Mind; the art of attaching the proper mechanism to the source of all power; the art of differentiating the formless into form; the art of becoming a channel for the flow of Infinite Wisdom; the art of visualizing perfection; the art of realizing the omnipresence of Omnipotence.

16. An understanding and appreciation of the fact that the infinite power is omnipresent and is therefore in the infinitely small as well as the infinitely large will enable us to absorb its essence; a further understanding of the fact that this power is spirit and therefore indivisible will enable us to appreciate its present at all points at the same time.

17. An understanding of these facts, first intellectually and then emotionally, will enable us to drink deeply from this ocean of infinite power. An intellectual understanding will be of no assistance; the emotions must be brought into action; thought without feeling is cold. The required combination is thought and feeling.

18. Inspiration is from within. The Silence is necessary, the senses must be stilled, the muscles relaxed, repose cultivated. When you have thus come into possession of a sense of poise and power you will be ready to receive the information or inspiration or wisdom which may be necessary for the development of your purpose.

19. Do not confuse these methods with those of the clairvoyant; they have nothing in common. Inspiration is the art of receiving and makes for all that is best in life; your business in life is to understand and command these invisible forces instead of letting them command and rule you. Power implies service; inspiration implies power; to understand and apply the method of inspiration is to become a superman.

20. We can live more abundantly every time we breathe, if we consciously breathe with that intention. The IF is a very important condition in this case, as the intention governs the attention, and without the attention you can secure only the results which every one else secures. That is, a supply equal to the demand.

21. In order to secure the larger supply your demand must be increased, and as you consciously increase the demand the supply will follow, you will find yourself coming into a larger and larger supply of life, energy and vitality.

22. The reason for this is not difficult to understand, but it is another of the vital mysteries of life which does not seem to be generally appreciated. If you make it your own, you will find it one of the great realities of life.

23. We are told that "In Him we live and move and have our being," and we are told that "He" is a Spirit, and again that "He" is Love, so that every time we breathe, we breathe this life, love, and spirit. This is Pranic Energy, or Pranic Ether, we could not exist a moment without it. It is the Cosmic Energy; it is the Life of the Solar Plexus.

24. Every time we breathe we fill our lungs with air and at the same time vitalize our body with this Pranic Ether which is Life itself, so that we have the opportunity of making a conscious connection with All Life, All Intelligence and All Substance.

25. A knowledge of your relation and oneness with this Principle that governs the Universe and the simple method whereby you can consciously identify yourself with it gives you a scientific understanding of a law whereby you may free yourself from disease, from lack or limitation of any kind; in fact, it enables you to breathe the "breath of life" into your own nostrils.

26. This "breath of life" is a superconscious reality. It is the essence of the "I am." It is pure "Being" or Universal Substance, and our conscious unity with it enables us to localize it, and thus exercise the powers of this creative energy.

27. Thought is creative vibration and the quality of the conditions created will depend upon the quality of our thought, because we cannot express powers which we do not possess. We must "be" before we can "do" and we can "do" only to the extent to which we "are," and so what we do will necessarily coincide with what we "are" and what we are depends upon what we "think."

28. Every time you think you start a train of causation which will create a condition in strict accordance with the quality of the thought which originated it. Thought which is in harmony with the Universal Mind will result in corresponding conditions. Thought which is destructive or discordant will produce corresponding results. You may use thought constructively or destructively, but the immutable law will not allow you to plant a thought of one kind and reap the fruit of another. You are free to use this marvelous creative power as you will, but you must take the consequences.

29. This is the danger from what is called Will Power. There are those who seem to think that by force of will they can coerce this law; that they can sow seed of one kind and by "Will Power" make it bear fruit of

another, but the fundamental principle of creative power is in the Universal, and therefore the idea of forcing a compliance with our wishes by the power of the individual will is an inverted conception which may appear to succeed for a while but is eventually doomed to failure — because it antagonizes the very power which it is seeking to use.

30. It is the individual attempting to coerce the Universal, the finite in conflict with the Infinite. Our permanent well-being will be best conserved by a conscious cooperation with the continuous forward movement of the Great Whole.

31. For your exercise this week, go into the Silence and concentrate on the fact that "In him we live and move and have our being" is literally and scientifically exact! That you ARE because He IS, that if He is Omnipresent He must be in you. That if He is all in all you must be in Him! That He is Spirit and you are made in "His image and likeness" and that the only difference between His spirit and your spirit is one of degree, that a part must be the same in kind and quality as the whole. When you can realize this clearly you will have found the secret of the creative power of thought, you will have found the origin of both good and evil, you will have found the secret of the wonderful power of concentration, you will have found the key to the solution of every problem whether physical, financial, or environmental.

PART 21

In paragraph 7 you will find that one of the secrets of success, one of the methods of organizing victory, one of the accomplishments of the Master Mind is to think big thoughts.

In paragraph 8 you will find that everything which we hold in our consciousness for any length of time becomes impressed upon our subconsciousness and so becomes a pattern which the creative energy will wave into our life and environment. This is the secret of the wonderful power of prayer.

We know that the universe is governed by law; that for every effect there must be a cause, and that the same cause, under the same conditions, will invariably produce the same effect.

Consequently, if prayer has ever been answered, it will always be answered, if the proper conditions are complied with. This must necessarily be true; otherwise the universe would be a chaos instead of a cosmos. The answer to prayer is therefore subject to law, and this law is definite, exact and scientific, just as are the laws governing gravitation and electricity. An understanding of this law takes the foundation of Christianity out of the realm of superstition and credulity and places it upon the firm rock of scientific understanding.

But, unfortunately, there are comparatively few persons who know how to pray.

They understand that there are laws governing electricity, mathematics, and chemistry, but, for some inexplicable reason, it never seems to occur to them that there are also spiritual laws, and that these laws are also definite, scientific, exact, and operate with immutable precision.

1. The real secret of power is consciousness of power. The Universal Mind is unconditional; therefore, the more conscious we become of our unity with this mind, the less conscious we shall become of conditions and limitations, and as we become emancipated or freed from conditions we come into a realization of the unconditional. We have become free!

2. As soon as we become conscious of the inexhaustible power in the world within, we begin to draw on this power and apply and develop the greater possibilities which this discernment has realized, because whatever we become conscious of, is invariably manifested in the objective world, is brought forth into tangible expression.

3. This is because the Infinite Mind, which is the source from which all things proceed, is one and indivisible, and each individual is a channel whereby this Eternal Energy is being manifested. Our ability to think is

our ability to act upon this Universal Substance, and what we think is what is created or produced in the objective world.

4. The result of this discovery is nothing less than marvelous, and means that mind is extraordinary in quality, limitless in quantity, and contains possibilities without number. To become conscious of this power is to become a "live wire"; it has the same effect as placing an ordinary wire in contact with a wire that is charged. The Universal is the live wire. It carries power sufficient to meet every situation which may arise in the life of every individual. When the individual mind touches the Universal Mind it receives all the power it requires. This is the world within. All science recognizes the reality of this world, and all power is contingent upon our recognition of this world.

5. The ability to eliminate imperfect conditions depends upon mental action, and mental action depends upon consciousness of power; therefore, the more conscious we become of our unity with the source of all power, the greater will be our power to control and master every condition.

6. Large ideas have a tendency to eliminate all smaller ideas so that it is well to hold ideas large enough to counteract and destroy all small or undesirable tendencies. This will remove innumerable petty and annoying obstacles from your path. You also become conscious of a larger world of thought, thereby increasing your mental capacity as well as placing yourself in position to accomplish something of value.

7. This is one of the secrets of success, one of the methods of organizing victory, one of the accomplishments of the Master-Mind. He thinks big thoughts. The creative energies of mind find no more difficulty in handling large situations, than small ones. Mind is just as much present in the Infinitely large as in the Infinitely small.

8. When we realize these facts concerning mind we understand how we may bring ourselves any condition by creating the corresponding conditions in our consciousness, because everything which is held for any length of time in the consciousness, eventually becomes impressed upon the subconscious and thus becomes a pattern which the creative energy will wave into the life and environment of the individual.

9. In this way conditions are produced and we find that our lives are simply the reflection of our predominant thoughts, our mental attitude; we see then that the science of correct thinking is the one science, that it includes all other sciences.

10. From this science we learn that every thought creates an impression on the brain, that these impressions create mental tendencies, and these tendencies create character, ability and purpose, and that the combined action of character, ability and purpose determines the experiences with which we shall meet in life.

11. These experiences come to us through the Law of Attraction; through the action of this law we meet in the world without the experiences which correspond to our world within.

12. The predominant thought or the mental attitude is the magnet, and the law is that "like attracts like," consequently the mental attitude will invariably attract such conditions as correspond to its nature.

13. This mental attitude is our personality and is composed of the thoughts which we have been creating in our own mind; therefore, if we wish a change in conditions all that is necessary is to change our thought; this will in turn change our mental attitude, which will in turn change our personality, which will in turn change the persons, things and conditions, or, the experiences with which we meet in life.

14. It is, however, no easy matter to change the mental attitude, but by persistent effort it may be accomplished; the mental attitude is patterned after the mental pictures which have been photographed on the brain; if you do not like the pictures, destroy the negatives and create new pictures; this is the art of visualization.

15. As soon as you have done this you will begin to attract new things, and the new things will correspond to the new pictures. To do this: impress on the mind a perfect picture of the desire which you wish to have objectified and continue to hold the picture in mind until results are obtained.

16. If the desire is one which requires determination, ability, talent, courage, power or any other spiritual power, these are necessary essentials for your picture; build them in; they are the vital part of the picture; they are the feeling which combines with thought and creates the irresistible magnetic power which draws the things you require to you. They give your picture life, and life means growth, and as soon as it beings to grow, the result is practically assured.

17. Do not hesitate to aspire to the highest possible attainments in anything you may undertake, for the mind forces are ever ready to lend themselves to a purposeful will in the effort to crystallize its highest aspirations into acts, accomplishments, and events.

18. An illustration of how these mind forces operate is suggested by the method in which all our habits are formed. We do a thing, then do it again, and again, and again, until it becomes easy and perhaps almost automatic; and the same rule applies in breaking any and all bad habits; we stop doing a thing, and then avoid it again, and again until we are entirely free from it; and if we do fail now and then, we should by no means lose hope, for the law is absolute and invincible and gives us credit for every effort and every success, even though our efforts and successes are perhaps intermittent.

19. There is no limit to what this law can do for you; dare to believe in your own idea; remember that Nature is plastic to the ideal; think of the ideal as an already accomplished fact.

20. The real battle of life is one of ideas; it is being fought out by the few against the many; on the one side is the constructive and creative thought, on the other side the destructive and negative thought; the

creative thought is dominated by an ideal, the passive thought is dominated by appearances. On both sides are men of science, men of letters, and men of affairs.

21. On the creative side are men who spend their time in laboratories, or over microscopes and telescopes, side by side with the men who dominate the commercial, political, and scientific world; on the negative side or men who spend their time investigating law and precedent, men who mistake theology for religion, statesmen who mistake might for right, and all the millions who seem to prefer precedent to progress, who are eternally looking backward instead of forward, who see only the world without, but know nothing of the world within.

22. In the last analysis there are but these two classes; all men will have to take their place on one side or the other; they will have to go forward, or go back; there is no standing still in a world where all is motion; it is this attempt to stand still that gives sanction and force to arbitrary and unequal codes of law.

23. That we are in a period of transition is evidenced by the unrest which is everywhere apparent. The complaint of humanity is as a roll of heaven's artillery, commencing with low and threatening notes and increasing until the sound is sent from cloud to cloud, and the lightning splits the air and earth.

24. The sentries who patrol the most advanced outposts of the Industrial, Political, and Religious world are calling anxiously to each other. What of the night? The danger and insecurity of the position they occupy and attempt to hold is becoming more apparent every hour. The dawn of a new era necessarily declares that the existing order of things cannot much longer be.

25. The issue between the old regime and the new, the crux of the social problem, is entirely a question of conviction in the minds of the people as to the nature of the Universe. When they realize that the transcendent force of spirit or mind of the Cosmos is within each individual, it will be possible to frame laws that shall consider the liberties and rights of the many instead of the privileges of the few.

26. As long as the people regard the Cosmic power as a power non-human and alien to humanity, so long will it be comparatively easy for a supposed privileged class to rule by Divine right in spite of every protest of social sentiment. The real interest of democracy is therefore to exalt, emancipate and recognize the divinity of the human spirit. To recognize that all power is from within. That no human being has any more power than any other human being, except such as may willingly be delegated to him. The old regime would have us believe that the law was superior to the law-makers; herein is the gist of the social crime of every form of privilege and personal inequality, the institutionalizing of the fatalistic doctrine of Divine election.

27. The Divine Mind is the Universal Mind; it makes no exceptions, it plays no favorites; it does not act through sheer caprice or from anger, jealousy or wrath; neither can it be flattered, cajoled or moved by sympathy or petition to supply man with some need which he thinks necessary for his happiness or even his existence. The Divine Mind makes no exceptions to favor any individual; but when the individual understands and realizes his Unity with the Universal principle he will appear to be favored because he will have found the source of all health, all wealth, and all power.

28. For your exercise this week, concentrate on the Truth. Try to realize that the Truth shall make you free, that is, nothing can permanently stand in the way of your perfect success when you learn to apply the scientifically correct thought methods and principles. Realize that you are externalizing in your environment your inherent soul potencies. Realize that the Silence offers an ever-available and almost unlimited opportunity for awakening the highest conception of Truth. Try to comprehend that Omnipotence itself is absolute silence, all else is change, activity, limitation. Silent thought concentration is therefore the true method of reaching, awakening, and then expressing the wonderful potential power of the world within.

PART 22

In Part Twenty-two you will find that thoughts are spiritual seeds, which, when planted in the subconscious mind, have a tendency to sprout and grow, but unfortunately the fruit is frequently not to our liking.

The various forms of inflammation, paralysis, nervousness and diseased conditions generally, are the manifestation of fear, worry, care, anxiety, jealousy, hatred and similar thought.

The life processes are carried on by two distinct methods; first, the taking up and making use of nutritive material necessary for constructing cells; second, breaking down and excreting the waste material.

All life is based upon these constructive and destructive activities, and as food, water and air are the only requisites necessary for the construction of cells, it would seem that the problem of prolonging life indefinitely would not be a very difficult one.

However strange it may seem, it is the second or destructive activity that is, with rare exception, the cause of all disease. The waste material accumulates and saturates the tissues, which causes autointoxication. This may be partial or general. In the first case the disturbance will be local; in the second place it will affect the whole system.

The problem, then, before us in the healing of disease is to increase the inflow and distribution of vital energy throughout the system, and this can only be done by eliminating thoughts of fear, worry, care, anxiety, jealousy, hatred, and every other destructive thought, which tend to tear down and destroy the nerves and glands which control the excretion and elimination of poisonous and waste matter.

"Nourishing foods and strengthening tonics" cannot bestow life, because these are but secondary manifestations to life. The primary manifestation of life and how you may get in touch with it is explained in the Part which I have the privilege of enclosing herewith.

1. Knowledge is of priceless value, because by applying knowledge we can make our future what we wish it to be. When we realize that our present character, our present environment, our present ability, our present physical condition are all the result of past methods of thinking, we shall begin to have some conception of the value of knowledge.

2. If the state of our health is not all that could be desired, let us examine our method of thinking; let us remember that every thought produces an impression on the mind; every impression is a seed which will sink into the subconscious and form a tendency; the tendency will be to attract other similar thoughts and before we know it we shall have a crop which must be harvested.

3. If these thoughts contain disease germs, the harvest will be sickness, decay, weakness, and failure; the question is, what are we thinking, what are we creating, what is the harvest to be?

4. If there is any physical condition which it is necessary to change, the law governing visualization will be found effective. Make a mental image of physical perfection, hold it in the mind until it is absorbed by the consciousness. Many have eliminated chronic ailments in a few weeks by this method, and thousands have overcome and destroyed all manner of ordinary physical disturbances by this method in a few days, sometimes in a few minutes.

5. It is through the law of vibration that the mind exercises this control over the body. We know that every mental action is a vibration, and we know that all form is simply a mode of motion, a rate of vibration. Therefore, any given vibration immediately modifies every atom in the body, every life cell is affected and an entire chemical change is made in every group of life cells.

6. Everything in the Universe is what it is by virtue of its rate of vibration. Change the rate of vibration and you change the nature, quality and form. The vast panorama of nature, both visible and invisible, is being constantly changed by simply changing the rate of vibration, and as thought is a vibration we can also exercise this power. We can change the vibration and thus produce any condition which we desire to manifest in our bodies.

7. We are all using this power every minute. The trouble is most of us are using it unconsciously and thus producing undesirable results. The problem is to use it intelligently and produce only desirable results. This should not be difficult, because we all have had sufficient experience to know what produces pleasant vibration in the body, and we also know the causes which produce the unpleasant and disagreeable sensations.

8. All that is necessary is to consult our own experience. When our thought has been uplifted, progressive, constructive, courageous, noble, kind or in any other way desirable, we have set in motion vibrations which brought about certain results. When our thought has been filled with envy, hatred, jealousy, criticism or any of the other thousand and one forms of discord, certain vibrations were set in motion which brought about certain other results of a different nature, and each of these rates of vibration, if kept up, crystallized in form. In the first case the result was mental, moral and physical health, and in the second case discord, in harmony and disease.

9. We can understand, then, something of the power which the mind possesses over the body.

10. The objective mind has certain effects on the body which are readily recognized. Someone says something to you which strikes you as ludicrous and you laugh, possibly until your whole body shakes, which shows that thought has control over the muscles of your body; or someone says

something which excites your sympathy and your eyes fill with tears, which shows that thought controls the glands of your body; or someone says something which makes you angry and the blood mounts to your cheek, which shows that thought controls the circulation of your blood. But as these experiences are all the results of the action of your objective mind over the body, the results are of a temporary nature; they soon pass away and leave the situation as it was before.

11. Let us see how the action of the subconscious mind over the body differs. You receive a wound; thousands of cells being the work of healing at once; in a few days or a few weeks the work is complete. You may even break a bone. No surgeon on earth can weld the parts together (I am not referring to the insertion of rods or other devices to strengthen or replace bones). He may set the bone for you, and the subjective mind will immediately begin the process of welding the parts together, and in a short time the bone is as solid as it ever was. You may swallow poison; the subjective mind will immediately discover the danger and make violent efforts to eliminate it. You may become infected with a dangerous germ; the subjective will at once commence to build a wall around the infected area and destroy the infection by absorbing it in the white blood corpuscles which it supplies for the purpose.

12. These processes of the subconscious mind usually proceed without our personal knowledge or direction, and so long as we do not interfere the result is perfect, but, as these millions of repair cells are all intelligent and respond to our thought, they are often paralyzed and rendered impotent by our thoughts of fear, doubt, and anxiety. They are like an army of workmen, ready to start an important piece of work, but every time they get started on the undertaking a strike is called, or plans changed, until they finally get discouraged and give up.

13. The way to health is founded on the law of vibration, which is the basis of all science, and this law is brought into operation by the mind, the "world within." It is a matter of individual effort and practice. Our world of power is within; if we are wise we shall not waste time and effort in trying to deal with effects as we find them in the "world without," which is only an external, a reflection.

14. We shall always find the cause in the "world within"; by changing the cause, we change the effect.

15. Every cell in your body is intelligent and will respond to your direction. The cells are all creators and will create the exact pattern which you give them.

16. Therefore, when perfect images are placed before the subjective, the creative energies will build a perfect body.

17. Brain cells are constructed in the same way. The quality of the brain is governed by the state of mind, or mental attitude, so that if undesirable mental attitudes are conveyed to the subjective they will in turn be transferred to the body; we can therefore readily see that if we wish the

body to manifest health, strength and vitality this must be the predominant thought.

18. We know then that every element of the human body is the result of a rate of vibration.

19. We know that mental action is a rate of vibration.

20. We know that a higher rate of vibration governs, modifies, controls, changes, or destroys a lower rate of vibration.

21. We know that the rate of vibration is governed by the character of brain cells, and finally,

22. We know how to create these brain cells; therefore,

23. We know how to make any physical change in the body we desire, and having secured a working knowledge of the power of mind to this extent, we have come to know that there is practically no limitation which can be placed upon our ability to place ourselves in harmony with natural law, which is omnipotent.

24. This influence or control over the body by mind is coming to be more and more generally understood, and many physicians are now giving the matter their earnest attention. Dr. Albert T. Shofield, who has written several important books on the subject, say, "The subject of mental therapeutics is still ignored in medical works generally. In our physiologies no references is made to the central controlling power that rules the body for its good, and the power of the mind over the body is seldom spoken of."

25. No doubt many physicians treat nervous diseases of functional origin wisely and well, but what we contend is that the knowledge they display was taught at no school, was learned from no book, but it is intuitive and empirical.

26. This is not as it should be. The power of mental therapeutics should be the subject of careful, special and scientific teaching in every medical school. We might pursue the subject of maltreatment, or want of treatment, further in detail and describe the disastrous results of neglected cases; but the task is an invidious one.

27. There can be no doubt that few patients are aware how much they can do for themselves. What the patient can do for himself, the forces he can set in motion are as yet unknown. We are inclined to believe that they are far greater than most imagine, and will undoubtedly be used more and more. Mental therapeutics may be directed by the patient himself to calming the mind in excitement, by arousing feelings of joy, hope, faith, and love; by suggesting motives for exertion, by regular mental work, by diverting the thoughts from the malady.

28. For your exercise this week concentrate on Tennyson's beautiful lines "Speak to Him, thou, for He hears, and spirit with spirit can meet, Closer is He than breathing, and nearer than hands and feet." Then try to realize that when you do "Speak to Him" you are in touch with Omnipotence.

29. This realization and recognition of this Omnipresent power will quickly destroy any and every form of sickness or suffering and substitute harmony and perfection. Then remember there are those who seem to think that sickness and suffering are sent by God; if so, every physician, every surgeon and every Red Cross nurse is defying the will of God and hospitals and sanitariums are places of rebellion instead of houses of mercy. Of course, this quickly reasons itself into an absurdity, but there are many; who still cherish the idea.

30. Then let the thought rest on the fact that until recently theology has been trying to teach an impossible Creator, one who created beings capable of sinning and then allowed them to be eternally punished for such sins. Of course the necessary outcome of such extraordinary ignorance was to create fear instead of love, and so, after two thousand years of this kind of propaganda, Theology is now busily engaged in apologizing for Christendom.

31. You will then more readily appreciate the ideal man, the man made in the image and likeness of God, and you will more readily appreciate the all originating Mind that forms, upholds, sustains, originates, and creates all there is.

PART 23

In the part which I have the honor to transmit herewith you will find that money weaves itself into the entire fabric of our very existence; that the law of success is service; that we get what we give, and for this reason we should consider it a great privilege to be able to give.

We have found that thought is the creative activity behind every constructive enterprise. We can therefore give nothing of more practical value than our thought.

Creative thought requires attention, and the power of attention is, as we have found, the weapon of the Super-man. Attention develops concentration, and concentration develops Spiritual Power, and Spiritual Power is the mightiest force in existence.

This is the science which embraces all sciences. It is the art which, above all arts, is relevant to human life. In the mastery of this science and this art there is opportunity for unending progression. Perfection in this is not acquired in six days, nor in six weeks, nor in six months. It is the labor of life. Not to go forward is to go backward.

It is inevitable that the entertainment of positive, constructive and unselfish thoughts should have a far-reaching effect for good. Compensation is the keynote of the universe. Nature is constantly seeking to strike an equilibrium. Where something is sent out something must be received; else there should be a vacuum formed.

By observance of this rule you cannot fail to profit in such measure as to amply justify your effort along this line.

1. The money consciousness is an attitude of mind; it is the open door to the arteries of commerce. It is the receptive attitude. Desire is the attractive force which sets the current in motion and fear is the great obstacle by which the current is stopped or completely reversed, turned away from us.

2. Fear is just the opposite from money consciousness; it is poverty consciousness, and as the law is unchangeable we get exactly what we give; if we fear we get what we feared. Money weaves itself into the entire fabric of our very existence; it engages the best thought of the best minds.

3. We make money by making friends, and we enlarge our circle of friends by making money for them, by helping them, by being of service to them. The first law of success then is service, and this in turn is built on integrity and justice. The man who at least is not fair in his intention is simply ignorant; he has missed the fundamental law of all exchange; he is impossible; he will lose surely and certainly; he may not know it; he may think he is winning, but he is doomed to certain defeat. He cannot

cheat the Infinite. The law of compensation will demand of him an eye for an eye and a tooth for a tooth.

4. The forces of life are volatile; they are composed of our thoughts and ideals and these in turn are molded into form; our problem is to keep an open mind, to constantly reach out for the new, to recognize opportunity, to be interested in the race rather than the goal, for the pleasure is in the pursuit rather than the possession.

5. You can make a money magnet of yourself, but to do so you must first consider how you can make money for other people. If you have the necessary insight to perceive and utilize opportunities and favorable conditions and recognize values, you can put yourself in position to take advantage of them, but your greatest success will come as you are enabled to assist others. What benefits one must benefit all.

6. A generous thought is filled with strength and vitality, a selfish thought contains the germs of dissolution; it will disintegrate and pass away. Great financiers are simply channels for the distribution of wealth; enormous amounts come and go, but it would be as dangerous to stop the outgo as the income; both ends must remain open; and so our greatest success will come as we recognize that it is just as essential to give as to get.

7. If we recognize the Omnipotent power that is the source of all supply we will adjust our consciousness to this supply in such a way that it will constantly attract all that is necessary to itself and we shall find that the more we give the more we get. Giving in this sense implies service. The banker gives his money, the merchant gives his goods, the author gives his thought, the workman gives his skill; all have something to give, but the more they can give, the more they get, and the more they get the more they are enabled to give.

8. The financier gets much because he gives much; he thinks; he is seldom a man that lets anyone else do his thinking for him; he wants to know how results are to be secured; you must show him; when you can do this he will furnish the means by which hundreds or thousands may profit, and in proportion as they are successful will he be successful. Morgan, Rockefeller, Carnegie and others did not get rich because they lost money for other people; on the contrary, it is because they made money for other people that they became the wealthiest men in the wealthiest country on the globe.

9. The average person is entirely innocent of any deep thinking; he accepts the ideas of others, and repeats them, in very much the same way as a parrot; this is readily seen when we understand the method which is used to form public opinion, and this docile attitude on the part of a large majority who seem perfectly willing to let a few persons do all their thinking for them is what enables a few men in a great many countries to usurp all the avenues of power and hold the millions in subjection. Creative thinking requires attention.

10. The power of attention is called concentration; this power is directed by the will; for this reason we must refuse to concentrate or think of anything except the things we desire. Many are constantly concentrating upon sorrow, loss and discord of every kind; as thought is creative it necessarily follows that this concentration inevitable leads to more loss, more sorrow and more discord. How could it be otherwise? On the other hand, when we meet with success, gain, or any other desirable condition, we naturally concentrate upon the effects of these things and thereby create more, and so it follows that much leads to more.

11. How an understanding of this principle can be utilized in the business world is well told by an associate of mine:

12. "Spirit, whatever else it may or may not be, must be considered as the Essence of Consciousness, the Substance of Mind, the reality underlying Thought. And as all ideas are phases of the activity of Consciousness, Mind or Thought, it follows that in Spirit, and in it alone, is to be found the Ultimate Fact, the Real Thing, or Idea."

13. This being admitted, does it not seem reasonable to hold that a true understanding of Spirit, and its laws of manifestation, would be about the most "practical" thing that a "practical" person can hope to find? Does it not seem certain that if the "practical" men of the world could but realize this fact, they would "fall all over themselves" in getting to the place in which they might obtain such knowledge of spiritual things and laws? These men are not fools; they need only to grasp this fundamental fact in order to move in the direction of that which is the essence of all achievement.

14. Let me give you a concrete example. I know a man in Chicago whom I had always considered to be quite materialistic. He had made several successes in life; and also several failures. The last time I had a talk with him he was practically "down and out," as compared with his former business condition. It looked as if he had indeed reached "the end of his rope," for he was well advanced into the stage of middle-age, and new ideas came more slowly, and less frequently to him than in former years.

15. He said to me, in substance: "I know that all things that "work out" in business are the result of Thought; any fool knows that. Just now, I seem to be short on thoughts and good ideas. But, if this "All-Mind" teaching is correct, it should be possible for the individual to attain a 'direct connection' with Infinite Mind; and in Infinite Mind there must be the possibility of all kinds of good ideas which a man of my courage and experience could put to practical use in the business world, and make a big success thereof. It looks good to me; and I am going to look into it."

16. This was several years ago. The other day I heard of this man again. Talking to a friend, I said: "What has come of our old friend X? Has he ever gotten on his feet again?" The friend looked at me in amazement. "Why," said he, "don't you know about X's great success? He is the Big Man in the '_____ Company' (naming a concern which has mad a

phenomenal success during the last eighteen months and is now well known, by reason of its advertisements, from one end of the country to another, and also abroad). He is the man who supplied the *big idea* for that concern. Why, he is about a half-million to the good and is moving rapidly toward the million mark; all in the space of eighteen months." I had not connected this man with the enterprise mentioned; although I knew of the wonderful success of the company in question. Investigation has shown that the story is true, and that the above stated facts are not exaggerated in the slightest.

17. Now, what do you think of that? To me, it means that this man actually made the "direct connection" with Infinite Mind — Spirit — and, having found it, he set it to work for him. He "used it in his business."

18. Does this sound sacrilegious or blasphemous? I hope not; I do not mean it to be so. Take away the implication of Personality, or Magnified Human Nature, from the conception of the "The Infinite," and you have left the conception of an Infinite Presence-Power, the Quintessence of which is Consciousness — in fact, at the last, Spirit. As this man, also, at the last, must be considered as a manifestation of Spirit; there is nothing sacrilegious in the idea that he, being Spirit, should so harmonize himself with his Origin and Source that he would be able to manifest at least a minor degree of its Power. All of us do this, more or less, when we use our minds in the direction of Creative Thought. This man did more, he went about it in an intensely "practical" manner.

19. I have not consulted him about his method of procedure, though I intend doing so at the first opportunity, but, he not only drew upon the Infinite Supply for the ideas which he needed (and which formed the seed of his success), but that he also used the Creative Power of Thought in building up for himself an Idealistic Pattern of that which he hoped to manifest in material form, adding thereto, changing, improving its detail, from time to time — proceeding from the general outline to the finished detail. I judge this to be the facts of the case, not alone from my recollection of the conversation a few years ago, but also because I have found the same thing to be true in the cases of other prominent men who have made similar manifestation of Creative Thought.

20. Those who may shrink from this idea of employing the Infinite Power to aid one in his work in the material world, should remember that if the Infinite objected in the least to such a procedure the thing could never happen. The Infinite is quite able to take care of itself.

21. "Spirituality" is quite "practical," very "practical," intensely "practical." It teaches that Spirit is the Real Thing, the Whole Thing, and that Matter is but plastic stuff, which Spirit is able to create, mold, manipulate, and fashion to its will. Spirituality is the most "practical" thing in the world — the only really and absolutely "practical" thing that there is!

22. This week concentrate on the fact that man is not a body with a spirit, but a spirit with a body, and that it is for this reason that his desires are incapable of any permanent satisfaction in anything not spiritual. Money is therefore of no value except to bring about the conditions which we desire, and these conditions are necessarily harmonious. Harmonious conditions necessitate sufficient supply, so that if there appears to be any lack, we should realize that the idea or soul of money is service, and as this thought takes form, channels of supply will be opened, and you will have the satisfaction of knowing that spiritual methods are entirely practical.

PART 24

The final lesson of this course.

If you have practiced each of the exercises a few minutes every day, as suggested, you will have found that you can get out of life exactly what you wish by first putting into life that which you wish, and you will probably agree with the student who said: "The thought is almost overwhelming, so vast, so available, so definite, so reasonable and so usable."

The fruit of this knowledge is, as it were, a gift of the Gods; it is the "truth" that makes men free, not only free from every lack and limitation, but free from sorrow, worry and care, and, is it not wonderful to realize that this law is no respecter of persons, that it makes no difference what your habit of thought may be, the way has been prepared.

If you are inclined to be religious, the greatest religious teacher the world has ever known made the way so plain that all may follow. If your mental bias is toward physical science, the law will operate with mathematical certainty. If you are inclined to be philosophical, Plato or Emerson may be your teacher, but in either case, you may reach degrees of power to which it is impossible to assign any limit.

An understanding of this principle, I believe, is the secret for which the ancient Alchemists vainly sought, because it explains how gold in the mind may be transmuted into gold in the heart and in the hand.

1. When the scientists first put the Sun in the center of the Solar System and sent the earth spinning around it, there was immense surprise and consternation. The whole idea was self-evidently false; nothing was more certain than the movement of the Sun across the sky, and anyone could see it descend behind the western hills and sink into the sea; scholars raged and scientists rejected the idea as absurd, yet the evidence has finally carried conviction in the minds of all.

2. We speak of a bell as a "sounding body," yet we know that all the bell can do is to produce vibrations in the air. When these vibrations come at the rate of sixteen per second, they cause a sound to be heard in the mind. It is also possible for the mind to hear vibrations up to the rate of 38,000 vibrations per second. When the number increases beyond this, all is silence again; so that we know that the sound is not in the bell, it is in our own mind.

3. We speak and even think of the Sun as "giving light." Yet we know it is simply giving forth energy which produces vibrations in the ether at the rate of four hundred trillion a second, causing what are termed light waves, so that we know that we call light is simply a form of energy and

that the only light there is, is the sensation caused in the mind by the motion of the waves. When the number increases, the light changes in color, each change in color being caused by shorter and more rapid vibrations; so that although we speak of the rose as being red, the grass as being green, or the sky as being blue, we know that the colors exist only in our minds, and are the sensations experienced by us as the result of the vibrations of light waves. When the vibrations are reduced below four hundred trillion a second, they no longer affect us as light, but we experience the sensation of heat. It is evident, therefore, that we cannot depend upon the evidence of the senses for our information concerning the realities of things; if we did we should believe that the sun moved, that the world was flat instead of round, that the stars were bits of light instead of vast suns.

4. The whole range then of the theory and practice of any system of metaphysics consists in knowing the Truth concerning yourself and the world in which you live; in knowing that in order to express harmony, you must think harmony; in order to express health you must think health; and in order to express abundance you must think abundance; to do this you must reverse the evidence of the senses.

5. When you come to know that every form of disease, sickness, lack and limitation are simply the result of wrong thinking, you will have come to know "the Truth which shall make you free." You will see how mountains may be removed. If these mountains consist only of doubt, fear, distrust or other forms of discouragement, they are none the less real, and they need not only to be removed but to be "cast into the sea."

6. Your real work consists in convincing yourself of the truth of these statements. When you have succeeded in doing this you will have no difficulty in thinking the truth, and as has been shown, the truth contains a vital principle and will manifest itself.

7. Those who heal diseases by mental methods have come to know this truth, they demonstrate it in their lives and the lives of others daily. They know that life, health and abundance are Omnipresent, filling all space, and they know that those who allow disease or lack of any kind to manifest, have as yet not come into an understanding of this great law.

8. As all conditions are thought creations and therefore entirely mental, disease and lack are simply mental conditions in which the person fails to perceive the truth; as soon as the error is removed, the condition is removed.

9. The method for removing this error is to go into the Silence and know the Truth; as all mind is one mind, you can do this for yourself or anyone else. If you have learned to form mental images of the conditions desired, this will be the easiest and quickest way to secure results; if not, results can be accomplished by argument, by the process of convincing yourself absolutely of the truth of your statement.

10. Remember, and this is one of the most difficult as well as most wonderful statements to grasp . . . remember that no matter what the difficulty is, no matter where it is, no matter who is affected, you have no patient but yourself; you have nothing to do but to convince yourself of the truth which you desire to see manifested.

11. This is an exact scientific statement in accordance with every system of Metaphysics in existence, and no permanent results are ever secured in any other way.

12. Every form of concentration, forming Mental Images, Argument, and Autosuggestion are all simply methods by which you are enabled to realize the Truth.

13. If you desire to help someone, to destroy some form of lack, limitation or error, the correct method is not to think of the person whom you wish to help; the intention to help them is entirely sufficient, as this puts you in mental touch with the person. Then drive out of your own mind any belief of lack, limitation, disease, danger, difficulty or whatever the trouble might be. As soon as you have succeeded is doing this the result will have been accomplished, and the person will be free.

14. But remember that thought is creative and consequently every time you allow your thought to rest on any inharmonious condition, you must realize that such conditions are apparent only, they have no reality, that spirit is the only reality and it can never be less than perfect.

15. All thought is a form of energy, a rate of vibration, but a thought of the Truth is the highest rate of vibration known and consequently destroys every form of error in exactly the same way that light destroys darkness; no form of error can exist when the "Truth" appears, so that your entire mental work consists in coming into an understanding of the Truth. This will enable you to overcome every form of lack, limitation or disease of any kind.

16. We can get no understanding of the truth from the world without; the world without is relative only; Truth is absolute. We must therefore find it in the "world within."

17. To train the mind to see Truth only is to express true conditions only, our ability to do this will be an indication as to the progress we are making.

18. The absolute truth is that the "I" is perfect and complete; the real "I" is spiritual and can therefore never be less than perfect; it can never have any lack, limitation, or disease. The flash of genius does not have origin in the molecular motion of the brain; it is inspired by the ego, the spiritual "I" which is one with the Universal Mind, and it is our ability to recognize this Unity which is the cause of all inspiration, all genius. These results are far reaching and have effect upon generations yet to come; they are the pillars of fire which mark the path that millions follow.

19. Truth is not the result of logical training or of experimentation, or even of observation; it is the product of a developed consciousness. Truth

within a Caesar, manifests in a Caesar's deportment, in his life and his action; his influence upon social forms and progress. Your life and your actions and your influence in the world will depend upon the degree of truth which you are enabled to perceive, for truth will not manifest in creeds, but in conduct.

20. Truth manifests in character, and the character of a man, should be the interpretation of his religion, or what to him is truth, and this will in turn be evidenced in the character of his possession. If a man complains of the drift of his fortune he is just as unjust to himself as if he should deny rational truth, though it stand patent and irrefutable.

21. Our environment and the innumerable circumstances and accidents of our lives already exist in the subconscious personality which attracts to itself the mental and physical material which is congenial to its nature. Thus our future being determined from our present, and if there should be apparent injustice in any feature or phase of our personal life, we must look within for the cause, try to discover the mental fact which is responsible for the outward manifestation.

22. It is this truth which makes you "free" and it is the conscious knowledge of this truth which will enable you to overcome every difficulty.

23. The conditions with which you meet in the world without are invariably the result of the conditions obtaining in the world within, therefore it follows with scientific accuracy that by holding the perfect ideal in mind you can bring about ideal conditions in your environment.

24. If you see only the incomplete, the imperfect, the relative, the limited, these conditions will manifest in your life; but if you train your mind to see and realize the spiritual ego, the "I" which is forever perfect and complete, harmonious; wholesome, and healthful conditions only will be manifested.

25. As thought is creative, and the truth is the highest and most perfect thought which anyone can think, it is self-evident that to think the truth is to create that which is true and it is again evident that when truth comes into being that which is false must cease to be.

26. The Universal Mind is the totality of all mind which is in existence. Spirit is Mind, because spirit is intelligent. The words are, therefore, synonymous.

27. The difficulty with which you have to contend is to realize that mind is not individual. It is omnipresent. It exists everywhere. In other words, there is no place where it is not. It is, therefore, Universal.

28. Men have, heretofore, generally used the word "God" to indicate this Universal, creative principle; but the word "God" does not convey the right meaning. Most people understand this word to mean something outside of themselves; while exactly the contrary is the fact. It is our very life. Without it we would be dead. We would cease to exist. The minute the spirit leaves the body, we are as nothing. Therefore, spirit is really, all there is of us.

29. Now, the only activity which the spirit possesses is the power to think. Therefore, thought must be creative, because spirit is creative. This creative power is impersonal and your ability to think is your ability to control it and make use of it for the benefit of yourself and others.

30. When the truth of this statement is realized, understood, and appreciated, you will have come into possession of the Master-Key, but remember that only those who are wise enough to understand, broad enough to weigh the evidence, firm enough to follow their own judgment, and strong enough to make the sacrifice exacted, may enter and partake.

31. This week, try to realize that this is truly a wonderful world in which we live, that you are a wonderful being that many are awakening to a knowledge of the Truth, and as fast as they awake and come into a knowledge of the "things which have been prepared for them" they, too, realize that "Eye hath not seen, nor ear heard, neither hath it entered into the heart of man," the splendors which exist for those who find themselves in the Promised Land. They have crossed the river of judgment and have arrived at the point of discrimination between the true and the false, and have found that all they ever willed or dreamed, was but a faint concept of the dazzling reality.

Mental Chemistry

Chemistry is the science which treats of the intra-atomic or the intra-molecular changes which material things undergo under various influences.

Mental is defined as "of or appertaining to the mind, including intellect, feeling, and will, or the entire rational nature."

Science is knowledge gained and verified by exact observation and correct thinking.

Mental chemistry is, therefore, the science which treats of the changes which material conditions undergo through the operations of the mind, verified by exact observation and correct thinking.

As the transformations which are brought about in applied chemistry are the result of the orderly combination of materials, it follows that mental chemistry brings about results in a like manner.

Any conceivable number may be formed with the Arabic numbers 1, 2, 3, 4, 5, 6, 7, 8, 9, 0.

Any conceivable thought may be expressed with the 26 letters of the alphabet.

Any conceivable thing can be organized with the 14 elements and always and only by the proper grouping of electrons into molecules.

When two or more molecules are grouped a new individuality is created, and this individuality which has been called into being possesses characteristics which are not possessed by either of the elements which gave it being.

Thus one atom of sodium and one of chlorine give us salt, and this combination alone can give us salt, and no other combination of elements can give us salt, and salt is something very different from either of the elements of which it is composed.

What is true in the inorganic world is likewise true in the organic—certain conscious processes will produce certain effects, and the result will invariably be the same. The same thought will always be followed by the same consequence, and no other thought will serve the purpose.

This must necessarily be true because the principle must exist independently of the organs through which they function. Light must exist—otherwise there could be no eye. Sound must exist—otherwise there could be no ear. Mind must exist—otherwise there could be no brain.

Mental action is therefore the interaction of the individual upon the Universal Mind, and as the Universal Mind is the intelligence which pervades all space and animates all living things, this mental action and reaction is the law of causation.

It is the Universal Chemist, but the principle of causation does not obtain in the individual mind but in the Universal Mind. It is not an objective faculty but a subjective process.

The individual may, however, bring the power into manifestation and as the possible combinations of thought are infinite, the results are seen in an infinite variety of conditions and experiences.

Primordial man, naked and bestial, squatting in gloomy caverns, gnawing bones, was born, lived, and died in a hostile world. His hostility and his wretchedness arose from his ignorance. His handmaidens were Hate and Fear. His sole reliance was his club. He saw in the beasts, forests, torrents, seas, clouds, and even in his fellow man, only enemies. He recognized no ties binding them one to another or to himself.

Modern man is born to comparative luxury. Love rocks his cradle and shields his youth. When he goes forth to struggle he wields a pencil, not a club. He relies upon his brain, now his brawn. He knows the physical as neither master nor equal, but as a useful servant. His fellow men and the forces of Nature are his friends—not his enemies.

These tremendous changes, from hate to love, from fear to confidence, from material strife to mental control, have been wrought by the slow dawn of Understanding. In direct proportion as he understands Cosmic Law is man's lot enviable or the reverse.

Thought builds organic structures in animals and men. The protoplasmic cell desires the light and sends forth its impulse; this impulse gradually builds an eye. A species of deer feed in a country where the leaves grow on high branches, and the constant reaching for their favorite food builds cell by cell the neck of the giraffe. The amphibian reptiles desire to fly in the open air above the water; they develop wings and become birds.

Experiments with parasites found on plants indicate that even the lowest order of life makes use of mental chemistry. Jacques Loeb, M. D., Ph. D., a member of the Rockefeller Institute made the following experiment: "In order to obtain the material, potted rose bushes are brought into a room and placed in front of a closed window. If the plants are allowed to dry out, the aphides (parasites), previously wingless, change to winged insects. After the metamorphosis, the insects leave the plants, fly to the window and then creep upward on the glass."

It is evident that these tiny insects found that the plants on which they had been thriving were dead, and that they could therefore secure nothing more to eat and drink from this source. The only method by which they could save themselves from starvation was to grow temporary wings and fly, which they did.

That the brain cells are directly affected by mental pictures, and that the brain cells in their turn can affect the entire being, was proven by Prof. Elmer Gates of the Smithsonian Institution at Washington. Guinea pigs were kept in enclosures with certain colors dominant; dissection showed their brains to be larger in the color area than those of the same class of guinea pigs kept in other enclosures. The perspiration of men in various mental moods was analyzed, and the resultant salts experimented with. Those of a man in an angry state were of an unusual color; a small portion put on the tongue of a dog produced evidences of poisoning.

Experiments at Harvard College with students on the weighing board proved that the mind moves the blood. When the student was told to imagine that he was running a foot race, the board sank down at the foot, and when a problem in mathematics was being worked the balanced board sank down at the head.

This shows that thought not only flashes constantly between mind and mind, with an intensity and swiftness far transcending electricity, but that it also builds the structures through which it operates.

Through the conscious mind we know ourselves as individuals, and take cognizance of the world about us. The subconscious mind is the storehouse of past thoughts.

We can understand the action of the conscious and subconscious minds by observing the process by which the child learns to play the piano. He is taught how to hold his hands and strike the keys, but at first he finds it somewhat difficult to control the movement of his fingers. He must practice daily, must concentrate his thoughts upon his fingers, consciously making the right movements. These thoughts, in time, become subconscious, and the fingers are directed and controlled in the playing by the subconsciousness. In his first months, and possibly first years of practice, the pupil can perform only by keeping his conscious mind centered upon the work; but later he can play with ease and at the same time carry on a conversation with those about him, because the subconscious has become so thoroughly imbued with the idea of right movements that it can direct them without demanding the attention of the conscious mind.

The subconscious cannot take the initiative. It carried out only what is suggested by the conscious mind. But these suggestions it carries out faithfully, and it is this close relation between the conscious and subconscious which makes the conscious thinking so important.

Man's organism is controlled by the subconscious thought; circulation, breathing, digestion, and assimilation are all activities controlled by the subconscious. The subconscious is continually getting its impulses from the conscious, and we have only to change our conscious thought to get a corresponding change in the subconscious.

We live in a fathomless sea of plastic mind substance. This substance is ever alive and active. It is sensitive to the highest degree. It takes form according to the mental demand. Thought forms the mold or matrix from which the substance expresses. Our ideal is the mold from which our future will emerge.

The Universe is alive. In order to express life there must be mind; nothing can exist without mind. Everything which exists is some manifestation of this one basic substance from which and by which all things have been created and are continually being recreated. It is man's capacity to think that makes him a creator instead of a creature.

All things are the result of the thought process. Man has accomplished the seemingly impossible because he has refused to consider it impossible. By concentration men have made the connection between the finite and the Infinite, the limited and the Unlimited, the visible and the Invisible, the personal and the Impersonal.

Great musicians have succeeded in thrilling the world by the creation of divine rhapsodies. Great inventors have made the connection and startled the world by their wonderful creations. Great authors, great philosophers, great scientists have secured this harmony to such an extent that though their writings were created hundreds of years ago, we are just beginning to realize their truth. Love of music, love of business, love of creation caused these people to concentrate, and the ways and means of materializing their ideals slowly but surely developed.

Throughout the entire Universe the law of cause and effect is ever at work. This law is supreme; here a cause, there an effect. They can never operate independently. One is supplementary to the other. Nature at all times is endeavoring to establish a perfect equilibrium. This is the law of the Universe and is ever active. Universal harmony is the goal for which all nature strives. The entire cosmos moves under this law. The sun, the moon, the starts are all held in their respective positions because of harmony. They travel their orbits, they appear at certain times in certain places, and because of the precision of this law, astronomers are able to tell us where various stars will appear in a thousand years. The scientist bases his entire hypothesis on this law of cause and effect. nowhere is it held in dispute except in the domain of man. Here we find people speaking of luck, chance, accident, and mishap; but is any one of these possible? Is the Universe a unit? If so, and there is law and order in one part, it must extend throughout all parts. This is a scientific deduction.

Like begets like on every plane of existence, and while people believe this more or less vaguely, they refuse to give it any consideration where they are concerned. This is due to the fact that heretofore man could never realize how he set certain causes in motion which related him with his various experiences.

It is only in the past few years that a working hypothesis could be formulated to apply this law to man—the goal of the Universe is harmony. This means a perfect balance between all things.

Ether fills all interplanetary space. This more or less metaphysical substance is the elementary basis of all matter. it is upon this substance that the messages of the wireless are transmitted through space.

Thought dropped into this substance causes vibrations which in turn unite with similar vibrations and react upon the thinker. All manifestations are the result of thought—but the thinking is on different planes.

We have one plane of thought constituting the animal plane. Here are actions and interactions which animals respond to, yet men know nothing of. Then we have the conscious thought plane. Here are almost limitless planes of thought to which man may be responsive. It is strictly the nature of our thinking that determines to which plane we shall respond. On this plane, we have the thoughts of the ignorant, the wise, the poor, the wealthy, the sick, the healthy, the very poor, the very rich, and so on. The number of thought planes is infinite, but the point is that when we think on a definite plane, we are responsive to thoughts on that plane, and the effect of the reaction is apparent in our environment.

Take for example one who is thinking on the thought plane of wealth. He is inspired with an idea, and the result is success. It could not be otherwise. He is thinking on the success plane, and as like attracts like, his thoughts attract other similar thoughts, all of which contribute to his success. His receiver is attuned for success thoughts only, all other messages fail to reach his consciousness, hence, he knows nothing of them; his antennae, as it were, reach into the Universal Ether and connect with the ideas by which his plans and ambitions may be realized.

Sit right where you are, place an amplifier to your ear, and you may hear the most beautiful music, or a lecture, or the latest market reports. What does this indicate, in addition to the pleasure derived from he music or the information received from the lecture or market reports?

It indicates first that there must be some substance sufficiently refined to carry these vibrations to every part of the world. Again it indicates that this substance must be sufficiently refined to penetrate every other substance known to man. The vibrations must penetrate wood, brick, stone or steel of any kind. They must go over, through and under rivers, mountains, above the earth, under the earth, everywhere and anywhere. Again it indicates that time and space have been annihilated. The instant a piece of music is broadcasted in Pittsburgh or anywhere else, by putting the proper mechanism to your ear you can get it as clearly and distinctly as though you were in the same room. This indicates that these vibrations proceed in every direction; wherever there is an ear to hear, it may hear.

If then there is a substance so refined that it will take up the human voice, and send it in every direction so that every human being who is equipped with the proper mechanism may receive the message, is it not possible that the same substance will carry a thought just as readily and just as certainly? Most assuredly. How do we know this? By experimentation. This is the only way to be certain of anything. Try it. Make the experiment yourself.

Sit right where you are. Select a subject with which you are fairly familiar. Begin to think. The thoughts will follow each other in rapid succession. One thought will suggest another. You will soon be surprised at some of the thoughts which have made you a channel of their manifestation. You did not know that you knew so much about the subject. You did not know that you could put them into such beautiful language. You marvel at the ease and rapidity with which the thoughts arrive. Where do they come from? From the One Source of all wisdom, all power. and all understanding. You have been to the source of all knowledge, for every thought which has ever been thought is still in existence, ready and waiting for someone to attach the mechanism by which it can find expression. You can therefore think the thoughts of every sage, every artist, every financier, every captain of industry who ever existed, for thoughts never die.

Suppose your experiment is not entirely successful; try again. Few of us are proud of our first effort at anything. We did not even make a very great success in trying to walk the first time we tried. If you try again, remember that the brain is the organ of the objective mind, that it is related to the objective world by the cerebro-spinal or voluntary nervous system; that this system of nerves is connected with the objective world by certain mechanism or senses. These are the organs with which we see, hear, feel, taste, and smell. Now, a thought is a thing which can neither be seen, nor heard; we cannot taste it, nor can we smell it, nor can we feel it. Evidently the five senses can be of no possible value in trying to receive a thought. They must therefore be stilled, because thought is a spiritual activity and cannot reach us through any material channel. We will then relax both mentally and physically and send out an S. O. S. for help and await the result. The success of our experiment will then depend entirely upon our ability to become receptive.

Scientists like to make use of the word Ether in speaking of the substance "In which we live and move and have our behaving," which is Omnipresent, which impenetrates everything, and which is the source of all activity. They like to use the word Ether because Ether implies something which can be measured and so far as the materialistic school of scientists is concerned, anything which cannot be measured does not exist; but who can measure an electron? And yet the electron is the basis for all material existence, so far as we know at present.

It would require 500,000,000 atoms placed side by side to measure one linear inch. A number of atoms equal to twenty-five million times the population of earth must be present in the test tube for a chemist to detect them in a chemical trace. About 125 septillions of atoms are in an inch cube of lead. And we cannot come anywhere near even seeing an atom through a microscope!

Yet the atom is as large as our solar system compared to the electrons of which it is composed. All atoms are alike in having one positive central sun of energy around which one or more negative charges of energy revolve. The number of negative electrons each atom contains determines the nature of the so-called "element" of which it is a part.

An atom of hydrogen, for instance, is supposed to have one negative electron as a satellite to its positive center. For this reason chemists accept it as a standard of atomic weight. The atomic weight of hydrogen is placed at 1.

The diameter of an electron is to the diameter of the atom as the diameter of our Earth is to the diameter of the orbit in which it moves around the sun. More specifically, it has been determined that an electron is one-eighteen-thousandth of the mass of a hydrogen atom.

It is clear therefore that matter is capable of a degree of refinement almost beyond the power of the human mind to calculate. We have not as yet been able to analyze this refinement beyond the electron, and even in getting thus far have had to supplement our physical observation of effects with imagination to cover certain gaps.

The building up of Matter from Electrons has been an involuntary process of individualizing intelligent energy.

Food, water and air are usually considered to be the three essential elements necessary to sustain life. This is very true, but there is something still more essential. Every time we breathe we not only fill our lungs with air which has been charged with magnetism by the Solar Orb, but we fill ourselves with Pranic Energy, the breath of life replete with every requirement for mind and spirit. This life giving spirit is far more necessary than air, food, or water, because a man can live for forty days without food, for three days without water, and for a few minutes without air; but he cannot live a single second without Ether. It is the one prime essential of life, and contains all the essentials of life, so that the process of breathing furnishes not only food for body building, but food for mind and spirit as well.

THE CHEMIST

Universal intelligence leaves its source to become embodied in material forms through which it returns to its source as an individual or entity. Mineral life animated by electro-magnetism is the first step of intelligence upward, toward its universal source. Universal energy is intelligent, and this involuntary process by which matter is built up, is an intelligent process of nature which has for its specific purpose the individualization of her intelligence.

Stockwell says: "The basis of life and consciousness lies back of the atoms, and may be found in the universal ether." Hemstreet says: "Mind in the ether is no more unnatural than mind in flesh and blood." Stockwell says: "The ether is coming to be apprehended as an immaterial superphysical substance, filling all space, carrying in its infinite, throbbing bosom the specks of aggregated dynamic force called worlds. It embodies the ultimate spiritual principle, and represents the unity of those forces and energies from which spring, as their source, all phenomena, physical, mental, and spiritual, as they are known to man." Dolbear, in his great work on the ether, says: "Besides the function of energy and motion, the ether has other inherent properties, out of which could emerge, under proper circumstances, other phenomena, such as life or mind or whatever may be in the substratum."

The microscopic cell, a minute speck of matter that is to become man, has in it the promise and germ of mind. May we not draw the inference that the elements of mind are present in those chemical elements—carbon, oxygen, hydrogen, nitrogen, sulphur, phosphorous, sodium, potassium, chlorine—that are found in the cell? not only must we do so; but we must go further, since we know that each of these elements, and every other, is built up of one invariable unit, the electron, and we must therefore assert that mind is potential in the unit of matter—the electron itself."

Atoms of mineral matter are attracted to each other to form aggregates or masses. This attraction is called Chemical Affinity. Chemical combinations of atoms are due to their magnetic relations to each other. Positive atoms will always attract negative atoms. The combination will last only so long as a still more positive force is not brought to bear on it to break it apart.

Two or more atoms brought into combination form a molecule, which is defined as "the smallest particle of a substance that can maintain its own identity." Thus a molecule of water is a combination of one atom of hydrogen and two atoms of oxygen (H_2O).

In building a plant, nature works with colloid cells rather than with atoms, for she has built up the cell as an entity just as she built the atom and the molecule as entities with which to work in mineral substance. The vegetable cell (colloid), has power to draw to itself from earth, air, and water whatever energies it needs for its growth. It therefore draws from mineral life and dominates it.

When vegetable matter is sufficiently refined to be receptive to still more of the universal intelligent energy, animal life appears. The plant cells have now become so plastic that they have additional capacities—those of individual consciousness, and also additional powers; those of sensational magnetism. It draws its life forces from both mineral and plant life, and therefore dominates them.

The body is an aggregate of cells animated by the spiritual magnetic life that tends toward organizing these cells into communities, and these communities into co-ordinated bodies which will operate the entire mass of the body as a conscious entity able to carry itself from one place to the other.

Atoms and molecules and their energies are now subordinated to the welfare of the cell. Each cell is a living, conscious entity, capable of selecting its own food, of resisting aggression, and of reproducing itself.

As each cell has its individual consciousness, intuition, and volition, so each federated group of cells has a collective individual consciousness, intuition, and volition. Likewise, each co-ordinated group of federations; until the entire body has one central brain where the great co-ordination of all the "brains" takes place.

The body of an average human being is composed of some twenty-six trillions (26,000,000,000,000) of cells; the brain and the spinal cord by themselves consist of some two billion.

The biogenic law proves that every vertebrate, like every other animal, evolves from a single cell. Even the human organism, according to Haeckel, is at first a simple nucleated globule of plasm, about 1.125 inch in diameter, barely visible to the naked eye as a tiny point. The ovum transmits to the child by heredity the personal traits of the mother, the sperm-cell those of the father; and this hereditary transmission extends to the finest characteristics of the soul as well as the body. What is plasm? What is this mysterious living substance that we find everywhere as the material foundation of the wonders of life? Plasm or protoplasm, is, as Huxley rightly said, the physical basis of organic life; to speak more precisely, it is a chemical compound of carbon that alone accomplishes the various processes of life. In its simplest form the living cell is merely a soft globule of plasm, containing a firmer nucleus. As soon as it is fertilized, it multiplies by division and forms a community or colony of many special cells.

These differentiate themselves, and by their specialization, or modifications, the tissues which compose the various organs are developed. the developed, many-celled organisms of man and all higher animals resemble, a social, civil community, the numerous single individuals of which are developed in various ways, but were originally only simple cells of one common structure.

All life on this earth, as Dr. Butler points out in "How the Mind Cures," began in the form of a cell which consisted of a body animated by a mind. In the beginning and long afterward the animating mind was the one we now call the subconscious. But as the forms grew in complexity and produced organs of sense, the mind threw out an addition, . . . forming another part, the one we now call the conscious. While at first all living creatures had but one guide that they must follow in all things, this later addition to mind gave the creature a choice. This was the formation of what has been termed Free Will.

Each cell is endowed with an individual intelligence, that helps it carry on, as by a miracle, its complex labors. The cell is the basis of man, and this fact must be constantly borne in mind in dealing with the wonders of mental chemistry.

As a nation is made up of a large number of living individuals, so the body is made up of a large number of living cells. The citizens of a country are engaged in varied pursuits—some in the work of production, in field, forest, mine, factory; some in the work of distribution, in transportation, in warehouse, store, or bank; some in the work of regulation, in legislative halls, on the bench, in the executive chair; some in the work of protection—soldiers, sailors, doctors, teachers, preachers. Likewise in the body some cells are working on production: mouth, stomach, intestines, lungs, supplying food, water, air; some are engaged in distribution of supplies and elimination of wastes: heart, blood, lymph, lungs, liver, kidneys, skin; some perform the office regulation: brain, spinal cord, nerves; some are occupied in protection; white blood corpuscles, skin, bone, muscle; there are also cells to which are entrusted the reproduction of species.

As the vigor and welfare of a nation depend fundamentally on the vitality and efficiency and co-operation of its citizens, so the health and life of the body depend upon the vitality, efficiency and co-operation of its myriad cells.

We have seen that the cells are gathered into systems and groups for the performance of particular functions essential to physical life and expression, such as we see in organs and tissues.

So long as the several parts all act together, in concord and due regard to one another and the general purposes of the organism, there is health and efficiency. But when from any cause discord arises, illness supervenes. Disease is lack of comfort and harmony.

In the brain and nervous system the cells are grouped in their action according to the particular functions which they are called upon to perform. It is in this way that we are able to see, to taste, to smell, to feel, and to hear. It is also in this way we are able to recall past experiences, to remember facts and figures, and so on.

In mental and physical health these various groups of neurons work in fine harmony, but in disease they do not. In normal conditions the ego holds all these individual cells and groups, as we as system of cells, in harmonious and co-ordinate action.

Disease represents dissociated organic action; certain systems or groups, each of which is made up of a vast number of microscopic cells, begin functioning independently, and hence inharmoniously; and thus upset the tone of the whole organism. A single organ or system can thus get out of tune with the rest of the body and do serious harm. this is one kind of disease.

In a federation of any sort, efficiency and concord of action depend upon the strength and confidence accorded the central administration of its affairs; and just in proportion to the degree of failure to maintain these conditions are discord and confusion sure to ensue.

Nels Quevli makes this clear in "Cell Intelligence;" he says, "The intelligence of man is the intelligence possessed by the cells in his brain. If man is intelligent and by virtue thereof is able to combine and arrange matter and force so as to effect structures such as houses and railroads, why is not the cell also intelligent when he is able to direct the forces of nature so as to effect the structures we see such as plants and animals. The cell is not compelled to act by reason of any chemical and mechanical force, any more than is man. He acts by reason of will and judgment of his own. He is a separate living animal. Bergson in his "Creative Evolution" seems to see in matter and life a creative energy. If we stood at a distance watching a skyscraper gradually grow into completeness, we would say there must be some creative energy back of it, pushing the construction and, if we could never get near enough to see the men and builders at work, we could have no other idea of how that skyscraper came into existence except that it was caused by some creative energy.

The cell is an animal, very highly organized and specialized. Take the single cell called amoeba for instance. He has no machinery with which he can manufacture starch. He does, however, carry with him building material with which he can in an emergency save his life by covering himself with a coat of armor. Other cells carry with them a structure which is called chromatophore. With this instrument, these cells are able to manufacture starch from the crude substances of earth, air and water by the aid of sunlight. From these facts, it must appear evident to the reader that the cell is a very highly organized and specialized individual, and that to look at him from the point of view of being mere matter and force is the same as to compare the actions of a stone rolling down a hill with that of an automobile moving over a smooth pavement. One is compelled to move by reason of the force of gravitation, while the other moves by virtue of the intellect that guides it. The structures of life, like plants and animals, are built from the materials taken from the earth, air, and water, just as are the structures man builds, like railroads and skyscrapers. If we were asked how it is possible for man to effect the construction of these railroads and buildings, we would say that it is by reason of the fact that he is an intelligent being.

If the cell has gone through the same process of social organization and evolution as man, why is it not also the same intelligent being as man? Did you ever stop to think what takes place when the surface of the body is cut or bruised? The white blood cells or corpuscles, as they are called, who are the general caretakers of the body, whose duty it is to look after everything in general, such as the fighting of bacteria and disease germs and the general repair work, will sacrifice their own lives by thousands if necessary to save the body. They live in the body, enjoying complete liberty. They do not float in the blood stream except when in a hurry to get somewhere, but move around everywhere as separate independent beings to see that everything goes right. If a bruise or cut happens, they are at once informed, and rush to the spot by thousands and direct the repair work and if necessary they change their own occupation and take a different job, that of making connective tissue in order to bind the tissues together. In nearly every open sore, bruise or cut, they are killed in great numbers in their faithful effort to repair and close up the wound. A text book on physiology briefly speaks of it as follows:

"When the skin is injured the white blood cells form new tissue upon the surface, while the epithelium spreads over it from the edges, stopping the growth and completing the healing processes."

There seems to be no particular center in the body around which intelligence revolves. Every cell seems to be a center of intelligence and knows what its duties are wherever it is placed and wherever we find it. Every citizen of the cell republic is an intelligent independent existence, and all are working together for the welfare of all. Nowhere can we find more absolute sacrifice of the lives of the individuals to the general welfare of all than we do in the cell republic. The results cannot be obtained in any other way nor at any less cost of individual sacrifice, so it is necessary to their social existence. The principle of individual sacrifice to common welfare has been accepted and agreed up as the right thing and as their common duty, impartially distributed among them, and they perform their allotted work and duties regardless of their own individual comfort.

Mr. Edison says, "I believe that our bodies are made up of myriads of units of life. Our body is not itself the unit of life or a unit of life. Let me give you as an example the S. S. Mauretania."

"The 'Mauretania' is not herself a living thing—it is the men in her that are alive. If she is wrecked on the coast, for instance, the men get out, and when the men get out it simply means that the 'life units' leave the ship. And so in the same way a man is not 'dead' because his body is buried and the vital principle, that is, the 'life units,' have left the body.

"Everything that pertains to life is still living and cannot be destroyed. Everything that pertains to life is still subject to the laws of animal life. We have myriads of cells and it is the inhabitants in these cells, inhabitants which themselves are beyond the limits of the microscope, which vitalize our body.

"To put it another way, I believe that these life-units of which I have spoken band themselves together in countless millions and billions in order to make a man. We have too facilely assumed that each one of us is himself a unit. This, I am convinced is wrong, even by the high-powered microscope, and so we have assumed that the unit is the man, which we can see, and have ignored the existence of the real life units, which are those we cannot see."

"No man today can set the line as to where 'life' begins and ends. Even in the formation of crystals, we see a definitely ordered plan of work. Certain solutions will always form a particular kind of crystal without variation. It is not impossible that these life entities are at work in the mineral and plant as in what we call the 'animal' world."

We have seen something of the chemist, something of his laboratory, something of his system of communication.

What about the product? This is a very practical age, an age of commercialism, if you please. If the chemist produces nothing of value, nothing which can be converted into cash, we are not interested.

But, fortunately the chemist in this case produces an article which has the highest cash value of any article known to man.

He provides the one thing which all the world demands, something which can be realized upon anywhere, at any time; it is not a slow asset; on the contrary, its value is recognized in every marked.

The product is thought; thought rules the world; thought rules every Government, every bank, every industry, every person and everything in existence, and is differentiated from everything else, simply and only because of thought.

Every person is what he is because of his method of thinking, and men and nations differ from each other only because they think differently.

What then is thought? Thought is the product of the chemical laboratory possessed by every thinking individual; it is the blossom, the combined intelligence which is the result of all previous thinking processes; it is the fruit and contains the best of all that the individual has to give.

There is nothing material about a thought, and yet no man would give up his ability to think for all the gold in Christendom; it is therefore of more value than anything which exists. As it is not material it must be spiritual. Here then is an explanation of the wonderful value of thought. Thought is a spiritual activity; in fact, it is the only activity which the spirit possesses. Spirit is the creative principle of the Universe, as a part must be the same in kind and quality as the whole, and can differ only in degree, thought must be creative also.

The Laboratory

The art of chemistry cannot proceed without a plant, or work-shop, and one of the most interesting features of the human system is its series of manufacturing plants in which are produced the chemical agents necessary to mobilize the constituents of food. And it is a part of the fine natural economy that the secretions containing these chemical agents should serve several other purposes also. In general, each may be said to have an alterative effect upon the others, or at least upon the activities of the other plants; also they act upon the inward bound nerve paths as exciters of effects in both the conscious and the subconscious activities.

Radiant energy, whether consciously or subconsciously released from the body, becomes the medium of sensory impressions that flash back to the perceptive centers and there set up reactions which are interpreted by these centers according to their stage of development of self, and therefore they interpret these messages exactly as they are received, without attempt to "think" about them, or to analyze them. The process is as mechanical as an impression made by the actinic rays of the sun on a photographic plate.

The general principle by which an idea is preserved is vibratory like all other phenomena of nature. Every thought causes vibration that will continue to expand and contract in wave circles, like the waves started by a stone dropped in a pool of water. Waves from other thoughts may countered it, or it may finally succumb of its own inanition.

Thought will instantly set in motion the finest of spiritual magnetism, and this motion will be communicated to the heavier and coarser densities, and will eventually affect the physical matter of the body.

Life is not created—it simply IS. All nature is animate with this force we call 'life.'" The phenomena of life on this physical plane, with which we are chiefly concerned, are produced by the involution of "energy" into "matter," and matter is, itself, an involution of energy.

But when the stage of matter is reached in the process of Nature's involution, matter then begins to evolve forms under the action upon it and within it. So that growth and life are the results of a simultaneous integration of matter and energy. Evolution starts with the lowest form of matter, and works upward through refining processes to serve as a matrix of energy.

The internal secretions constitute and determine much of the inherited powers of the individual and their development. They control physical and mental growth, and all metabolic processes of fundamental importance. They dominate all the vital functions of man. they co-operate in an intimate relationship which may be compared to an interlocking directorate. A derangement of their functions, causing an insufficiency of them, an excess or an abnormality upsets the entire equilibrium of the body, with transformed effect upon the mind and the organs. Blood chemistry of our time is a marvel undreamed of a generation ago.

These achievements are a perfect example of accomplished fact contradicting all former prediction and criticism. One of the greatest advances of modern medicine has been the study of the processes and secretions of the hitherto obscure ductless glands; endocrinology, as this study is called, has thrown much valuable light upon certain abnormal physical conditions about which science had until now been in the dark. We now know that most of the freaks of nature we see on exhibition are such owing to endocrine disturbance—the disturbance of the ductless glands. The bearded lady, a victim of pogoniasis; the victims of obesity and of skeletonization; of acromegalis, or giantism; of micromegalie or liliputianism—all such evolutional deviations are due to subnormalities or abnormalities of the chemical elements which the glands produce and send into the blood-stream.

These are no mere theories, for they have been rigorously tested in the laboratories of science. As Sir William Osler, one of the world's most illustrious luminaries of knowledge, has said: "For man's body, too, is a humming hive of working cells, each with its specific function, all under central control of the brain and heart, and all dependent on materials called hormones (secreted by small, even insignificant looking structures) which lubricate the wheels of life. For example, remove the thyroid gland just below the adam's apple, and you deprive man of the lubricants which enable his thought-engines to work. It is as if you cut off the oil-supply of a motor, and gradually the stored acquisitions of his mind cease to be available, and within a year he sinks into dementia. The normal processes of the skin cease, the hair falls, the features bloat, and the paragon of animals is transformed into a shapeless caricature of humanity.

These essential lubricators, of which a number are now known, are called hormones—you will recognize from its derivation how appropriate is the term. The name is derived from the he Greek verb meaning "to rouse or set in motion." The name was given by Starling and Bayliss, two great Englishmen noted for their research work in endocrinology. Cretins—dwarfed imbeciles—can be cured by the administration, internally, of the thyroid glands of sheep, with truly miraculous results; because cretinism is caused by the lack or absence of thyroid gland secretions.

As an instance of the fascination of these studies, consider the conception that the thyroid played a fundamental part in the change of sea creatures into land animals. Feeding the Mexican axolotl, a purely aquatic newt, breathing through gills, on thyroid, quickly changes it into the ambystoma, a terrestrial salamander, breathing by means of lungs.

The endocrine glands produce secretions which enter the blood-stream and vitally affect the bodily structure and functions. The pituitary is a small gland, located near the center of the head, directly under the third ventricle of the brain, where it rests in a depression in the bony floor-plate of the skull. Its secretions have an important part in the mobilizing of carbohydrates, maintaining blood-pressure, stimulating other glands, and maintaining the tonicity of the sympathetic nerve system. Its under, or over, activity during childhood, will produce marked characteristics in the body structure, and what concerns us more, equally marked characteristics of mental development and function.

The thyroid gland is located at the frontal base of the neck, extending upward in a sort of semicircle on both sides, with the parathyroids near the tips. The thyroid secretion is important in mobilizing both proteins and carbohydrates; it stimulates other glands, helps resist infections, affects the hair growth, and influences the organs of digestion and elimination. It is a strongly determining factor in the all-around physical development, and also in the mental functioning. A well-balanced thyroid goes a long way toward insuring an active, efficient, smoothly co-ordinated mind and body.

The adrenal glands are located just above the small of the back. These organs have been called by some writers the "decorative glands," since one of their functions appears to be that of keeping the pigments of the body in proper solution and distribution. But of greater importance is the agency of the adrenal secretion in other directions. It contains a most valuable blood-pressure agent; it is a tonic to the sympathetic nerve system, hence to the involuntary muscles, heart, arteries, intestines, and so on; as well as to the perceptive paths. It responds to certain emotional excitements by an immediate increase in volume of secretion, thus increasing the energy of the whole system, and preparing it for effective response.

The cerebro-spinal nervous system is the telephone system of the conscious mind; it is a very complete wiring system for communication from the brain to every part of the body, especially the terminals. It is the intelligence department of self-conscious man.

The sympathetic nervous system is the system of the subconscious mind. Behind the stomach, and in front of the spine, is the center of the system known as the "Solar Plexus." It is composed of two masses of brain substance, each in the shape of a crescent. They surround an artery whose function it is to equalize the blood pressure of all the abdominal organs.

Just as the brain and the voluntary nervous system constitute the apparatus of self-conscious man, in like manner the solar plexus and the sympathetic system comprise the special apparatus of the subconscious mind.

The function of the sympathetic nervous system is to maintain the equilibrium of the body, to act as a balance wheel, to prevent over or under action of the cerebro-spinal system. As it is directly affected by emotional states such as fear, anger, jealousy or hatred, these may easily throw out of gear the operation of the automatic functions of the body. That is to say, that emotional states such as joy, fear, anger and hatred may upset such functions of the body as digestion, blood circulation, general nutrition, and so forth.

"Nerves," and all the unpleasant experiences that follow in the way of bodily discomfort and ill health, are caused by negative emotions, such as fear, anger, hatred and the like; they break down the resistance which has been offered by the various plexii which, when in normal working order, have a definite capacity to inhibit the effect of such emotions.

The sympathetic system is the apparatus whose function it is to maintain the body in normal and healthy working order and to replace the wastage due to ordinary wear and tear, both emotional and physical. The kind of emotions which we entertain is therefore of great importance; if positive, they are constructive; if negative, they are destructive.

ATTRACTION

Mental chemistry is a power which is sweeping through eternity, a living stream of relative action in which the basic principle is ever active; it embraces the past and carries it forward into the ever widening future; a movement where relative action, cause, and effect go hand in hand; where law dovetails into law and where all laws are the ever willing handmaids of this great creative force.

This power stretches beyond the utmost planets, beyond a beginning, beyond an ending, and on into a beginningless and endless eternity; it causes the things we see to take form and shape. It brings the fruit from the he blossom and the sweetness to the honey; it measures the sweep of the countless orbs; it lurks in the sparkle in the diamond, and in the amethyst and in the grape; it works in the seen and in the unseen, and it permeates the all.

It is the source of perfect justice, perfect unity, perfect harmony, and perfect truth; while its constant activity brings perfect balance, perfect growth, and perfect understanding.

Perfect justice, because it renders equal retribution.

Perfect unity, because it has oneness of purpose.

Perfect harmony, because in it all laws blend.

Perfect truth, because it is the one great truth of all existence.

Perfect balance, because it measures unerringly.

Perfect growth, because it is a natural growth.

Perfect understanding, because it solves every problem of life.

The reality of this law lies in its activity, for only through action, and constant change, can this law come to be; and only through inaction can it cease to be; but as there is no inaction, there can be no cessation.

The one purpose of this law is unchangeable; in the silence of darkness, in the glory of light, in the turmoil of action and the pain of reaction, it moves ever forward toward the fulfillment of its one great purpose—perfect harmony.

We see and feel its urge in the myriads and myriads of plant forms on hill and in dale, as they push forth from the same darkness into one light; and though bathed by the same waters and breathed upon by same air, yet all varieties maintain their own individuality—that is, the rose is always a rose and differs from the violet, which is always a violet; the acorn gives to the world the oak and never a willow or any other variety of tree; and though all send out roots into the same soil, and blossom in the same sunshine, yet some are frail, some are strong, some are bitter, and some are sweet; while others are repulsive, some are beautiful; thus all varieties draw to themselves through their own roots and from the same elements, that which differ entiates them from each other; and this great law of life, this constant urge, this hidden force in the plant causing it to manifest, to grow, and to attain, is this Law of Attraction bearing forward in silent majesty, bring all fruition; dictating nothing, yet making each unit of growth true to its own individual nature.

In the Mineral world it is the cohesion in the rock, sand, and clay; it is the strength in the granite, the beauty in the marble, the sparkle in the sapphire, and the blood in the ruby.

Thus do we find it working in the things we see; but its unseen power, as it works in the mind of man, is greater.

This Law of Attraction is neither good nor evil, neither moral nor immoral; it is a neutral law that always flows in conjunction with the desires of the individual; we each choose our own line of growth, and there are as many lines of growth as there are individuals; and although no two of us are exactly alike, yet many of us move along similar lines.

These lines of growth are made up of past, present, and future desires, manifesting in the ever forming present, where they establish the central line of our being along which we advance; the nature of these desires has no power to check the action of this, for its function is to bring to maturity the bitter as well as the sweet.

An illustration of the neutrality and action of this law is found in the grafting of an apple tree bud into an osage orange tree, where we find in due time eatable and uneatable fruits growing together on the same tree; that is, wholesome and unwholesome fruits nourished and brought to maturity by the same sap.

In applying this illustration to ourselves, we find that the apples and oranges represent our different desires, while the sap represents this Law of Growth; and just the sap brings to maturity the different kinds of fruit, just so will this Law bring to fruitfulness our different kinds of desires; and whether they be wholesome or unwholesome, it matters not to the law, for its place in life is to bring to our minds a conscious realization of the results that follow all desires we hold, as well as of their nature, their effect and their purpose.

In man's division of the Law, we come into contact with a larger activity, one that is utterly unknown to the primitive mind, which leads us to a conscious awakening of a newer power in a larger field of action—in other words, a larger truth, a greater understanding, and a deeper insight.

We are touching a greater reality, for let us understand that reality lies in activity and not outside of it; to exist is to be alive to the action of the laws about us; the hidden urge in the plant is its reality, and not the outer form we see.

True knowledge comes to us through our own activities, borrowed knowledge through the activities of others; both together evolves our intellects. And slowly we are forming an unique self, an individualizing unit.

As we move out into the power of our growing intellects, into an ever moving consciousness we are learning to seek for the wherefore and why of things, and in this search we think and imagine that we are original, when in fact we are only students of established beliefs, notions, and facts, gathered throughout generations of tribal and national life.

We live in a state of fear and uncertainty, until we find, and make use of, the unvarying uniformity running though all laws; this is a central truth that we must know and use before we can become masters of self, or masters of conditions. The Law of Growth ripens collectively, for its one function is: "to act upon that which we give it to act upon."

As the nature of the cause governs the effect, so does thought precede and predetermine action. Each one must use this Law knowingly, consciously; otherwise we use it blindly—use it we must.

In our growth from primitive man to conscious man, there are three seeming divisions or sections. First, our growth through the savage or unconscious state; second, our growth through the intellectual and conscious growing state; and third, our growth into, and conscious recognition of, our conscious state.

We all know that the bulb must first send out roots before it can send out shoots, and it must send out shoots before it can come to blossom in the sunlight. It is just so with us, like the plant, we must first send out roots (our roots are our thoughts), before we can evolve from our primitive or animal bulb-like state into the intellectual and conscious growing state.

Next we, like the plant, must send forth shoots before we can evolve from a purely intellectual state of conscious growing, into a conscious state of conscious knowing; otherwise we would always remain only creatures of the law and never masters of the law.

Lastly, we, like the plant, must individualize, must come to full blossom; in other words, must give forth the radiating beauty of a perfected life, must stand revealed to ourselves and to others, as a unit of power and a master over those laws that govern and control our growth. Each has a force within itself, and this force is the action of law set into activity by ourselves; it is through this consciousness that we begin to master laws, and to bring results through our conscious knowledge of their operation.

Life is a rigid conformity to laws, where we are the conscious or unconscious chemists of our own life; for when life is truly understood it is found to be made up of chemical action. As we breathe in oxygen, chemical action takes place in our blood; as we consume food and water, chemical action takes place in our digestive organs; in our use of thought chemical action takes place in both mind and body; in the change called death, chemical action takes place and disintegration sets in; so we find that physical existence is chemical action.

Life is made up of laws and as we make use of these laws, so do we get results.

If we think distress we get distress; if we think success, we get success. When we entertain destructive thought we set up a chemical action that checks digestion, which in turn irritates other organs of the body and reacts upon the mind, causing disease and sickness; when we worry, we churn a cesspool of chemical action, causing fearful havoc to both mind and body; on the other hand, if we entertain constructive thoughts, we set up a healthy chemical action.

When we entertain negative thoughts, we put into action a poisonous chemical activity of a disintegrating nature, that stupefies our sensibilities and deadens our nerve actions, causing the mind and body to become negative and therefore subject to many ills; on the other hand, if we are positive, we put into action a healthy chemical activity of a constructive nature, causing the mind and body to be come free from the many ills due to discordant thoughts.

These analyses can be carried through every avenue of life, but enough has been shown to indicate that life is largely chemical action, and that the mind is the chemical laboratory of thought, and that we are the chemists in the workshop of mental action where everything is prepared for our use, and where the product turned out will be in proportion to the material used; in other words, the nature of the thought we use determines the kind of conditions and experiences with which we meet; what we put into life we get out of life—no more, no less.

Life is an orderly advancement, governed by the "Law of Attraction." our growth is through three seeming sections. In the first we are creatures of law, in the second users of law, and in the third we are masters of law. In the first we are unconscious users of thought power, in the second conscious users of thought power, and in the third we are conscious users of conscious power. So long as we persist in using only the laws of the first section we are held in bondage to them; so long as we remain satisfied with the laws and growth of the second section we shall never become conscious of a greater advancement. In the third section we awaken to our conscious power over laws of the first and second sections, and become fully awake to the laws governing the third.

When rightly understood, life is found not to be a question of chance; not a question of creed; not a question of nationality; not a question of social standing; not a question of wealth; not a question of power, NO—all of these have a place to fill in the growth of the individual, but we must all eventually come to know that Harmony comes only as the result of a compliance with Natural Law.

This rigid exactness and stability in the nature of law is our greatest asset, and when we become conscious of this available power, and use it judiciously, we shall have found the Truth which will make us Free!

Science has of late made such vast discoveries, has revealed such an infinity of resources, have unveiled such enormous possibilities and such unsuspected forces, that scientific men more and more hesitate to affirm certain theories as established and indubitable, or to deny certain other theories as absurd or impossible; and so a new civilization is being born; customs, creeds and cruelty are passing; vision, faith and service are taking their place. The fetters of tradition are being melted off from humanity, and as the dross of militarism and materialism are being consumed, thought is being liberated and truth is rising full orbed before an astonished multitude.

"We have caught only a glimpse of the possibility of the rule of mind which means the rule of spirit. We have just begun to realize in a small degree what this newly discovered power may do for us. That it can bring success in this world's affairs is beginning to be understood and practiced by thousands."

"The whole world is on the eve of a new consciousness, a new power and a new realization of resources within the self. The last century saw the most magnificent material progress in history. May the new century produce the greatest progress in mental and spiritual power."

VIBRATION

Before any environment, harmonious or otherwise, can be created, action of some kind is necessary, and before any action is possible, there must be thought of some kind, either conscious or unconscious, and as thought is a product of mind, it becomes evident that Mind is the creative center from which all activities proceed.

It is not expected that any of the inherent laws which govern the modern business world as it is at present constituted can be suspended or repealed by any force on the same plane, but it is axiomatic that a higher law may overcome a lower one. Tree life causes the sap to ascend, not by repealing the law of gravity, but by surmounting it.

The naturalist who spends much of his time in observing visible phenomena is constantly creating power in that portion of his brain set apart for observation. The result is that he becomes very much more expert and skillful in knowing what he sees, and grasping an infinite number of details at a glance, than does his unobserving friend. He has reached this facility by exercise of his brain. He deliberately chose to enlarge his brain power in the line of observation, so he deliberately exercised that special faculty, over and over, with increasing attention and concentration. Now we have the result—a man learned in the lore of observation far above his fellow. Or, on the other hand, one can be stolid in action, allow the delicate brain matter to harden and ossify until his whole life is barren and fruitless.

Every thought tends to become a material thing. Our desires are seed thoughts that have a tendency to sprout and grow and blossom and bear fruit. We are sowing these seeds every day. What shall the harvest be? Each of us today is the result of his past thinking. Later we shall be the result of what we are now thinking. We create our own character, personality and environment by the thought which we originate, or entertain. Thought seeks its own. The law of mental attraction is an exact parallel to the law of atomic affinity. Mental currents are as real as electric, magnetic or heat currents. We attract the currents with which we are in harmony.

Lines of least resistance are formed by the constant action of the mind. The activity of the brain reacts upon the particular faculty of the brain employed. The latent power of the mind is developed by constant exercise. Each form of its activity becomes more perfect by practice. Exercises for the development of the mind present a variety of motives for consideration. They involve the development of the perceptive faculties, the cultivation of the emotions, the quickening of the imagination, the symmetrical unfoldment of the intuitive faculty, which without being able to give a reason frequently impels or prohibits choice, and finally the power of mind may be cultivated by the development of the moral character.

"The greatest man," said Seneca, "is he who chooses right with invincible determination." The greatest power of mind, then, depends upon its exercise in moral channels, and therefore requires that every conscious mental effort should involve a moral end. A developed moral consciousness modifies consideration of motives, and increases the force and continuity of action; consequently the well developed symmetrical character necessitates good physical, mental and moral health, and this combination creates initiative, power, resistless force, and necessarily success.

It will be found that Nature is constantly seeking to express Harmony in all things, is forever trying to bring about an harmonious adjustment, for every discord, every wound, every difficulty; therefore when thought is harmonious, Nature begins to create the material conditions, the possession of which are necessary in order to make up an harmonious environment.

When we understand that mind is the great creative power, what does not become possible? With Desire as the great creative energy, can we not see why Desire should be cultivated, controlled and directed in our lives and destinies? Men and women of strong mentality who dominate those around them, and often those far removed from them, really emanate currents charged with power which, coming in contact with the minds of others, cause the desires of the latter to be in accord with the mind of the strong individuality. Great masters of men possess this power to a marked degree. Their influence is felt far and near, and they secure compliance with their wishes by making others "want" to act in accord with them. In this way men of strong Desire and Imagination may and do exert powerful influence over the minds of others, leading the latter in the way desired.

No man is ever created without the inherent power in himself to help himself. The personality that understands its own intellectual and moral power of conquest will assert itself. It is this truth which an enfamined world craves today. The possibility of asserting a slumbering intellectual courage that clearly discerns, and a moral courage that grandly undertakes in open to all. There is a divine potency in every human being.

We speak of the sun as "rising" and "setting," though we know that this is simply an appearance of motion. To our senses the earth is apparently standing still, and yet we know it is revolving rapidly. We speak of a bell as a "sounding body," yet we know that all that the bell can do is to produce vibrations in the air. When these vibrations come at the rate of sixteen a second they cause a sound to be heard in the mind. It is possible for the mind to hear vibrations up to the rate of 38,000 a second. When the number increases beyond this all is silence again; so that we know that the sound is not in the bell; it is in our own mind.

We speak and even think of the sun as "giving light," yet we know it is simply giving forth energy which produces vibrations in the ether at the rate of four hundred trillion a second, causing what are termed light waves, so that we know that what we call light is simply a mode of motion, and the only light existent, is the sensation caused in the mind by the motion of these waves. When the number of vibrations increases, the light changes in color, each change in color being caused by shorter and more rapid vibrations; so that although we speak of the rose as being red, the grass as being green, or the sky as being blue, we know that these colors exist only in our minds, and are the sensations experienced by us as the result of the vibrations of light. When the vibrations are reduced below four hundred trillion a second, they no longer affect us as light, but we experience the sensation of heat.

So we have come to know that appearances exist for us only in our consciousness. Even time and space become annihilated, time being but the experience of succession, there being no past or future except as a thought relation to the present. In the last analysis, therefore, we know that one principle governs and controls all existence. Every atom is forever conserved; whatever is parted with must inevitably be received somewhere. It cannot perish and it exists only for use. It can go only where it is attracted, and therefore required. We can receive only what we give, and we may give only to those who can receive; and it remains with us to determine our rate of growth and the degree of harmony that we shall express.

The laws under which we live are designed solely for our advantage. These laws are immutable and we cannot escape from their operation. All the great eternal forces act in solemn silence, but it is within our power to place ourselves in harmony with them and thus express a life of comparative peace and happiness.

Difficulties, in harmonies, obstacles, indicate that we are either refusing to give out what we no longer need, or refusing to accept what we require. Growth is attained through an exchange of the old for the new, of the good for the better; it is a conditional or reciprocal action, for each of us is a complete thought entity and the completeness makes it possible for us to receive only as we give. We cannot obtain what we lack if we tenaciously cling to what we have.

The Principle of Attraction operates to bring to us only what may be to our advantage. We are able to consciously control our conditions as we come to sense the purpose of what we attract, and are able to extract from each experience only what we require for our further growth. Our ability to do this determines the degree of harmony or happiness we attain.

The ability to appropriate what we require for our growth continually increases as we reach higher planes and broader visions, and the greater our ability to know what we require, the more certain we shall be to discern its presence, to attract it and to absorb it. Nothing may reach us except what is necessary for our growth. All conditions and experiences that come to us do so for our benefit. Difficulties and obstacles will continue to come until we absorb their wisdom and gather from them the essentials of further growth. That we reap what we sow, is mathematically exact. We gain permanent strength exactly to the extent of the effort required to overcome our difficulties.

The inexorable requirements of growth demand that we exert the greatest degree of attraction for what is perfectly in accord with us. Our highest happiness will be best attained through our understanding of and conscious co-operation with natural laws.

Our mind forces are often bound by the paralyzing suggestions that come to us from the crude thinking of the race, and which are accepted and acted upon without question. Impressions of fear, of worry, of disability and of inferiority are given us daily. These are sufficient reasons in themselves why men achieve so little—why the lives of multitudes are so barren of results, while all the time there are possibilities within them which need only the liberating touch of appreciation and wholesome ambition to expand into real greatness.

Women, perhaps even more than men, have been subject to these conditions. This is true because of their finer susceptibilities, making them more open to thought-vibrations from other minds, and because the flood of negative and repressive thoughts has been aimed for especially at them.

But it is being overcome. Florence Nightingale overcame it when she rose in the Crimea to heights of tender sympathy and executive ability previously unknown among women. Clara Barton, the head of the Red Cross, overcame it when she wrought a similar work in the armies of the Union. Jenny Lind overcame it when she shoed her ability to command enormous financial rewards while at the same time gratifying the passionate desire of her nature and reaching the front rank of her day in musical art. And there is a long list of women singers, philanthropists, writers and actresses who have proved themselves capable of reaching the greatest literary, dramatic, artistic and sociological achievement.

Women as well as men are beginning to do their own thinking. They have awakened to some conception of their possibilities. They demand that if life holds any secrets, these shall be disclosed. At no previous time has the influence and potency of thought received such careful and discriminating investigation. While a few seers have grasped the great fact that mind is the universal substance, the basis of all things, never before has this vital truth penetrated the more general consciousness. Many minds are now striving to give this wonderful truth definite utterance. Modern science has taught us that light and sound are simply different intensities of motion, and this has led to discoveries of forces within man that could not have been conceived of until this revelation was made.

A new century has dawned, and now, standing in its light man sees something of the vastness of the meaning of life—something of its grandeur. Within that life is the germ of infinite potencies. One feels convinced that man's possibility of attainment cannot be measured, that boundary lines to his onward march are unthinkable. Standing on this height he finds that he can draw new power to himself from the Infinite energy of which he is a part.

Some men seem to attract success, power, wealth, attainment, with very little conscious effort; others conquer with great difficulty; still others fail altogether to reach their ambitions, desires and ideals. Why is this so? Why should some men realize their ambitions easily, others with difficulty, and still others not at all? The cause cannot by physical, else the most perfect men physically would be the most successful. The difference, therefore, must be mental—must be in the mind; hence mind must be the creative force, must constitute the sole difference between men. It is mind, therefore, which overcomes environment and every other obstacle in the path of man.

When the creative power of thought is fully understood, its effect will seem to be marvelous. But such results cannot be secured without proper application, diligence and concentration. The laws governing in the mental and spiritual world are as fixed and infallible as in the material world. To secure the desired results, then, it is necessary to know the law and to comply with it. A proper compliance with the law will be found to produce the desired result with invariable exactitude.

Scientists tell us that we live in the universal ether. This is formless, of itself, but it is pliable, and forms about us, in us and around us, according to our thought and word. We set it into activity by that which we think. Then that which manifests to us objectively is that which we have thought or said.

Thought is governed by law. The reason we have not manifested more faith is because of lack of understanding. We have not understood that everything works in exact accordance with definite law. The law of thought is as definite as the law of mathematics, or the law of electricity, or the law of gravitation. When we begin to understand that happiness, health, success, prosperity and every other condition or environment are results, and that these results are created by thinking, either consciously or unconsciously, we shall realize the importance of a working knowledge of the laws governing thought.

Those coming into a conscious realization of the power of thought find themselves in possession of the best that life can give; substantial things of a higher order become theirs, and these sublime realities are so constituted that they can be made tangible parts of daily personal life. They realize a world of higher power, and keep that power constantly working. This power is inexhaustible, limitless, and they are therefore carried forward from victory to victory. Obstacles that seem insurmountable are overcome. Enemies are changed to friends, conditions are overcome, elements transformed, fate is conquered.

The supply is inexhaustible, and the demand can be made along whatever lines we may desire. This is the mental law of demand and supply.

Our circumstances and environment are formed by our thoughts. We have, perhaps, been creating these conditions unconsciously. If they are unsatisfactory the remedy is to consciously alter our mental attitude and see our circumstances adjust themselves to the new mental condition. There is nothing strange or supernatural about this; it simply the Law of Being. the thoughts which take root in the mind will certainly produce fruit after their kind. The greatest schemer cannot "gather grapes of thorns, or figs of thistles." To improve our conditions we must first improve ourselves. Our thoughts and desires will be the first to show improvement.

To be in ignorance of the laws of Vibration is to be like a child playing with fire, or a man manipulating powerful chemicals without a knowledge of their nature and relations. This is universally true because Mind is the one great cause which produces all conditions in the lives of men and women.

Of course, mind creates negative conditions just as readily as favorable conditions, and when we consciously or unconsciously visualize every kind of lack, limitation and discord, we create these conditions; this what many are unconsciously doing all the time.

This law as well as every other law is no respecter of persons, but is in constant operation and is relentlessly bringing to each individual exactly what he has created; in other words, "Whatsoever a man soweth, that shall he also reap."

Arthur Brisbane says, "Thought and its work include all the achievements of man."

Compare spirit and thought to the genius of the musician and the sound which issues from the musical instrument.

What the instrument is to the musician the brain of the man is to the spirit that inspires thought.

However great the musician, the genius must depend for its expression upon the instrument which gives it reality in the physical world, through sound waves produced in the material atmosphere, striking nerves that carry music to the brain.

Give Paderewski a piano out of tune and he can give you only discord and lack of harmony. Or give to Paganini, the greatest violinist that ever lived, a violin out of tune, and in spite of the genius of the musician you will hear only hideous, disagreeable sounds. The spirit of music must have the right instruments for its expression.

The spirit that inspires thought, the spirit of man, must have the right brain for its expression.

The more complicated and highly developed the instrument, the more displeasing to the ear is the result when the instrument is out of tune.

Among human beings a highly developed brain out of tune—for instance, the insane ravings of a powerful genius like Nietzsche, with his mind broken down—is infinitely more painful and shocking than in the case of a human being with a mind in comparison feeble and simple.

Our minds are so little accustomed to deal with the abstract, we live so much in the material world, inanimate objects have so much meaning for us that many human beings live and die without ever thinking at all of the spirit, yet the spirit is the only real thing in the universe.

And thought is the expression of spirit, working through a more or less imperfect human brain.

Bring yourself to think for some time earnestly of the nature and mysterious power of spirit. There is no thought more inspiring, fascinating, bewildering.

Consider the Falls of Niagara, with their tremendous power, the vast moving machinery, the cities that are lighted, the blazing streets, the moving cars, all due apparently to the power in Niagara. Yet not due to that power in reality so much as to the spirit expressed in the thought of man. It was spirit that harnessed Niagara. It was spirit transferred the power of the Falls to distant cities.

Yet that spirit has neither shape nor weight, size nor color, taste nor smell. You ask a man "What is the Spirit?" and he must answer that it is nothing, since it occupies no space, and cannot be seen or felt. And yet he must answer also that the spirit is everything. The world only exists as it is because we see it in the eyes of the spirit. The optic nerve takes a picture, sends it to the brain and the spirit sees the picture.

It was the spirit acting on the brain of Columbus, and through him upon others, that brought the first ship to America.

It is the spirit working and expressing itself through the thought of brains more and more highly developed that has gradually brought man from hi former condition of savagery to his present comparative degree of civilization. And that same spirit, working in future ages through brains infinitely superior to any that we can now conceive, will establish real harmony on this planet.

Yet you know that spirit exists, and that it is you, and that except for that spirit which animates you, picks you up when you fall, inspires you in success and comforts you in failure and misfortune, there would be nothing at all in this life, and you would not be different from one of the stones in the field, or some of the dummies that the tailor sets in front of his store.

Compare the spirit and the material world as you see it with the genius that dwells in the brain of the great painter and the works which the painter has to do.

every statue, painting and church that Michael Angelo created already existed in his spirit. But the spirit could not be content with that existence. It had to visualize itself; it had to see itself created.

The spirit really lives completely only when it sees itself reflected in the material world. All the mother love is in the spirit of woman. But it has complete existence only when the mother holds the child in her arms and sees in reality, in flesh and blood, the being that she loves and has created.

The achievements of the greatest men are all locked up within them from the first, but the spirit of such men can reach full realization only when the spirit, acting through the brain and expressing itself through thought, creates the work.

We know that all useful work is the result of sound thought. If we realize that thought itself is the expression of the spirit, we are moved by a sense of duty to give to that spirit the best possible expression of which we are capable, the best chance that it can have, dwelling in imperfect bodies and speaking through imperfect minds such as those we possess.

It is an inspiration to realize that men here on earth, gradually improving, become less animal and more spiritual as the centuries pass, are destined to develop in their own physical bodies, instruments capable of interpreting properly the spirit that animates us.

Human beings improve from generation to generation—that we know. The improvement is due to the affection of fathers and mothers for each other and for their children.

This race of ours one hundred thousand years ago was made up of animal-like creatures, with huge, projecting jaws, enormous teeth, small foreheads and hideously shaped bodies. Gradually through the centuries we have changed, the brute has gradually disappeared, the prognathous face of man as become fatter. The jaw has gone in, the forehead has come out, and behind the forehead, gradually, thanks to the devotion and patient labor of women, we are developing a brain that will ultimately give decent and adequate expression to spirit.

Spirit and thought are identical in the sense that the genius of the musician and the sound that you hear when his music is played are identical. In music the sound represents and interprets the musician's spirit. And the interpretation and the accuracy of that interpretation depend upon the orchestra, the violin or the piano. When the instruments are out of tune it is not the genius of the musician, but a misinterpretation that you hear.

And with our human brains, most of them out of tune, most of them incapable of expressing anything but the merest, faintest reflection of true spiritual life, there is as yet very little harmony.

Through the perfected brain of man, the cosmic sprit, in which each of us is a conscious atom, will speak clearly, and then this earth, our little corner in the universe, will be truly harmonious, governed by the spirit distinctly expressed instantly obeyed.

This cosmic spirit can and frequently does, operate through the brain of another. Many a man seems to be doing something very wonderful when in reality another man—another mind, not visible in the work, but actually at the work—does the heavy pulling.

You may see the salesman, the editor, the floor walker, the engineer, the architect—any kind of a man engaged in any kind of work—apparently doing something wonderful.

Yet he is not doing it all. An unseen power—another man, another brain, perhaps some little man with a small body and a big head, who keeps out of sight—is doing the work.

Every one of us without exception is pulled along or pushed ahead by some force unseen. It may be the man in the inside office, usually invisible. It may be the woman at home setting a good example, giving to the man at work the inspiration and the power that no one else could give. It may be paternal affection, enabling a man to do for a child what he could not possibly do for himself.

Very often the power is one that has long disappeared from the earth, a father or a mother whose energy and inspiration persists and does in the life of the son at work what the man could never have accomplished of his own accord."

TRANSMUTATION

Abundance is a natural law of the universe. The evidence of this law is conclusive; we see it on every hand. Everywhere Nature is lavish, wasteful, extravagant. Nowhere is economy observed in any created thing. The millions and millions of trees and flowers and plants and animals and the vast scheme of reproduction where the process of creating and re-creating is forever going on, all indicate the lavishness with which nature has made provision for man. That there is an abundance for everyone is evident; but that many seem to have been separated from this supply is also evident; they have not yet come into realization of the universality of all substance and that mind is the active principle which starts causes in motion whereby we are related to the things we desire.

To control circumstances, a knowledge of certain scientific principles of mind-action is required. Such knowledge is a most valuable asset. It may be gained by degrees and put into practice as fast as learned. Power over circumstances is one of its fruits; health, harmony and prosperity are assets upon its balance sheet. It costs only the labor of harvesting its great resources.

All wealth is the offspring of power; possessions are of value only as they confer power. Events are significant only as they affect power; all things represent certain forms and degrees of power.

The discovery of a reign of law by which this power could be made available for all human efforts marked an important epoch in human progress. It is the dividing line between superstition and intelligence; it eliminated the element of caprice in men's lives and substituted absolute, immutable universal law.

A knowledge of cause and effect as shown by the laws governing steam, electricity, chemical affinity and gravitation enables men to plan courageously and to execute fearlessly. These laws are called Natural Laws, because they govern the physical world, but all power is not physical power; there is also mental power, and there is moral and spiritual power.

Thought is the vital force or energy which is being developed and which has produced such startling results in the last half century, as to bring about a world which would be absolutely inconceivable to a man existing only 50 or even 25 years ago. If such results have been secured by organizing these mental powerhouses in 50 years, what may not be expected in another 50 years?

Some will say, if these principles are true, why are we not demonstrating them; as the fundamental principle is obviously correct, why do we not get proper results? We do; we get results in exact accordance with our understanding of the law and our ability to make the proper application. We did not secure results from the laws governing electricity until someone formulated the law and showed us how to apply it. Mental action inaugurates a series of vibrations in the ether, which is the substance from which all things proceed, which in their turn induce a corresponding grosser vibration in the molecular substance until finally mechanical action is produced.

This puts us in an entirely new relation to our environment, opening out possibilities hitherto undreamt of, and this by an orderly sequence of law which is naturally involved in our new mental attitude.

It is clear, therefore, that thoughts of abundance will respond only to similar thoughts; the wealth of the individual is seen to be what he inherently is. Affluence within is found to be the secret of attraction for affluence without. The ability to produce is found to be the real source of wealth of the individual. It is for this reason that he who has his heart in his work is certain to meet with unbounded success. He will give and continually give, and the more he gives the more he will receive.

Thought is the energy by which the law of attraction is brought into operation, which eventually manifests in abundance in the lives of men.

The source of all power, as of all weakness, is from within; the secret of all success as well as all failure is likewise from within. All growth is an unfoldment from within. This is evident from all Nature; every plant, every animal, every human is a living testimony to this great law, and the error of the ages is in looking for strength or power from without.

A thorough understanding of this great law which permeates the Universe leads to the acquirement of that state of mind which develops and unfolds a creative thought which will produce magical changes in life. Golden opportunities will be strewn across your path, and the power and perception to properly utilize them will spring up within you, friends will come unbidden, circumstances will ad just themselves to changed conditions; you will have found the "Pearl of greatest price."

Wisdom, strength, courage and harmonious conditions are the result of power, and we have seen that all power is from within; likewise every lack, limitation or adverse circumstance is the result of weakness, and weakness is simply absence of power; it comes from nowhere; it is nothing—the remedy, then is simply to develop power.

This is the key with which many are converting loss into gain, fear into courage, despair into joy, hope into fruition.

This may seem to be too good to be true, but remember that within a few years, by the touch of a button or the turn of a lever, science has placed almost infinite resources at the disposal of man. Is it not possible that there are other laws containing still great possibilities?

Let us see what are the most powerful forces in Nature. In the mineral world everything is sold and fixed. In the animal and vegetable kingdom it is in a state of flux, forever changing, always being created and recreated. In the atmosphere we find heat, light and energy. Each realm becomes finer and more spiritual as we pass from the visible to the invisible, from the coarse to the fine, from the low potentiality to the high potentiality. When we reach the invisible we find energy in its purest and most volatile state.

And as the most powerful forces of Nature are the invisible forces, so we find that the most powerful forces of man are his invisible forces, his spiritual force, and the only way in which the spiritual force can manifest is through the process of thinking. Thinking is the only activity which the spirit possesses, and thought is the only product of thinking.

Addition and subtraction are therefore spiritual transactions; reasoning is a spiritual process; ideas are spiritual conceptions; questions are spiritual searchlights and logic, argument and philosophy are parts of the spiritual machinery.

Every thought brings into action certain physical tissue, parts of the brain, nerve or muscle. This produces an actual physical change in the construction of the tissue. Therefore it is only necessary to have a certain number of thoughts on a given subject in order to bring about a complete change in the physical organization of a man.

This is the process by which failure is changed to success. Thoughts of courage, power, inspiration, harmony, are substituted for thoughts of failure, despair, lack, limitation and discord, and as these thoughts take root, the physical tissue is changed and the individual sees life in a new light, old things have actually passed away; all things have become new; he is born again, this time born of the spirit; life has anew meaning for him; he is reconstructed and is filled with joy, confidence, hope, energy. He sees opportunities for success to which he was heretofore blind. He recognizes possibilities which before had no meaning for him. The thoughts of success with which he has been impregnated are radiated to those around him, and they in turn help him onward and upward; he attracts to him new and successful associates, and this in turn changes his environment; so that by this simple exercise of thought, a man changes not only himself, but his environment, circumstances and conditions.

You will see, you must see, that we are at the dawn of a new day; that the possibilities are so wonderful, so fascinating, so limitless as to be almost bewildering. A century ago any man with an aeroplane or even a Gattling gun could have annihilated a whole army equipped with the implements of warfare then in use. So it is at preset. Any man with a knowledge of the possibilities of modern metaphysics has an inconceivable advantage over the multitude.

Mind is creative and operates through the law of attraction. We are not to try to influence anyone to do what we think they should do. Each individual has a right to choose for himself, but aside from this we would be operating under the laws of force, which is destructive in its nature and just the opposite of the law of attraction. A little reflection will convince you that all the great laws of nature operate in silence and that the underlying principle is the law of attraction. It is only destructive processes, such as earthquakes and catastrophies, that employ force. Nothing good is ever accomplished in that way.

To be successful, attention must invariably be directed to the creative plane; it must never be competitive. You do not wish to take anything away from any one else; you want to create something for yourself, and what you want for yourself you are perfectly willing that every one else should have.

You know that it is not necessary to take from one to give to another, but that the supply for all is abundant. Nature's storehouse of wealth is inexhaustible and if there seems to be a lack of supply anywhere it is only because the channels of distribution are as yet imperfect.

Abundance depends upon a recognition of the laws of Abundance. Mind is not only the creator, but the only creator of all there is. Certainly nothing can be created before we know that it can be created and then make the proper effort. There is no more Electricity in the world today than there was fifty years ago, but until someone recognized the law by which it could be made of service, we received no benefit; now that the law is understood, practically the whole world is illuminated by it. So with the law of Abundance; it is only those who recognize the law and place themselves in harmony with it, who share in its benefits.

A recognition of the law of abundance develops certain mental and moral qualities, among which are Courage, Loyalty, Tact, Sagacity, Individuality and Constructiveness. These are all moods of thought, and as all thought is creative, they manifest in objective conditions corresponding with the mental condition. This is necessarily true because the ability of the individual to think is his ability to act upon the Universal Mind and bring it into manifestation; it is the process whereby the individual becomes a channel for the differentiation of the Universal. Every thought is a cause and every condition an effect.

This principle endows the individual with seemingly transcendental possibilities, among which is the mastery of conditions through the creation and recognition of opportunities. This creation of opportunity implies the existence or creation of the necessary qualities or talents which are thought forces and which result in a consciousness of power which future events cannot disturb. It is this organization of victory or success within the mind, this consciousness of power within, which constitutes the responsive harmonious action whereby we are related to the objects and purposes which we seek. This is the law of attraction in action; this law, being the common property of all, can be exercised by any one having sufficient knowledge of its operation.

Courage is the power of the mind which manifests in the love of mental conflict; it is a noble and lofty sentiment; it is equally fitted to command or obey; both require courage. It often has a tendency to conceal itself. There are men and women, too, who apparently exist only to do what is pleasing to others, but when the time comes and the latent will is revealed, we find under the velvet glove an iron hand, and no mistake about it. True courage is cool, calm, and collected, and is never foolhardy, quarrelsome, ill-natured or contentious.

Accumulation is the power to reserve and preserve a part of the supply which we are constantly receiving, so as to be in a position to take advantage of the larger opportunities which will come as soon as we are ready for them. Has it not been said, "To him that hath shall be given"? All successful business men have this quality, well developed. James J. Hill, who recently died, leaving an estate of over fifty-two million dollars said: "If you want to know whether you are destined to be a success or failure in life, you can easily find out. The test is simple and it is infallible: Are you able to save money? If not, drop out. You will lose. You may think not, but you will lose as sure as you live. The seed of success is not in you."

This is very good so far as it goes, but any one who knows the biography of James J. Hill knows that he acquired his fifty million dollars by following the exact methods we have given. In the first place, he started with nothing; he had to use his imagination to idealize the vast railroad which he projected across the western prairies. He then had to come into a recognition of the law of abundance in order to provide the ways and means for materializing it; unless he had followed out this program he would never had anything to save.

Accumulativeness acquires momentum; the more you accumulate the more you desire, and the more you desire the more you accumulate, so that it is but a short time until the action and reaction acquire a momentum that cannot be stopped. It must, however, never be confounded with selfishness, miserliness or penuriousness; they are perversions and will make any true progress impossible.

Constructiveness is the creative instinct of the mind. It will be readily seen that every successful business man must be able to plan, develop or construct. In the business world it is usually referred to as initiative. It is not enough to go along in the beaten path. New ideas must be developed, new ways of doing things. It manifests in building, designing, planning, inventing, discovering, improving. It is a most valuable quality and must be constantly encouraged and developed. Every individual possesses it in some degree, because he is a center of consciousness in that infinite and Eternal Energy from which all things proceed.

Water manifests on three planes, as ice, as water and as steam; it is all the same compound; the only difference is the temperature, but no one would try to drive an engine with ice; convert it into steam and it easily takes up the load. So with your energy; if you want it to act on the creative plane, you will have to begin by melting the ice with the fire of imagination, and you will find the stronger the fire, and the more ice you melt, the more powerful your thought will become, and the easier it will be for you to materialize your desire.

Sagacity is the ability to perceive and co-operate with Natural Law. True Sagacity avoids trickery and deceit as it would the leprosy; it is the product of that deep insight which enables on to penetrate into the heart of things and understand how to set causes in motion which will inevitably create successful conditions.

Tact is a very subtle and at the same time a very important factor in business success. It is very similar to intuition. To possess tact one must have a fine feeling, must instinctively know what to say or what to do. In order to be tactful one must possess Sympathy and Understanding, the understanding which is so rare, for all men see and hear and feel, but how desperately few "understand." Tact enables one to foresee what is about to happen and calculate the result of actions. Tact enables us to feel when we are in the presence of physical, mental and moral cleanliness, for these are today invariably demanded as the price of success.

Loyalty is one of the strongest links which bind men of strength and character. It is one which can never be broken with impunity. The man who would lose his right hand rather than betray a friend will never lack friends. The man who will stand in silent guard, until death, if need be, besides the shrine of confidence or friendship of those who have allowed him to enter will find himself linked with a current of cosmic power which will attract desirable conditions only. It is conceivable that such a person should ever meet with lack of any kind.

Individuality is the power to unfold our own latent possibilities, to be a law unto ourselves, to be interested in the race rather than the goal. Strong men care nothing for the flock of imitators who trot complacently behind them. They derive no satisfaction in the mere leading of large numbers, or the plaudits of the mob. This pleases only petty natures and inferior minds. Individuality glories more in the unfolding of the power within than in the servility of the weakling.

Individuality is a real power inherent in all and the development and consequent expression of this power enables one to assume the responsibility of directing his own footsteps rather than stampeding after some self-assertive bell-wether.

Inspiration is the art of imbibing, the art of self realization, the art of adjusting the individual mind to that of the Universal Mind, the art of attaching the proper mechanism to the source of all power, the art of differentiating the formless into form, the art of becoming a channel for the flow of Infinite Wisdom, the art of visualizing perfection, the art of realizing the Omnipresence of Omnipotence.

Truth is the imperative condition of all well being. To be sure, to know the truth and to stand confidently on it, is a satisfaction beside which no other is comparable. Truth is the underlying verity, the condition precedent to every successful business or social relation.

Every act not in harmony with Truth, whether through ignorance or design, cuts the ground from under our feet, leads to discord, inevitable loss, and confusion, for while the humblest mind can accurately foretell the result of every correct action, the greatest, most profound and penetrating mind loses its way hopelessly and can form no conception of the result due to a departure from correct principles.

Those who establish within themselves the requisite elements of true success have established confidence, organized victory, and it only remains for them to take such steps from time to time as the newly-awakened thought force will direct, and herein rests the magical secret of all power.

Less than 10 per cent of our mental processes are conscious; the other 90 per cent are subconscious and unconscious, so that he who would depend upon his conscious thought alone for results is less than 10 per cent efficient. Those who are accomplishing anything worth while are those who are enabled to take advantage of this greater storehouse of mental wealth. It is in the vast domain of the subconscious mind that great truths are hidden, and it is here that thought finds its creative power, its power to correlate with its object, to bring out of the unseen the seen.

Those familiar with the laws of Electricity understand the principle that electricity must always pass from a higher to a lower potentiality and can therefore make whatever application of the power they desire. Those not familiar with this law can effect nothing; and so with the law governing in the Mental World; those who understand that Mind penetrates all things, is Omnipresent and is responsive to every demand, can make use of the law and can control conditions, circumstances and environment; the uninformed cannot use it because they do not know it.

The fruit of this knowledge is as it were, a gift of the Gods; it is the "truth" that makes men free, not only free from every lack and limitation, but free from sorrow, worry and care, and, is it not wonderful to realize that this law is no respecter of persons, that it makes no difference what your habit of thought may be, the way has been prepared?

With the realization that this mental power controls and directs every other power which exists, that it can be cultivated and developed, that no limitation can be placed upon its activity, it will be come apparent that it is the greatest fact in the world, the remedy for every ill, the solution for every difficulty, the gratification of every desire; in fact, that it is the Creator's magnificent provision for the emancipation of mankind.

Attainment

The nervous system is matter. Its energy is mind. It is therefore the instrument of the Universal Mind. It is the link between matter and spirit, between our consciousness and the Cosmic-Consciousness. It is the gateway of Infinite Power.

Both the Cerebro-spinal and the Sympathetic nervous systems are controlled by nervous energy that is alike in kind; and the two systems are so interwoven that their impulses can be sent from one to the other. Every activity of the body, every impulse of the nervous system, every thought, uses up nervous energy.

The system of nerves may be compared to a telegraph system; the nerve cells corresponding to the batteries, the fibres to the wires. In the batteries is generated electricity. The cells, however, do not generate nervous energy. They transform it and the fibres convey it. This energy is not a physical wave like electricity, light, or sound. It is *mind*.

It hears the same relationship to the mind as a piano does to its player. The Mind can only have perfect expression when the instrument through which it functions is in order.

The organ of the Cerebro-spinal Nervous System is the Brain, the organ of the Sympathetic Nervous System is the Solar Plexus. The first is the voluntary or Conscious, the latter the involuntary or Subconscious.

It is through the Cerebro-spinal Nervous System and the Brain that we become conscious of possessions, hence all possession has its origin in consciousness. The undeveloped consciousness of a babe, or the inhibited consciousness of an idiot, cannot possess.

This mental condition—consciousness—increases in direct proportion to our acquisition of knowledge. Knowledge is acquired by observation, experience, and reflection. We become conscious of these possessions by the mind; so that we recognize that possession is based on consciousness; this consciousness we designate the world within. Those possessions of Form that we acquire are of the world without.

That which possesses in the world within is Mind. That which enables us to possess in the world without is also Mind. Mind manifests itself as thoughts, mental pictures, words, and actions. Thought is therefore Creative. Our power to use Thought to create the conditions, surroundings, and other experiences of life, depends upon our habit of thinking. What we do depends upon what we are; what we are is the result of what we habitually think. Before we can Do, we must BE; before we can BE we must control and direct the force of Thought within us.

Thought is Force. There are but two things in the universe; Force and Form. When we realize that we possess this Creative Power, and that we can control and direct it, and by it act on the forces and forms in the objective world, we shall have made our first experiment in Mental Chemistry.

The Universal Mind is the 'Substance' of all force and form, the Reality that underlies ALL. In accordance with fixed laws, from Itself, and by Itself, is ALL brought into being and sustained. It is the Creative Power of Thought in its perfect expression. The Universal Mind is All Consciousness, All Power, and is Everywhere Present. It is essentially the same at every point of its presence, all mind is one mind. This explains the order and harmony of the universe. To apprehend this statement is to possess the ability to understand and solve every problem of life.

Mind has a two-fold expression—conscious or objective, and subconscious or subjective. We come into relationship with the world without by the objective mind; and with the world within by the subconscious mind. Though we are making a distinction between the conscious and the subconscious minds, such a distinction does not really exist; but this arrangement will be found convenient. All Mind is One Mind; in all phases of the mental life there is an indivisible unity and oneness.

The sub-conscious mind connects us with the Universal Mind, and thus we are brought into direct relationship with all power. In the sub-consciousness is stored up the observations and experiences of life that have come to it through the conscious mind. It is the storehouse of memory. The sub-conscious mind is a great seed plot in which thoughts have been dropped, or experiences conveyed by observation, or happenings planted, to come up again into consciousness with the fruitage of their growth.

Consciousness is the inner, and Thought is the outward expression of power. The two are inseparable; it is impossible to be conscious of a thing without thinking of it.

We have captured the lightning and changed its name to electricity. We have harnessed the waters and made the remorseless flood our servant. By the miracle of thought we have quickened water into vapor to bear the burdens, and move the commerce of the world. We have called into being floating palaces that plough the highways of the deep. We have triumphed in our conquest of the air. Although we are moored in the silvern archepelago of the Milky Way, we have conquered time and space.

When two electric wires are in close proximity, the first carrying a heavier load of electricity than the second, the second will receive by induction some current from the first. This will illustrate the attitude of mankind to the Universal Mind. They are not consciously connected with the source of power.

If the second wire were attached to the first, it would become charged with as much electricity as it could carry. When we become conscious of Power, we become a 'life wire,' because consciousness we are connected with the Power. In proportion to our ability to use power, we are enabled to meet the various situations which arise in life.

The Universal Mind is the source of all power and all form. We are channels through which this power is being manifested; consequently within us is power unlimited, possibilities without end, and all under the control of our own thought. Because we have these powers, because we are in living union with the Universal Mind, we may adjust or control every experience which may come to us.

There are no limitations to the Universal Mind, therefore the better we realize our oneness with this mind, the less conscious will we be of any limitation or lack, and the more conscious of power.

The Universal Mind is the same at every point of its presence, whether in the infinitely large or the infinitely small. The difference in the power relatively manifested lies entirely in the ability of expression. A stick of clay and a stick of dynamite of equal weight contain much the same amount of energy. But in the one it is readily set free, whereas in the other we have not yet learned how to release it.

In order to express we must create the corresponding condition in our consciousness. Either in the Silence or by repetition we impress this condition upon the subconsciousness.

Consciousness apprehends, and Thought manifests the conditions desired. Conditions in our life and in our environment are but the reflection of our predominant thoughts. So the importance of correct thinking cannot be over-estimated. "Having eyes and seeing not, having ears and hearing not, neither do they understand," is another way of expressing the truth that without consciousness there can be no apprehension.

Thought constructively used creates tendencies in the subconsciousness, these tendencies manifest themselves as character. The primary meaning of the word character is an engraved mark, as on a seal; and means: The peculiar qualities impressed by nature or habit on a person, which separates the person possessing them from all others. Character has an outward and an inward expression; the inward being Purpose, and the outward Ability.

Purpose directs the mind towards the ideal to be realized, the object to be accomplished, or the desire to be materialized. Purpose gives quality to thought. Ability is the capacity to co-operate with Omnipotence—although this may be done unconsciously. Our purpose and our ability determine our experiences in life. It is important that purpose and ability be balanced; when the former is greater than the latter 'the Dreamer' is produced; when ability is greater than purpose, impetuosity is the result, producing much useless activity.

By the law of attraction our experiences depend upon our mental attitude. Like is attracted to like. Mental attitude is as much the result of character as character is of mental attitude. Each acts and reacts on the other.

"Chance," "Fate," "Luck," and "Destiny" seem to be blind influences at work behind every experience. This is not so, but every experience is governed by immutable laws, which may be controlled so as to produce the conditions which we desire.

Everything visible and tangible in the universe is composed of matter, which is acted upon by force. As matter is known to us by its external appearances, we shall designate it as form.

Form may be dived into four classes: That possessing Form only or the in-organic, as for example, Iron, Marble, etc. Form that is living or the organic which has sensation and voluntary motion, as in Animals. Form that in addition is Conscious of its own being, and its possessions, as Man.

The fundamental principle underlying every successful business relation or social condition is the recognition of the difference between the world within and the world without, the subjective world and the objective world.

Around you, as the center of it, the world without revolves. Matter, organized life, people, thoughts, sounds, light and other vibrations, the universe itself with its numberless millions of phenomena; sending out vibrations toward you, vibrations of light, of sound, of touch; loudness, softness; of love, hate, of thoughts, good and bad, wise and unwise, true and untrue. These vibrations are directed toward you—your ego—by the smallest, as well as by the greatest, the farthest and the nearest. A few of them reach your world within, but the rest pass by, and as far as you are immediately concerned, are lost.

Some of these vibrations or forces are essential to your health, your power, your success, your happiness. How is it that they have passed you by, and have not been received in your world within?

When making a gramophone record, certain conditions must be observed. Everything coming within range of the transmitter will be recorded, provided that the disc to receive the vibrations has been properly prepared, and the requisite conditions are observed.

Assuming that the transmitter is perfect, any defect in the recording disc, will make a corresponding deficient record. For example: the disc may not be perfectly flat, or may not be moving at the correct speed, or the wax may be too soft, or too hard, or the contact of the needle may be imperfect.

The world within possesses sensibility, a faculty that catches the vibrations from the world without, and conveys them to the world within. It is the link that joins the two worlds. This sensibility is a form of consciousness.

Considering consciousness as a general term, we may say that it is the result of the world without acting on the world within. This takes place continuously whether we are awake or asleep. Consciousness is the result of sensing or feeling.

We easily recognize three phases of consciousness, between each of which there are enormous differences.

Simple consciousness, which all animals posses in common. It is the sense of existence, by which we recognize that "we are," and "that we are where we are;" and by which we perceive the various objects and varied scenes and conditions.

Self-consciousness, possessed by all mankind, except infants, and the mentally deficient. This gives us the power of self contemplation, I. e., the effect of the world without upon our world within. "Self contemplates self." Amongst many other results, language has thus come into existence, each word being a symbol for a thought or an idea.

Cosmic-consciousness, this form of consciousness is as much above self-consciousness as self-consciousness is above simple consciousness. It is as different from either as sight is different from hearing or touching. The blind can get no true notion of color, however keen his hearing or sensitive his touch.

Neither by simple consciousness nor by self-consciousness can one get any notion of cosmic-consciousness. it is not like either of them, any more than sight is like hearing. A deaf man can never learn of the value of music by means of his senses of sight or of touch.

Cosmic-consciousness is all forms of consciousness. It overrides time and space, for apart from the body and the world of matter, these do not exist.

The immutable law of consciousness is: that in the degree that the consciousness is developed, so is the development of power in the subjective, and its consequent manifestation in the objective.

Cosmic-consciousness is the result of the creation of the necessary conditions, so that the Universal Mind may function in the direction desired. All vibrations in harmony with the Ego's well being are caught and used.

When truth is directly apprehended, or becomes a part of consciousness, without the usual process of reasoning or observation, it is intuition. By intuition the mind instantly perceives the agreement or the disagreement between two ideas. The Ego always so recognizes truth.

By intuition the mind transforms knowledge into wisdom, experience into success, and takes into the world within the things that have been waiting for us in the world without. Intuition, then, is another phase of the Universal Mind that presents truth as facts of consciousness.

INDUSTRY

All the lost mines of Mexico, all the argosies that ever sailed from the Indies, all the gold and silver-laden ships of the treasure fleets of storied Spain, count no more in value than a beggar's dole compared to the wealth that is created every eight hours by modern business ideas.

Opportunity follows perception, action follows inspiration, growth follows knowledge, environment follows progress, always the mental first, then the transformation into the illimitable possibilities of character and achievement.

The progress of the United States is due to two per cent of its population. In other words, all our railroads, all our telephones, our automobiles, our libraries, our newspapers, and a thousand other conveniences, comforts and necessities are due to the creative genius to two per cent of the population.

As a natural consequence, the same two percent are the millionaires of our country. Now, who are these millionaires, these creative geniuses, these men of ability and energy, to whom we owe practically all the benefits of civilization? The same authority tells us that thirty per cent of them are the sons of poor preachers who had never earned more than $1,500 a year; twenty-five per cent were the sons of teachers, doctors, and country lawyers; and only five per cent were the sons of bankers.

We are interested, therefore, in ascertaining why the two per cent succeeded in acquiring all that is best in life, and the ninety-eight per cent remain in perpetual want. We know that this is not a matter of chance, because the universe as we know it, is governed by law. Law governs solar systems, sun, stars, planets. Law governs every form of light, heat, sound, and energy. Law governs every material thing and every immaterial thought. Law covers the earth with beauty and fills it with bounty—shall we then not be certain that it also governs the distribution of this bounty?

Financial affairs are governed by law just as surely, just as positively, just as definitely as health, growth, harmony, or any other condition in life, and the law is one with which anyone can comply.

Many are already unconsciously complying with this law; others are consciously coming into harmony with it.

Compliance with the law means joining the ranks of the two per cent; in fact, the new ear, the golden age, the industrial emancipation, means that the two per cent is about to expand until the prevailing conditions shall have been reversed—the two per cent will soon become the ninety-eight per cent.

In seeking the truth we are seeking ultimate cause; we know that every human experience is an effect; therefore, if we may ascertain the cause, and if we shall find that this cause is one which we can consciously control, the effect or the experience will be within our control also.

Human experience will then no longer be the football of fate; a man will not be the child of fortune; but destiny, fate and fortune will be controlled as readily as a captain controls his vessel, or an engineer his train.

All things are finally resolvable into the same element, and as they are thus translatable, one into the other, they must ever be in relation and many never be in opposition to one another.

In the physical world there are innumerable contrasts, and these may, for the sake of convenience, be designated by distinctive names. There are surfaces, colors, shades, dimensions, or ends to all things. There is a North Pole; and a South Pole; an inside and an outside; a seen and an unseen; but these expressions merely serve to place extremes in contrast.

They are names given to two different parts or aspects of the same quantity. The two extremes are relative; they are not separate entities, but are two parts or aspects of one whole.

In the mental world we find the same law. We speak of knowledge and ignorance, but ignorance is but a lack of knowledge and is therefore found to be simply a word to express the absence of knowledge; it has no principle in itself.

In the moral world we speak of good and evil, but upon investigation, we find that good and evil are but relative terms. Thought precedes and predetermines action; if this action results in benefit to ourselves and others, we call this result good. If this result is to the disadvantage of ourselves and others, we call it evil. Good and evil are therefore found to be simply words which have been coined to indicate the result of our actions, which in turn are the result of our thoughts.

In the Industrial World, we speak of Labor and Capital as if there were two separate and distinct classes, but Capital is wealth and wealth is a product of Labor, and Labor necessarily includes Industry of every kind—physical, mental, executive, and professional. Every man or woman who depends in whole or in part for his or her income upon the results of their effort in the Industrial World must be classed as Labor. We therefore find that in the Industrial World there is but one Principle and that is Labor, or Industry.

There are many who are seriously and earnestly trying to find the solution to the present industrial and social chaos, and we hear much of production, waste, efficiency—and sometimes something in regard to constructive thinking.

The thought that humanity is one the borderland of a new idea, that the dawn of a new era is at hand, that a new epoch in the history of the world is about to take place, is rapidly spreading from mind to mind, and is changing the preconceived ideas of man and his relation to Industry.

We know that every condition is the result of a cause, and that the same cause invariably produces the same result. What has been the cause of similar changes in the thought of the world; the Renaissance, the Reformation, the Industrial Revolution? Always the discovery and discussion of new knowledge.

The elimination of competition by the centralization of industry into corporations and trusts, and the economies resulting therefrom, have set man to thinking.

He sees that competition is not necessary to progress and he is asking: "What will be the outcome of the evolution which is taking place in the Industrial World?" And gradually the thought begins to dawn, the thought which is rapidly germinating, which is about to burst forth in the minds of all men everywhere, the thought which is carrying men off their feet and crowding out every selfish idea, the thought that the emancipation of the Industrial World is at hand.

This is the thought which is arousing the enthusiasm of mankind as never before; this is the thought which is centralizing force and energy, and which will destroy every barrier between itself and its purpose. It is not a vision of the future; it is a vision of the present; it is at the door—and the door is open.

The creative instinct in the individual is his spiritual nature; it is a reflection of the Universal Creative Principle; it is therefore instinctive and innate; it cannot be eradicated; it can only be perverted.

Owing to the changes which have taken place in the Industrial World, this creative instinct no longer finds expression; a man cannot build his own house; he can no longer make his own garden; he can by no manner of means direct his own labor; he is therefore deprived of the greatest joy which can come to the individual, the joy of creating, of achievement; and so this great power for good is perverted and turned into destructive channels; becoming envious, he attempts to destroy the works of his more fortunate fellows.

Thought results in action. If we wish to change the nature of the action, we must change the thought, and the only way to change the thought is to substitute a healthy mental attitude for the chaotic mental conditions existing at present.

It is evident that the power of thought is by far the greatest power in existence; it is the power which controls every other power, and while this knowledge has until recently been the possession of the few, it is about to become the priceless privilege of the many. Those who have the imagination, the vision, will see the opportunity of directing this thought into constructive and creative channels; they will encourage and foster the spirit of mental adventure; they will arouse, develop and direct the creative instinct, in which case we shall soon see such an industrial revival as the world has never before experienced.

Henry Ford visions the approach of the new Era in The Dearborn Independent. He says: "The human race is now on the border line between two periods, the period when to use is to lose, and the period when not to use is to waste. For a long time mankind has been conscious of somehow coming to the end of irresponsible childhood; the provision made by the Parent of mankind has seemed to be coming to the end of its lavishness. That is, there has been a sense that the more we used the less we had in reserve. This feeling has been expressed in the popular adage," you can't eat your cake and have it."

But now that man is learning enough to plant his supply as well as reap it, to make his supply a recurrent crop instead of a slowly diminishing original store of natural resources, the time is coming when instead of being afraid of wasting our resources by using them we shall be afraid of wasting them by not using them. The stream of supply will be so full and constant that when people worry it will not be worry about not having enough, but about not using enough.

If you can imagine a world in which the source of supply will be so plentiful that people will worry about not using enough of it, instead of worrying as we do now about using too much, you will have a picture of the world that is soon to be. We have long depended on the resources which nature long ago stored up, the resources which can be exhausted. We are entering an ear when we shall create resources which shall be so constantly renewed that the only loss will be not to use them. There will be such a plenteous supply of heat, light and power, that it will be sin not to use all we want. This era is coming in now. And it is coming by way of Water.

With the fuel question settled, and the light question settled, and the heating question settled, and the power question settled, on such terms as actually liberate the whole world from the crushing weight of these four great burdens; and not only that, but with the whole fuel and light and heat and power situation turned around so that people will have to use all that they want, in order to prevent waste—don't you see how economic life will swing loose and breathe deeply, as if a new spring day had downed for humanity?

That is the era we are approaching. There is no question about that. There will be, of course, the usual preliminary skirmish between selfishness and service, but service will win. The ownership of a coal mine located on a man's property may easily be granted to private parties but the ownership of a river? Nature itself rebukes the man who would claim ownership of a river.

Our next period is before us, not the first period of reckless waste, nor the second period of anxious accounting, but the third period of overlapping abundance which compels us to use and use and use, to fulfill every need."

Thought is mind in motion, just as wind is air in motion. Mind is spiritual activity; in fact, it is the only activity which the spiritual man possesses, and Spirit is the creative Principle of the Universe.

Therefore, when we think, we start a train of causation; the thoughts go forth and meet other similar thoughts; they coalesce and form ideas; the ideas now exist independently of the thinker; they are the invisible seeds which exist everywhere, and which sprout and grow and bring forth fruit, some an hundred—and some a thousandfold.

We have been led to believe, and many still seem to think, that Wealth is something very material and tangible; that we can secure and hold it for our own exclusive use and benefit. We somehow forget that all the gold in the world only amounts to a very few dollars per capita. The entire supply of gold for the world is only eight billion dollars.

This includes all the gold coined or in bars in the various banks or Government treasuries of the world. This quantity of gold could be easily contained in a sixty-foot cube. If we depended upon the supply of gold it would be exhausted in a single day, and yet with this as a basis we spend hundreds and thousands, millions and now billions, of dollars daily, and yet the original supply of gold is not altered. The gold is simply a measure, a rule; with one ruler we may measure thousands and hundreds of thousands of feet, so with one $5 bill hundreds and thousands and millions of people may have the use of it by simply passing it from one to the other.

So it is that if we can only keep the tokens of wealth, which we call money, circulating, everyone could have all he or she might want; there need be no lack. The sense of lack comes only when we begin to hoard, when we are seized with fear and panic and fail to give out, to release.

It is therefore evident that the only way we can get any benefit from wealth is by its use, and to use it we must give it out, so that someone else can get the benefit of it; we are then co-operating for our mutual benefit and putting the law of abundance into practical operation.

We also see that wealth is by no means as substantial and tangible as many supposed, but that, on the contrary, the only way to get it is to keep it going; as soon as there is any concerted movement whereby there is any danger of stopping the circulation of this medium of exchange there is stagnation, fever, panic, and industrial death.

It is this intangible nature of wealth that makes it peculiarly susceptible to the power of thought and has enabled many men to secure fortunes in a year or two which others could not hope to acquire in a lifetime of effort. This is due to the creative power of mind.

Helen Wilmans gives an interesting description of the practical operation of this law in "The Conquest of Poverty." She says:

"There is an almost universal reaching out for money. This reaching out is from the acquisitive faculties only, and it operations are confined to the competitive realm of the business world. it is a purely external proceeding; its mode of action is not rooted in the knowledge of the inner life, with its finer, more just, and spiritualized wants. It is but an extension of animality into the realm of the human, and no power can lift it to the divine plane the race is now approaching.

"For all lifting on this plane is the result of spiritual growth. It is doing just what Christ said we must do in order to be rich. It is first seeking the kingdom of heaven within, where alone it exists. After this kingdom is discovered, then all these things (external wealth) shall be added.

"What is there within a man that can be called the kingdom of heaven? When I answer this question not one reader out of ten will believe me—so utterly bankrupt of knowledge of their own internal wealth are the great majority of people. But I shall answer it, nevertheless, and it will be answered truly.

"Heaven exists within us in the faculties latent in the human brain, the superabundance of which no man has ever dreamed. The weakest man living has the powers of a God folded within his organization; and they will remain folded until he learns to believe in their existence, and then tries to develop them. Men generally are not introspective, and this is why they are not rich. They are poverty-stricken in their own opinions of themselves and their powers, and they put the stamp of their belief on everything they come in contact with. If a day laborer, let us say, does but look within himself long enough to perceive that he has an intellect that can be made as great and far reaching as that of the man he serves; if he sees this, and attaches due importance to it, the mere fact of his seeing it, has, to a degree, loosened his bonds and brought him face to face with better conditions.

"But there is wanted something more than the fact of knowing that he is, or may become, by recognition of self, his employer's intellectual equal. There remains the fact that he needs also to know the Law and claims its provisions; namely, that his superior knowing relates him to a superior position. He must know this and trust it; for it is by holding this truth in faith and trust that he beings to ascend bodily. Employers everywhere hail with delight the acquisition of employees who are not mere machines—they want brains in their business and are glad to pay for them. Cheap help is often the most expensive, in the sense of being the least profitable. As brain growth or development of thought power in the employee increases his value to the employer, and as the employee grows to the degree of strength where he is capable of doing for himself, there will be another not yet grown so strong to take his place.

"The gradual recognition by a man of his own latent powers is the heaven within that is to be brought forward in the world and established in these conditions which correlate it.

"A mental poor-house projects from itself the spirit of a visible poor-house, and this spirit expresses itself in visible externals correlated to its character.

"A mental palace sends forth the spirit of a visible with results that correlate it. And the same may be said of sickness and sin, of health and goodness."

ECONOMICS

Senator Wadsworth recently said: "I pray that the time will come when American public opinion will come to any appreciation of what organic chemistry means, of what research means, in the way of progress. We have been interested as a propel in the development of material resources—the digging of iron and coal from the ground, the raising of crops upon the surface, and the engaging in transportation and other forms of commercial effort. As a people we have paid little attention and given little encouragement to scientific research, but Mr. President and Senators, the progress of the future depends upon scientific research. It is the man working in the chemical laboratory who is to blaze the way for human progress."

He went on to say: "I believe that in organic chemistry lies the solution of the secrets of the past and of the future. I believe that its establishment and maintenance in this country, even under an embargo, means the happiness, the progress, and the security of 100,000,000 people."

Senator Frelinghuysen added: "When we realize that it was due to the genius of the German chemists, and the advance in the science by the German industries, that enabled Germany to get almost to the channel ports; when we realize that the next war will be fought with chemicals, I think it is our patriotic duty to give this industry the highest protection that can be imposed."

It is true that many of the more important discoveries in science are due to the genius of German Chemists; it is also true that the next war, if there be one, will be fought with chemicals, but the next and all future wars will be won by an understanding of mental chemistry.

Try to realize the situation, think for a moment, see an army of men pass in review, four abreast, all men in the prime of life, see them march on and on, men from Germany, men from France, from England, from Belgium, from Austria, from Russia, from Poland, from Rumania, from Bulgaria, from Servia, from Turkey, yes and from China and Japan, India, New Zealand, Australia, Egypt and America, on they go, marching all day long, all the next day and the day after, all the week they keep coming and the next week, and the next week, and the next month, for if we would take months for this army of ten million men to pass any given point. All dead, and dead only because a few men in high places were more concerned about organic chemistry than they were about mental chemistry.

They did not know that force can always be met with equal or superior force; they did not know that a higher law always controls a lower law, and because intelligent men and women allowed a few men in high places to control their thinking processes, the entire world must sit in sack-cloth and ashes, for the living will find it necessary to work the rest of their lives in order to even pay the interest on the obligations assumed and their children will find these obligations an inheritance, and they in turn will pass them on to their children and their children's children.

Marion Leroy Burton, President of the University of Michigan, says: "Perhaps the most solemn question that can be put to a person today is, 'Can you think?' The test of individual efficiency and usefulness to society centers in a man's ability to use his mind. Emerson never erected a more arresting danger signal than when he exclaimed: 'Beware when the great God lets loose a thinker on the planet.' If we could only harness the mental power of America today we could solve the gigantic problems of the world.

Not by appeals to prejudice and class interest, not by the hurling of epithets, not by the ready acceptance of half truths, not by superficial, but by careful, painstaking, scientific scholarly thought combined with wise and timely action, will civilization be rescued and human freedom made secure. Upon Education depends the future of Democracy. Therefore, every loyal citizen, every self-respecting person, must utilize his opportunities to strengthen his grip on knowledge and to stimulate his mind. The truth has always made men free, and truth is available only for him who thinks."

That people are beginning to think is evident; formerly when men were discontented or dissatisfied they met in a near-by saloon, had a few drinks and promptly forgot their discontent and dissatisfaction. The situation is very different under existing conditions, men spend their time reading, studying and thinking, and the more they think the less satisfied they become.

Leaders of men all know this, for this reason England has her ale, Scotland her whiskey, France her absinthe, Germany her beer and we of America who are recruited from all of these have had all forms of alcohol, it is by far the easiest way of keeping the people "happy and contented." A man who has access to a fair percentage of alcohol, will not ask too many questions, if he does give him another drink.

This method of reducing the citizens of a country to a kind of idiotic servility has the additional advantage in that it produces enormous revenues which may be used for reducing them to economic slavery as well as spiritual slavery, for the man who cannot think has but small prospect of ever coming into any understanding of spiritual truth.

But because the opium traffic furnishes millions of revenue of Englishmen, millions of Chinese must be sacrificed, and because the sale and distribution of alcohol furnishes million dollar accounts for large banks and trust companies, $100,000.00 fees for corporation attorneys, because it makes it possible to lead large masses of men to the polls for the purpose of voting for political parties who are both morally and politically bankrupt, there are those who would again inflict this deadly curse upon the citizens of our country.

Dr. Woods Hutchinson tells us that the death rate for the United States has fallen in the last three years from 14.2 to 12.3 a thousand, which represents a saving of over 200,000 lives a year since the brewers' business was closed down. "Almost unanimous reports from public school teachers, school and district nurses, welfare workers among the poor, intelligent police chiefs and heads of charitable organizations, show that never, in all their experience, has there been so striking an improvement in the feeding, the clothing, the general comfort and welfare of school children as within the last two years.

And yet there are those who favor the modification of the Volstead act. There is probably not a single individual in existence whose thinking processes are in such an infantile stage of development that he does not know that when a door has been partly opened it requires but the pressure of the little finger to push it wide open, so that modification is but another word for annulment with all of its physical, mental, moral and spiritual degradation and disaster, and all of the sorrow, suffering, infamy, shame and horror which this most monstrous curse has inflicted upon suffering humanity.

"There can be no argument on the assertion that this country is in need of constructive legislation and administration as never before. There never was a time in our history when sound judgment, broad vision, great knowledge, and practical initiative were so necessary to the preservation and promotion of our national and individual welfare. There never was a time when statesmanship and leadership of the highest qualities were so essential to our advancement and prosperity. The country has before it, and has long had, an impressive proof of the futility of mediocrity in Government under the conditions that have oppressed us since the war. It has seen a Congress without leadership, hopelessly confused by the tremendous problems that confront it, accomplishing little toward their solution, and that little badly. There never has been a time, we repeat, when able, constructive statesmanship was so greatly needed and there never has been a time when there was so little of that quality of statesmanship in office.

The following editorial entitled "Where are we going?" recently appeared in the St. Louis Globe-Democrat:

"Whose fault is this? Who is primarily to blame for the fact that our resources are so small when our needs are so great? There can be no other answer to that. The people of the United States. The men who are responsible for legislation and administration are chosen by the people. Within the people rests the sole power of election. That is the fundamental principle of our Government, and we have no right to complain when our affairs are badly managed if we do nothing to obtain better managers. But what do we see in this perilous situation? Are the people seeking and supporting men whose brains and judgment and knowledge and character justify expectation of improvement in our governmental conditions? Most conspicuously they are not. On the contrary, they are turning to men who are most lacking in the qualities needed for this emergency, to men, indeed, whose qualities are the opposite, men who are mainly distinguished, if distinguished at all, by their abilities as obstructionists and destructionists, or if they are new aspirants, by their capacity to condemn whatever is and to propose strange and weird political nostrums for popular enticement.

"How is the Government of the world's greatest nation to function greatly and maintain its greatness with such materials? How is construction, the supreme need of this time, to be accomplished by men who know not how to build, who do not want to build, and whose counsels are but confusion? And what is the meaning of this popular trend which sets these men in the high places of Government? Undoubtedly, we think, it is the voicing of a great protest against present conditions, a great outpouring of popular discontent over many things that disturb and irritate the public. That there are numerous reasons for dissatisfaction is not to be questioned, but far from providing a remedy for these conditions the course taken by the people must inevitably make them worse. The problems that are pressing upon us must somehow be solved before we can be restored and resume our progress, and their solution can only come from constructive minds. There can be no disagreement as to that. Yet it is not constructive but destructive statesmanship to which we are trusting our affairs. What is to be the outcome?"

The unit of the Nation is the individual. The Government represents only the average intelligence of the unites comprising that Nation. Therefore, our work is with the unit. When the thought of the individual changes, the collective thought will take care of itself, but we try to reverse the process. We try to change Governments instead of individuals. But with a little intelligent organized effort, the present destructive thought could be readily charged into a constructive thought, in which case the situation would rapidly change.

Ten years ago the securities of German corporations, sold side by side with those of England and America, no one dreamed that they were not absolutely safe. The Municipal bonds of any large German city sold freely on a 4 per cent basis in London, Paris and New York. The mark was as stable as the dollar or pound sterling.

The interest is still being paid upon these securities and the principal will be paid at maturity, but in money that is hardly worth the paper it is printed upon, and so the conservative German investor, the man who made only "safe" investments, who was careful to buy only first mortgage bonds that yielded not more than 4 or 5 per cent is practically penniless, but as a compensation he can reflect that a liberal Government allowed the people to have plenty of beer, and when men have plenty of beer they will usually be glad to let some one else do the thinking for them, for the use of beer is not calculated to produce deep, clear, sustained or logical thought.

And so we find that during the past week in November, 1922, there were issued 61,644,000,000 of these marks, which was exceeded only by the number issued during the preceding week, which was 67,579,000,000. The value of a German mark is now something like one one-hundredth part of one cent.

Thousand and tens of thousands of American citizens are slowly and painfully creating a fund which they hope will protect them in the days to come, is it impossible that they, too, will be paid in valueless dollars ten years from now?

The reason that the dollar will probably remain at par is because we do not desire the kind of personal liberty that enriches a few at the expense of the many, the kind of liberty that attempts to reduce American citizens to automatons in order that a few may dictate the destiny of the nation.

Happiness, prosperity and contentment are the result of clear thinking and right action, for the thought precedes and predetermines the nature of the action. A little artificial stimulation in the form of intoxicating liquor may temporarily still the senses and thus serve to confuse the issue, but as in economics and mechanics every action is followed by a reaction, so in human relations every action is followed by an equal reaction, and so we have come to know that the value of things depends upon the recognition of the value of person. Whenever a creed becomes current that things are of more importance than people programs become fixed which set the interest of wealth above the interests of people, this action must necessarily be followed by a reaction.

We of America must remember that the large business of life is not economically conducted unless we succeed in transforming our resources into the highest grade of physical, mental and moral persons evolvable. Then and then only shall we know that our investments are safe.

The question is how may this be accomplished, what combinations of thought shall be made in order to bring about the chemicalization which will result in the greatest good for the greatest number. Shall we encourage the spirit of anarchy and discontent and follow the example of Italy by turning over the machinery of Government to those who are interested only in the exaltation of personality, for in Italy there is today no authority but that of Mussolini, the Chamber has none, the Senate has none, the King has none, his power is absolute. He may abrogate all laws appertaining to finance and apply new laws of his own making, already he has indicated that he will levy a tax upon workmen drawing high wages, "not so much for fiscal reasons as for political and moral reasons."

This is the result of fostering a spirit of discontent, disorder and social unrest, and nowhere do these conditions obtain except in countries where it has been easy to mislead the people through the distribution of alcoholic beverages which destroy the power to think.

A celebrated European statesman visions the present situation as follows:

"Unfortunately, the ills of a war like that of 1914-1918 are repaired but with difficulty. Given even the entire good faith of the conquered, if the latter by conscientious labor genuinely desired to help the world out of its sanguinary nightmare and back to normal life, that world would none the less remain for a long time hopelessly adrift and at sea. We are assisting today at the prolongation of a war which is not even likely to approach a conclusion unless there is a new orientation of a peace-time energy. Finances upside down, budgets artificially met, rates of exchange giving 65 francs to the pound and 14 to the dollar, and terribly distorted fiduciary circulation, an ever-increasing cost of living, strikes, rapid changes in the stock markets, making commerce and industry impossible; accumulation of stocks—such is the ransom of these four years of war. It was materially impossible that either for conqueror or conquered aught else should result from this world catastrophe than complete chaos for all. Millions of men are not consecrated for 52 months to a work of death and destruction for the world to be re-established on the morrow of peace. Such rapidity reacquired equilibrium is beyond the bounds of human practicability."

It will be remember that the Master Metaphysician said the same thing in somewhat different language many years ago:

"Then shall be great tribulation such as never was since the beginning of the world, nor never shall be afterwards, and if that period would not be shortened no flesh at all would be saved, but for the elect's sake that period will be shortened."—Matt. 24:21,22.

The stomach is the great organ of accelerated circulation to the blood, of elasticity to the animal spirits, of pleasurable or painful vibration to the nerves, of vigor to the mind, and of fullness to the cheerful affections of the soul. Here is the silver cord of life, and the golden bowl at the fountain, and the wheel at the cistern; and as these fulfill their duty, the muscular and mental and moral powers act in unison, and fill the system with vigor and delight. But as these central energies are enfeebled, the strength of mind and body declines, and lassitude and depression and melancholy and sighing succeed to the high beating of health and the light of life becomes as darkness.

Experience has decided that any stimulus applied statedly to the stomach, which raises its muscular tone above the point at which it can be sustained by food and sleep, produces, when it has passed away, debility—a relaxation of the overworked organ proportioned to its preternatural excitement. The life-giving power of the stomach falls of course as much below the tone of cheerfulness and health, as it was injudiciously raised above it. If the experiment be repeated often, it produces an artificial tone of stomach, essential to cheerfulness and muscular vigor, entirely above the power of the regular sustenance of nature to sustain, and creates a vacuum which nothing can fill but the destructive power which made it; and when protracted use has made the difference great between the natural and this artificial tone, and habit has made it a second nature, the man is a drunkard, and in ninety-nine instances in a hundred is irretrievably undone.

Beer has been recommended as a substitute, and a means of leading back the captive to health and liberty. But though it may not create intemperate habits as soon, it has no power to allay them. It will even finish what alcohol has begun, and with this difference only, that it does not rasp the vital organs with quite so keen a file, and enables the victim to come down to his grave by a course somewhat more dilatory, and with more of the good-natured stupidity of the idiot and less of the demoniac frenzy of the madman.

Wine has been prescribed as a means of decoying the intemperate from the ways of death. But habit cannot be thus cheated out of its dominion, nor ravening appetite be amused down to a sober and temperate demand. It is not true that wine will restore the intemperate, or stay the progress of the disease. Enough must be taken to screw up nature to the tone of cheerfulness, or she will cry, "Give," with an importunity not to be resisted; and long before the work of death is done, wine will fail to minister a stimulus of sufficient activity to rouse the flagging spirits, or will become acid on the enfeebled stomach, and whisky and brandy will be called in to hasten to its consummation the dilatory work of self-destruction. So that if no man becomes a sot upon wine, it is only because it hands him over to more fierce and terrible executions of Heaven's delayed vengeance.

To the action of a powerful mind, a vigorous muscular frame is, as a general rule, indispensable. Like heavy ordnance, the mind, in its efforts, recoils on the body, and will soon shake down a puny frame.

The history of the world confirms this conclusion. Egypt, once at the head of nations, has, under the weight of her own effeminacy, gone down to the dust. The victories of Greece let in upon her the luxuries of the East, and covered her glory with a night of ages. And Rome, who iron foot trod down the nations and shook the earth, witnessed in her latter days faintness of heart and the shield of the mighty vilely cast away.

MEDICINE

The attitude of the practitioners of medicine toward mental chemistry has always been most catholic. To quote from Dr. Osler: "The psychical method has always played an important, though largely unrecognized, part in therapeutics. It is from faith, which buoys up the spirits, sets the blood flowing more freely, and the nerves playing their parts without disturbance, that a large part of all cures arise. Despondency or lack of faith will often sink the stoutest constitution almost to death's door; faith will enable a bread pill or a spoonful of clear water to do almost miracles of healing, when the best medicines have been given over in despair. The basis of the entire profession of medicine is faith in the doctor and his drugs and his methods."

F. W. Clarke has fitly summed up the relation of modern chemistry to progressive medicine: "Medicine is indebted to chemistry for almost a new pharmacopoeia, for not only have new medicines been created, but in place of old drugs, crude and bulky, the compact and more elegant active principles are now employed. Anaesthetics, such as ether, chloroform and nitrous oxide; hypnotics like chloral; the remedies derived from coal-tar; and alkaloids like quinine, morphine, and cocaine, are a few of the contributions with which chemistry has enriched medical practice. Even antiseptic surgery depends upon chemical preparations for its success."

On the other hand, Dr. Osler admits that, "We have not as yet made as many additions to the stock of panaceas as we might. But chemistry has done vast service for us, and will probably do far more. Aside from the discovery of new substances like cocaine, it has given us the active principles of calculable strength and purity, in place of crude drugs of varying strength at best, and of varying purity and age, and there is no reason why we may not have new specifics as sure (and for as important diseases) as quinine."

Our problem would be more simple, and the doctors, with their wide knowledge and splendid service, would have solved the problem long ago, had it been a purely physical one; but unfortunately it is a mental problem long before it becomes a physical one; as we continue to exercise our capacity for response we shall find it necessary to treat our thoughts and emotions if we are to establish health upon a firm basis.

For instance, it is commonly recognized that worry or continued negative emotional excitement will disorganize digestion. When the digestion is normal the feeling of hunger will stop, will be inhibited when we have eaten as much as we need, nor will we feel hunger again until we actually require food. in such cases our inhibiting center is working properly. But if we get dyspeptic, this inhibiting center has ceased to function, and we are hungry all the time, with the consequent tendency to overwork an already impaired digestive apparatus. Mankind is continually experiencing such small disturbances. They are strictly local and attract but small attention at the great center. They come and go—and properly so—without drawing from the organism as a whole much consideration. But if the disorder has grown out of a deep-rooted cause which cannot easily be removed, disease of a more serious nature will ensue. Under such circumstances, by reason of its seriousness and long continuance, the trouble involves all parts of the organism and may threaten its very life. When it reaches this point, if the administration at the grand center is vigorous and determined and wise, the disturbance cannot long endure; but if there is weakness at the center the whole federation may go down with a crash.

Dr. Lindlahr says that "Nature Cure Philosophy presents a rational concept of evil, its cause and purpose, namely: that it is brought on by violation of Nature's laws, that it is corrective in its purpose that it can be overcome only by compliance with the Law. There is no suffering, disease or evil of any kind anywhere unless the law has been transgressed somewhere by someone."

These transgressions of the law may be due to ignorance, to indifference, or to willfulness and viciousness. The effect will always be commensurate with the causes.

The science of natural living and healing shows clearly that what we call disease is primarily Nature's effort to eliminate morbid matter and to restore the normal functions of the body; that the processes of disease are just as orderly in their way as everything else in Nature; that we must not check or suppress them, but co-operate with them. Thus we con, slowly but laboriously, the all-important lesson that "obedience to the law" is the only means of prevention of disease, and the only cure.

The Fundamental Law of Cure, the Law of Action, and Reaction, and the Law of Crisis, as revealed by the Nature Cure Philosophy, impress upon us the truth that there is nothing accidental or arbitrary in the processes of health, disease and cures; that every changing condition is either in harmony or in discord with the laws of our being; that only by complete surrender and obedience to the law can we master the law, and attain and maintain perfect physical health.

In our study of the cause and character of disease we must endeavor to begin at the beginning, and that is *Life* itself; for the processes of health, disease and cure are manifestations of that which we call life and vitality.

There are two prevalent, but widely differing conceptions of the nature of life or vital force: the material and the vital.

The former looks upon life or vital force with all its physical mental and psychical phenomena as manifestations of the electric, magnetic and chemical activities of the physical-material elements composing the human organism. From this view point, life is a sort of "spontaneous combustion," or, as one scientist expressed it, a "succession of fermentations."

This materialistic conception of life, however, has already become obsolete among the more advanced biologists as a result of the discoveries of modern science, which are fast bridging the chasm between the material and the spiritual realms of being.

The vital conception of Life or Vital Force on the other hand, regards it as the primary force of all forces, coming from the central source of all power.

This force, which permeates, warms and animates the entire created universe, is the expression of the Divine Will, the Logos, the Word, of the Great Creative Intelligence. it is this Divine Energy which sets in motion the whirls in the ether, the electric corpuscles and ions that make up the different atoms and elements of matter.

These corpuscles and ions are positive and negative forms of electricity. Electricity is a form of energy. It is intelligent energy; otherwise it could not move with that unvarying wonderful precision in the electrons of the atoms as in the suns and planets of the sidereal universe.

If t his supreme intelligence should withdraw its energy—the electrical charges (forms of energy)—and with it the atoms, elements, and the entire material universe, would disappear in the flash of a moment.

From this it appears that crude matter, instead of being the source of life and of all its complicated mental and spiritual phenomena is only an expression of the Life Force, itself a manifestation of the Great Creative Intelligence which some call God, other Nature, the Oversoul, Brahma, Prana, etc., each one according to his understanding.

It is this supreme power and intelligence, acting in and through every atom, molecule, and cell in the human body, which is the true healer, this "vis medicatrix naturae" which always endeavors to repair, to heal, and to restore the perfect type. all that the physician can do is to remove obstructions and to establish normal condition within and about the patient, so that the power within can do its work to the best advantage.

In the final analysis, all things in Nature, from a fleeting thought or emotion to the hardest piece of diamond or platinum, are modes of motion or vibration. A few years ago physical science assumed that an atom was the smallest imaginable part of a given element of matter; that although infinitesimally small, it still represented solid matter. Now, in the light of better evidence, we have good reason to believe that there is no such thing as solid matter; that every atom is made up of charges of negative and positive electricity acting in and upon an omnipresent ether; that the difference between an atom of iron and of hydrogen, of any other element, consists solely in the number of electrical charges or corpuscles it contains, and on the velocity with which these vibrate around one another.

Thus the atom, which was thought to be the ultimate particle of solid matter, is found to be a little universe in itself in which corpuscles of electricity rotate or vibrate around one another like the suns and planets in the sidereal universe. This explains what we mean when we say life and matter are vibratory.

What we call "Inanimate Nature" is beautiful and orderly because it plays in tune with the score of the Symphony of Life. Man alone can play out of tune. This is his privilege, or his curse, as he chooses, by virtue of his freedom of choice and action.

We can now better understand the definitions of health and of disease, given in the catechism of Nature Cure as follows:

"Health is normal and harmonious vibration of the elements and forces composing the human entity on the physical, mental, moral, and spiritual planes of being, in conformity with the constructive principle of Nature applied to individual life."

"Disease is abnormal or inharmonious vibration of the elements and forces composing the human entity on one or more planes of being, in conformity with the destructive principle of Nature applied to individual life."

The question naturally arising here is, "Normal or abnormal vibration with what?" The answer is that the vibratory conditions of the organism must be in harmony with Nature's established harmonic relations in the physical, mental, moral, spiritual, and psychical realms of human life and action.

MENTAL MEDICINE

In "The Law of Mental Medicine," Thomson Jay Hudson, says:

"Like all the laws of nature, the law of mental medicine is universal in its application; and, like all the others, it is simple and easily comprehended. Granted that there is an intelligence that controls the functions of the body in health, it follows that it is the same power or energy that fails in case of disease. Failing, it requires assistance; and that is what all therapeutic agencies aim to accomplish. No intelligent physician of any school claims to be able to do more than to "assist nature" to restore normal conditions of the body.

That it is a mental energy that thus requires assistance, no one denies; for science teaches us that the whole body is made up of a confederation of intelligent entities, each of which performs its functions with an intelligence exactly adapted to the performance of its special duties as a member of the confederacy. There is, indeed, no life without mind, from the lowest unicellular organism up to man. It is, therefore, a mental energy that actuates every fibre of the body under all its conditions. That there is a central intelligence that controls each of those mind organisms, is self-evident.

Whether, as the materialistic scientists insist, this central intelligence is merely the sum of all the cellular intelligences of the bodily organism, or is an independent entity, capable of sustaining a separate existence after the body perishes, is a question that does not concern us in the pursuance of the present inquiry. It is sufficient for us to know that such an intelligence exists, and that, for the time being, it is the controlling energy that normally regulates the action of the myriad cells of which the body is composed.

it is, then, a mental organism that all therapeutic agencies are designed to energize, when, for any cause, it fails to perform its functions with reference to any part of the physical structure. It follows that mental therapeutic agencies are the primary and normal means of energizing the mental organism. That is to say, mental agencies operate more directly than any other, because more intelligibly, upon a mental organism; although physical agencies are by no means excluded, for all experience shows that a mental organism responds to physical as well as to mental stimuli.

All that can be reasonably claimed is that, in therapeutics, a mental stimulus is necessarily more direct and more positive in its effects, other things being equal, than a physical stimulus can be, for the simple reason that it is intelligent on the one hand and intelligible on the other. It must be remarked, however, that it is obviously impossible wholly to eliminate mental suggestion even in the administration of material remedies. Extremists claim that the whole effect of material remedies is due to the factor of mental suggestion; but this seems to be untenable. The most that can be claimed with any degree of certainty is that Material remedies, when they are not in themselves positively injurious, are good and legitimate forms of suggestions, and, as such, are invested with a certain therapeutic potency, as in the administration of the placebo. It is also certain that, whether the remedies are material or mental, they must, directly or indirectly, energize the mental organism in control of the bodily functions. Otherwise the therapeutic effects produced cannot be permanent.

It follows that the therapeutic value of all remedial agencies, material or mental, is proportioned to their respective powers to produce the effect of stimulating the subjective mind to a state of normal activity, and directing its energies into appropriate channels. We know that suggestion fills this requirement more directly and positively than any other known therapeutic agent; and this is all that needs to be done for the restoration of health in any case outside of the domain of surgery. It is all that can be done. No power in the universe can do more than energize the mental organism that is the seat and source of health within the body. A miracle could do no more.

Professor Clouston, in his inaugural address to the Royal Medical Society in 1896, says:

"I would desire this evening to lay down or enforce a principle that is, I think, not sufficiently, and often not at all, considered in practical medicine and surgery. It is founded on a physiological basis, and it is of the highest practical importance. The principle is that the brain cortex, and especially the mental cortex, has such a position in the economy that it has to be reckoned with more or less as a factor for good or evil in all diseases of every organ, in all operations, and in all injuries. Physiologically the cortex is the great regulator of all functions, the ever-active controller of every organic disturbance. We know that every organ and every function are represented in the cortex, and are so represented that they all may be brought into the right relationship and harmony with each other, and so they all may be converted into a vital unity through it.

"Life and mind are the two factors of that organic unity that constitute a real animal organism. The mental cortex of man is the apex of the evolutionary pyramid, whose base is composed of the swarming pyramids of bacilli and other monocellular germs which we now see to be almost all-pervading in nature. It seems as if it has been the teleological aim of all evolution from the beginning. In it every other organ and function find their organic end. In histological structure—so far as we yet know this—it far exceeds all other organs in complexity.

"When we fully know the structure of each neuron, with its hundreds of fibres and its thousands of dendrites, and the relation of one neuron to another, when we can demonstrate the cortical apparatus for universal intercommunication of nervous energy, with its absolute solidarity, its partial localization, and its wondrous arrangements for mind, motion, sensibility, nutrition, repair, and drainage—when we fully know all this, there will be no further question of the dominance of the brain cortex in the organic hierarchy, nor of its supreme importance in disease."

"The Lancet" records a case of Dr. Barkas of a woman (58) with supposed disease of every organ, with pains everywhere, who tried every method of cure, but was at least experimentally cured by mental therapeutics pure and simple. Assured that death would result from her state, and that a certain medicine would infallibly cure her, provided it was administered by an experienced nurse, one tablespoonful of pure distilled water was given her at 7, 12, 5 and 10, to the second with scrupulous care; and in less than three weeks all pain ceased, all diseases were cured, and remained so. This is a valuable experiment as excluding every material remedy whatever, and proving that it is the mental factor alone that cures; however, it may be generally associated with material remedies.

Dr. Morrison, of Edinburgh, discovered that a lady who had constant violent hysterical attacks had given her hand to one man and her heart to another. A little direct common-sense talk in this case formed an agreeable substitute for the distilled water in the other, and the patient never had another attack.

Many seem to think that only nervous or functional diseases are cured by Mental or Spiritual methods, but Alfred T. Scholfield, M. D., tells in "The force of Mind:"

In one long list of 250 published cases of disease cured we find five "consumption," one "diseased hip," five "abscess," three "dyspepsia," four "internal complaint," two "throat ulcer," seven "nervous debility," nine "rheumatism," five "diseased heart," two "withered arm," four "bronchitis," three "weak eyes," one "ruptured spine," five "pains in the head." And these are the results in one year at one small chapel in the north of London.

What about the "cures" at home and Continental spas, with their eternal round of sulphur and iron waters and baths?

Does the doctor attached to the spa, in his heart of hearts believe that all the cures which in these cases he cheerfully certifies to are effected by the waters, or even the waters and the diet, or even the waters and the diet and the air; or does he not think there must be a "something else" as well? And to come nearer home and into the center of all things, and the chamber of all his secrets: In his own consulting room and in his own practice, is not the physician brought face to face with cures, aye, and diseases, too, the cause of which he cannot account for; and is he not often surprised to find a continuation of the same treatment originated by the local practitioners is, when continued by his August self, efficacious? And is not the local practitioner not only surprised but disgusted as well to find such is the case?

Does any practical medical man, after all, really doubt these mental powers? Is he not aware of the ingredient "faith," which, if added to his prescriptions, makes them often all-powerful for good? Does he know experimentally the value of strongly asserting that the medicine will produce such and such effects as a powerful means of securing them?

If, then, this power is so well known, why in the name of common sense is it ignored? It has its laws of action, its limitations, its powers for good and for evil; would it not clearly help the medical student if these were indicated to him by his lawful teachers, instead of his gleaning them uncertainly from the undoubted successes of the large army of irregulars?

We are, however, inclined to think that, after all, a silent revolution is slowly taking place in the minds of medical men, and that our present text-books on disease, content with merely prescribing any mental cure in a single line as unworthy of serious consideration, will in time be replaced by others containing views more worthy of the century in which we live."

ORTHOBIOSIS

Virgil says: "Happy is he who has found the cause of things."

It was Metchnikoff who tried, after his investigations into the physical, to apply ethics to life, so that life might be lived to the full, which is the true wisdom. He called this condition orthobiosis. He held that the end of science is to rid the world of its scourges, through hygiene and other measures of prophylaxis.

Our manner of life, says Mm. Metchnikoff, transcribing her husband's idea, will have to be modified and directed according to rational and scientific date if we are to run through the normal cycle of life—orthobiosis. The pursuit of that goal will ever influence the basis of morals. Orthobiosis cannot be accessible to all until knowledge, rectitude and solidarity increase among men, and until social conditions are kinder.

Like all faculties, faith has a center through which it functions—the pineal gland. Faith is therefore physical, just as disease may be spiritual; spirit and body are but parts of a glorious whole. The cure of disease requires the use of Cosmic Force; and who shall say that that force—whether we call it God, Nature, Oversoul, Brahma, Vis Medicatrix Naturae, Prana, Logos, Divine Will does not manifest itself through material means, as well as spiritual?

"Plato," Dr. Butler tells us, "said that man is a plant rooted in heaven, and we agree to this, that he is also rooted in the earth." In fact, man may be said to have two origins, one earthly and physical, the other spiritual, though the former originates in the latter-so that ultimately the origin is one. . . .

Man is an organism. De Quincey defines an organism as a group of parts which act upon the whole, the whole in turn acting upon all parts. This is simple and true.

"It is paradoxical that mind, though a principal and usually a determining part of a human organism's actions and reactions, has by formal medicine been disregarded as a primary cause in pretty much all of those bodily disorders which are not produced by contagion. But of late years autointoxication and disturbances of the ductless glands have come into increased consideration. Their operations are being gradually traced to origins beyond the physical body, and definitely located in states of mind. These states are coming within the scope of diagnostics; enlightened medical art brings them under treatment."

Recognition of the influence of mind upon the body was recognized even of old, as far back as Hippocrates, and probably anterior to him. Mondeville, in the 14th century, approved of the custom of reciting certain verses of the psalms when taking medicine; nor was he averse to pilgrimages undertaken in search of health—he held that no harm could be done, while the potentialities of good were great. The value of the physical exercise in going on a pilgrimage, usually on foot, with most of the time spent in the open air, need scarcely be pointed out. Many a cure of lethargy and obesity in the middle ages and after owed its efficacy to the insistence of famous physicians that the patients, no matter how wealthy or high-born, were to come from their dwellings on foot, in all humility, refusing to extend treatment otherwise.

Ignatius of Loyola is credited with saying: "Do everything you can with the idea that everything depends on you, and then hope for results just as if everything depended on God."

It will be found that the sanest, most catholic and liberal exponents of each school of healing generously admit the value of other schools and the limitations of their own. The responsible healer of the future, who truly respects his honorable calling, will employ all beneficial, constructive agencies at the disposal of science. Thus, we have an eminent occultist saying:

"In cases of misplacement, dislocation, or broken bones, the quickest way to obtain relief is to send for a competent physician or anatomist and have an adjustment made of the injured member or organ. In cases of disruptions of blood-vessels or muscles, a surgeon's aid should be immediately sought; not because mind is unable to cure any or all of these cases, but because of the fact that at the present time, even among educated people, mind is many times impotent through misuse or non-use. Mental treatment should follow these physical treatments in order to obviate unnecessary suffering and to obtain rapid recovery."

We can not do better than to quote, Sir William Osler, Bt., M. D., F. R. Sx.:

"The salvation of science lies in a recognition of a new philosophy—the scientia scientiarum of which Plato speaks: 'Now when all these studies reach the point of intercommunion and connection with one another and come to be considered in their mutual affinities, then, I think, and not till then, will the pursuit of them have a value.'" "The Old Humanities and the New Science."

Scientists assume that there is one substance only, and therefore their deduced science is the science of that substance, and none other; and yet they are confronted with the fact that their one substance is differentiated, and that when they come to the finest degree thereof, as for instance bioplasm, we are brought face to face with the operation of higher laws than they are familiar with, or can adequately explain.

Many scientists, however, with a broader view, are beginning to glimpse a "fourth dimension," and recognize the fact that there may be degrees of matter which are utterly beyond their chemical tests and microscopic lens.

But a new day is dawning, the telephone, the telegraph and the wireless are now coming into general use and it is now possible to make use of every avenue of information and knowledge. It is therefore but a question of time when the sick will have the benefit of all that is known in the art of healing.

The physician frequently loses his patient because he refuses to recognize the spiritual nature of the patient, and that because of his spiritual nature there are certain fundamental laws governing in the spiritual world, and that these laws continue to operate whether he recognizes them or not, and the metaphysician frequently loses his patient because he refuses to recognize that the body of the patient is the material manifestation of the spirit within, and that the condition of the body is but an expression of the spirit.

But all this iconoclasm is but the result of a certain conservatism which is both human and natural. With the wisdom which the years are bringing there will soon be no one who cannot see that the germ is not only the cause of disease but the result of disease, that bacteria is the result of impure water not the cause of impure water, and so with everything else.

What we can see, handle or touch are never causes, but always effects, and if it is our purpose to simply substitute one form of distress for another we shall continue to deal with effects and effects only, but if it is our purpose to bring about a remedy, we shall seek the cause by which alone every effect is brought into existence, and this cause will never be found in the world of effects.

In the new era, abnormal, mental and emotional conditions will be immediately detected and corrected. Tissue in process of destruction will be eliminated or reconstructed by the constructive methods at the disposal of the physician. Abnormal lesions will be corrected by manipulative treatment, but above and beyond all of this will be the primary and essential idea, the idea upon which all results will depend and that is that no inharmonious or destructive thought shall be allowed to reach the patient, that every thought for him or about him shall be constructive, for every physician, every nurse, every attendant, every relative will eventually come to know that thoughts are spiritual things, which are ever seeking manifestation, and that as soon as they find fertile soil they begin to germinate.

Not all thoughts find expression in the objective world and especially in the health and environment of the patient. This is because not all patients are responsive, but when the patient finds that these invisible guests come laden with precious gifts, they will be given a royal welcome. This welcome will be subconscious because the thoughts of others are received subconsciously.

The conscious mind receives thought only through the organs of perception, which are its method of contact with the objective world; which are the five senses, seeing, hearing, feeling, tasting and smelling.

Subconscious thought is received by any organ of the body affected and think of the mechanism which has been provided and which can and does objectify the thought received. First the millions of cell chemists ready and waiting to carry out all instructions received. Next the complete system of communication, consisting of the vast sympathetic nervous system reaching every fibre of the being and ready to respond to the slightest emotion of joy or fear, of hope or despair, of courage or impotence.

Next the complete manufacturing plant consisting of a series of glands wherein are manufactured all the secretions necessary for the use of the chemists in carrying out the instructions which have been given.

Then there is the complete digestive tract wherein food, water and air are converted into blood, bone, skin, hair and nails.

Then there is the supply department which constantly sends a supply of Oxygen, Nitrogen and Ether into every part of the being, and the wonder of it all is that this Ether holds in solution everything necessary for the use of the chemist, for the Ether holds in pure form, and food, water, and air in the secondary form every element necessary for the use of the chemist in the production of a perfect man.

Why then do not these chemists produce a perfect specimen of manhood? The reply is simple, the prescriptions which consist of thoughts received by the subconscious call for nothing of the kind, in fact, they usually call for exactly the reverse.

The subconscious is also provided with a complete equipment for the elimination of waste and useless material as well as a complete repair department. In addition to this there is a complete system of wireless whereby it is connected with every other subconscious entity in existence.

We are not usually conscious of the operation of this wireless, but the same thing is true concerning the operation of the Marconi System. There may be messages of all kinds all about us, but unless we make use of an amplifier, we receive no message, and so with our subconscious wireless. Unless we try to co-ordinate the conscious and the subconscious we fail to realize that the subconscious is constantly receiving messages of some kind and just as constantly objectifying the messages in our life and environment.

This then is the mechanism devised and planned by the Creator, Himself, and it has been placed under the supervision of the subconscious instead of the conscious mind, but let us not forget that the subconscious mind with all of its wonderful mechanism can be controlled and dominated by the conscious mind when it becomes attuned to the Universal Mind, where all that is, or ever was, or ever shall be is held in solution waiting to come forth and manifest in form.

BIOCHEMISTRY

Biochemistry is a science, whose concern is with vital processes, and which has availed itself of the cell theory and of the principle of the infinite divisibility of matter. It also makes use of the homeopathic dose. The dose must be proportionate to the patient, the cell; for, as Virchow has pointed out, "the essence of disease is the cell, changed pathogenically.

Dr. Schuessler, the originator of Biochemistry, arrived at his conclusions by studying the elements, nature, and functions of human blood. The cells receive their sustenance, their life-supply, from the blood and lymph, which, in their turn, derive their supply from the elements taken in as food. Normalcy in the supply of these elements means health; any deviation, a disturbance of health.

Dr. Schuessler placed the number of mineral combinations in the human body at twelve; in the last edition, 1895, he reduced the number to eleven. These all-necessary cell-salts are:

Potassium Chloride, Potassium Phosphate, Potassium Sulphate, Sodium Chloride, Sodium Phosphate, Sodium Sulphate, Phosphate of Lime, Flouride of Lime, Phosphate of Magnesia, Phosphate of Iron, Silica.

Milk contains all these elements; other foods can give them in combination. Cremation reduces the body to these elements.

Each kind of cell depends upon a different salt, or combination of salts, for its food; a lack of any of these salts is shown by certain symptoms; the proper tissue salts, in right proportions are given to remove the symptoms, since a removal of the symptoms implies a removal of the need, or disease, in the cell.

It must be remembered, however, that the cells are not fed, they feed themselves; and any attempt to compel them to accept more than they require causes disaster. They voluntarily accept what is necessary and they reject what they do not need.

The difference in the cells consists in the kind and quality of the inorganic tissue salts of which they are composed.

Health, therefore, requires the requisite quantity of cell salts, and a lack of some one of these organic tissue salts results in imperfect cell action and diseased tissue.

The controlling principle which underlies every manifestation of form may be epitomized as follows: "In the apportionment and grouping of the elements that constitute a thing lies the cause, not only of the form, but also of its functions and qualities."

Dr. Charles W. Littlefield, M. D., the author of "The Beginning and the Way of Life," gives some very beautiful illustrations of the application of this law, in the chapter on the "Elements and Compounds of Nature," in which he says:

"Within the scope and application of this principle of grouping of electrons, as the law of origin of elements, molecules, tissues, organs and forms, will be found a practical solution to every problem in biology from the origin and differentiation of species to every modification of form and configuration of outline that mark individuals with characteristic personalities, both physical and mental . . . . It is well known in chemistry that the molecule is the smallest part of any substance that can exist separately and still retain its properties.

Since the nature of the molecule is determined by the polarities, number and arrangement of the "electrons" which compose it, and since all structures in the mineral, vegetable and animal kingdoms are molecular, it follows that in the last analysis the grouping and apportionment of negative and positive "electrons" in the molecule determine in turn the nature and physical conditions of the form, whether it be perfect or imperfect. Deformity, personal likes and dislikes, are only questions of being "electronically" balanced or unbalanced, through supply or lack of supply of the forms of molecules that compose the organism. Only the spirit-mind-image of man, however, can make this grouping of molecules for the perfecting of a human form. To bring humanity to a state of primitive perfection, therefore, not only must the same material, prepared in the same manner, be supplied, but the environment of forces must be the same as those employed by the Creative Spirit in the beginning.

"Since then, we are able to trace every elemental form of matter back to some definite grouping of negative and positive electrons, that is, through varying numbers and arrangements of these; and since we find life manifesting through various forms as determined by different molecular groupings—by law of composition—and since it is rational to place Divine Mind behind this physical process, we are justified in assuming that Divine Mind—Images of living things preceded their physical development.

Therefore, in the ultimate science of being, idealism is more probable than materialism. But, while mind may thus exist alone there in the realm of cause, here in the realm of phenomena, we always have a psycho-physical parallelism, a realism, where everything must be explained by mind and matter, but by neither alone. While the spiritual entity which constitutes the real self may well be assumed to be akin to the Supreme Mind, being a particular mind-image thereof in the line of descent, having power of choice and therefore of independent action, it is unquestionably limited, by bodily conditions.

In "The Chemistry of Life," Dr. George W. Carey says:

"So-called disease is neither a "person, place nor thing.""

The symptoms of sensation, called disease, are the results of lacking material—a deficiency in the dynamic molecules that carry on the orderly procedure of life. The effect of the deficiency causes unpleasant sensations, pains, exudations, swellings; or overheated tissue caused by increased motion of blood.

The increased motion is the effort nature or chemical law, makes to restore equilibrium with the diminished molecules of blood builders. By the law of conservation of energy the increased motion is changed to heat. We call this effect fever.

Biochemistry means the Chemistry of Life, or the union of inorganic and organic substances whereby new compounds are formed.

In its relation to so-called disease this system uses the inorganic salts, known as Cell-salts, or tissue builders.

The constituent parts of man's body are perfect principles, namely, oxygen, hydrogen, carbon, lime, iron, potash, soda, silica, magnesia, etc. These elements, gases, etc., are perfect per se, but may be endlessly diversified in combination as may the planks, bricks, or stones with which a building is to be erected.

Symptoms, called disease, disappear or cease to manifest when the food called for is furnished.

The human body is a receptacle for a storage battery, and will always run right while the chemicals are present in proper quantity and combination, as surely as an automobile will run when charged and supplied with the necessary ingredients to vibrate or cause motion.

The cell-salts are found in all our food, and are thus carried into the blood, where they carry on the process of life, and by the law of Chemical Affinity keep the human form, bodily functions, materialized. When a deficiency occurs in any of these workers through a non-assimilation of food, poor action of liver or digestive process, dematerialization of the body commences. So disease is a deficiency in some of the chemical constituents that carry on the chemistry of life.

Biochemists have shown that food does not form blood, but simply furnishes the mineral base by setting free the inorganic or cell-salts contained in all food stuff. The organic part, oil, fibrin, albumen, etc., contained in food is burned or digested in the stomach and intestinal tract to furnish motive power to operate the human machine and draw air into lungs, thence into arteries, i.e., air carriers.

Therefore, it is clearly proven that air (spirit) united with the minerals and forms blood, proving that the oil, albumen, etc., found in blood, is created every breath.

Increase the rate of activity of the brain cells by supplying more of the dynamic molecules of the blood known as mineral or cell -salts of lime, potash, sodium, iron, magnesia, silica, and we see mentally, truths that we could not sense at lower or natural rates of motion, although the lower rate may manifest ordinary health.

Natural man, or natural things must be raised from the level of nature to supernatural, in order to realize new concepts that lie waiting for recognition.

By this regenerative process millions of dormant cells of the brain are resurrected and set in operation, and then man no longer "sees through a glass darkly," but with the Eye of Spiritual understanding."

SUGGESTION

Mr. C. Harry Brooks tells of a very interesting and instructive visit to the clinic of Dr. Emile Coue in a book entitled the Practice of Auto-suggestion, published by Dodd, Mead & Co. The clinic is situated in a pleasant garden attached to Dr. Coue's house at the end of the rue Jeanne d'Arc, in Nancy. He states that when he arrived the room reserved for patients was already crowded, but in spite of that, eager newcomers constantly tried to gain entrance. The window sills on the ground floor were beset and a dense knot had formed in the door. The patients had occupied every available seat and were sitting on camp stools and folding chairs.

He then tells of the man remarkable cures which Dr. Coue proceeded to effect by no other means than suggestion to the patient that the power of healing lies within the patient himself. There was also a children's clinic in charge of Mademoiselle Kauffmant who devotes her entire time to this work.

Mr. Brooks thinks that "Coue's" discoveries may profoundly affect our life and education because it teaches us that the burdens of life are, at least in a large measure, of our own creating. We reproduce in ourselves and in our circumstances the thoughts of our minds. It goes further, it offers us a means by which we can change these thoughts when they are evil and foster them when they are good, so producing a corresponding betterment in our individual life. But the process does not end with the individual.

The thoughts of society are realized in social conditions, the thoughts of humanity in world conditions. What would be the attitude towards our social and international problems of a generation nurtured from infancy in the knowledge and practice of auto-suggestion? If each person found happiness in his own heart, would the illusory greed for possession survive? The acceptance of auto-suggestion entails a change of attitude, a revaluation of life. If we stand with our faces westward we see nothing but clouds and darkness, yet by a simple turn of the head we bring the wide panorama of the sunrise into view."

The New York Times, under date of Aug. 6, 1922, published an excellent likeness of Emile Coue and a review of his work by Van Buren Thorne, M. D. He says that the keynote to the system of treatment of mental and physical ills devised and elaborated by Emile Coue of Nancy, France, can be described in a single paragraph:

"The individual is possessed of two minds, called the conscious and the unconscious. The latter is referred to by some psychologists as the subconscious mind, and is literally the humble and obedient servant of the conscious mind. The unconscious mind is the director and overseer of our internal economy. By means of its activities the processes of digestion and assimilation of foods are carried on, repairs are made, wastes are eliminated, our vital organs function and life itself persists.

When the thought arises in the conscious mind that extra efforts toward the repair of some deficiency, either physical or mental are needed, all the individual has to do, in the opinion of Dr. Coue, is audibly to enunciate that thought in the form of a direct suggestion to the unconscious mind, and that humble obedient servant immediately, and without questioning the dictates of its conscious master, proceeds to obey instructions."

Dr. Coue, Mr. Brooks, and large numbers of persons of repute in France, England, and elsewhere in Europe, have declared that the results in many cases under their direct observation have been nothing short of marvelous. Those who have not witnessed the benefits of this form of treatment—hence may incline to be skeptical—are more likely to give attention to what follows when they are informed of three facts regarding the Nancy practice. First, Dr. Coue has never accepted a penny for his treatments in the many years of his ministration; second, he is in the habit of explaining to his patients that he possesses no healing powers, has never healed a person in his life, and that they must find the instruments of their own well-being in themselves; third, that any individual can treat himself without consulting any other person.

It may be added that a child who is capable of comprehending the fact of the conscious and subconscious mind, and is competent to issue orders from one to the other, is quite capable of the self-administration of the treatment.

"For what man knoweth the things of a man save the spirit of the man which is in him?" Mr. Brooks quotes from First Corinthians for his title page. Doubtless this was selected as an apt biblical reference to the existence of the conscious and unconscious minds. But neither the treatment, nor this book about it, dwells at length upon any possible religious significance of the methods employed or the results obtained.

The single thing that has contributed largely to the recent rapid spread of knowledge concerning Dr. Coue's method of practice at Nancy is his insistence upon the benefits to be derived from the frequent repetition of this formula: "Day by day, in every way, I'm getting better and better." As I remarked, no great stress is laid upon the religious significance of his alleged cures; yet, says Mr. Brooks, "religious minds who wish to associate the formula with God's care and protection might do so after this fashion: 'Day by day, in every way, by the help of God, I'm getting better and better.'" The secret of success in the treatment is to so beget confidence in the conscious mind that what it repeats is accepted at its face value by the unconscious mind, and as Mr. Brooks puts it: "Every idea which enters the conscious mind, if it is accepted by the unconscious, is transformed by it into a reality and forms henceforth a permanent element in our life."

But let us see how this book came to be written, and then watch Dr. Coue at work.

Mr. Brooks is an Englishman who became interested in Dr. Coue's work at Nancy and went there to observe it at first hand. In his foreword to the volume, Dr. Coue says that Mr. Brooks visited him for several weeks last summer, and that he was the first Englishman who came to Nancy with the express purpose of studying methods of conscious auto-suggestion. He attended Dr. Coue's consultations and obtained a full mastery of the method. Then the two men threshed out a good deal of the theory on which the treatment rests.

Dr. Coue says that Mr. Brooks skillfully seized on the essentials and he has put them forward in the volume in a manner that seems to him both simple and clear.

"It is a method," says Dr. Coue, "which every one should follow—the sick to obtain healing, the healthy to prevent the coming of disease in the future. By its practice we can insure for ourselves, all our lives long, an excellent state of health, both of the mind and the body."

Now let us enter Dr. Coue's clinic with Mr. Brooks. Back of the house there is a pleasant garden with flowers, strawberry beds, and laden fruit trees. Groups of patients occupy the garden seats. There are two brick buildings—the waiting and consultation rooms. These are crowded with patients—men, women and children.

Coue tells him he is going to get better, and adds: "You have been sowing bad seed in your Unconscious; now you will sow good seed. The power by which you have produced such ill-effects will in the future produce equally good ones."

"Madame," he tells a woman who breaks into a torrent of complaint, "you think too much about your ailments, and in thinking of them you create fresh ones."

He tells a girl with headaches, a youth with inflamed eyes, and a laborer with varicose veins, that auto-suggestion should bring complete relief. He comes to a neurasthenic girl who is making her third visit to the clinic and who has been practicing the method at home for ten days. She says she is getting better. She can now eat heartily, sleep soundly, and is beginning to enjoy life.

A big peasant, formerly a blacksmith, next engages his attention. He says he has not been able to raise his right arm above the level of his shoulder for nearly ten years. Coue predicts a complete cure. For forty minutes he keeps on with the interrogation of patients.

Then he pays attention to those who have come to tell him of the benefits they have received. Here is a woman who has had a painful swelling in her breast, diagnosed by the doctor (in Coue's opinion, wrongly), as cancerous. She says that, with three weeks' treatment, she has completely recovered. Another has overcome her anaemia and has gained nine pounds in weight. A third says he has been cured of varicose ulcer; while a fourth, a lifelong stammerer, announces a complete cure in one sitting.

Coue now turns to the former blacksmith and says: "For ten years you have been thinking that you could not lift your arm above your shoulder; consequently, you have not been able to do so, for whatever we think becomes true for us. Now think: 'I can lift it.'"

The man looks doubtful, says half-heartedly, "I can," makes an effort, and says it hurts.

"Keep it up,' Coue commands in a tone of authority, "and think 'I can, I can!' Close your eyes and repeat with me as fast as you can, 'ca passe, ca passe.'"

After half a minute of this, Coue says, "Now think well that you can lift your arm."

"I can," says the man with conviction and proceeds to raise it to full height, where he holds it in triumph for all to see.

"My friend," observes Dr. Coue quietly. "You are cured."

"It is marvelous," says the bewildered blacksmith, "I believe it."

"Prove it," says Coue, "by hitting me on the shoulder," whereupon the blows fall in regular sequence.

"Enough," cautions Coue, wincing from the sledge-hammer blows. "Now you can go back to your anvil."

Now he turns to patient No. 1, the tottering man. The sufferer seems inspired with confidence by what he has seen. Under Coue's instructions he takes control of himself, and in a few minutes he is walking about with ease.

"When I get through with the clinic," says Coue, "you shall come for a run in the garden."

And so it happens; very soon this patient is trotting around the enclosure at five miles an hour.

Coue then proceeds to the formulation of specific suggestions. The patients close their eyes and he speaks in a low, monotonous voice. Here is an example:

"Say to yourself that all the words I am about to utter will be fixed, imprinted and engraved in your minds; that they will remain fixed, imprinted and engraven there, so that without your will and knowledge, without your being in any way aware of what is taking place, you yourself and your whole organism will obey them. I tell you first that every day, three times a day, morning, noon and evening, at meal times, you will be hungry; that is to say, you will feel that pleasant sensation which makes us think and say: "How I should like something to eat.' You will then eat with excellent appetite, enjoying your food, but you will never eat too much.

You will eat the right amount, neither too much nor too little, and you will know intuitively when you have sufficient. You will masticate your food thoroughly, transforming it into a smooth paste before swallowing it.

In these conditions you will digest it well, and so feel no discomfort of any kind either in the stomach or in the intestines. Assimilation will be perfectly performed, and your organism will make the best possible use of the food to create blood, muscle, strength, energy, in a word—Life."

"They (Dr. Coue and Mlle. Kauffmant)," says Mr. Brooks, "have placed not only their private means, but their whole life at the service of others. Neither ever accepts a penny-piece for the treatments they give, but I have never seen Coue refuse to give a treatment at however awkward an hour the subject may have asked it. The fame of the school has now spread to all parts, not only France, but of Europe and America. Coue's work has assumed such proportions that his time is taken up often to the extent of fifteen or sixteen hours a day. He is a living monument to the efficacy of "Induced Autosuggestion."

In "Regeneration," Mr. Weltmer says:

"The last battle in which the race is engaged is now on. It is not a battle of cannon and sword, but it is a conflict of ideas. It is not going to be destructive, but constructive. It will not be a destroying warfare, but a fulfilling. It will not promote discord, but will insure harmony. It will not knit the human family together in combinations and associations, lodges and congregations, but will individualize the race, and each person will stand alone, recognizing within himself all the potentialities that exist, recognizing within himself all the Divine principles, constituting a part of the perfect whole.

"When man sees himself thus, he will see this kingdom within, is not within him only, but within all men. We must assume that the power to do, to act, or to perform the work we give our minds to do, exists in the mind; but before we entrust the mind with this work, we must have a clear conception of what is to be done. In order to regenerate the body we must conclude or assume to be true, that the power to generate life and health is in us; we must know where it is generated and how to generate it.

"Could we but comprehend it, could the veil of ignorance that enshrouds us be lifted, and we be allowed to look into the storehouse of knowledge, such as the prophet or seer was allowed to look upon, could we but climb where Moses stood, and view the landscape o'er, could we experience what Paul did during the time when he says: 'I know not whether I was in the body or out of the body,' we would be able to comprehend what he means when he says: 'Eye hath not seen, nor ear heard, nor hath it entered into the heart of man, the glory that shall be revealed in us.'"

The brain is an organ through which we communicate our thoughts to other organs in our bodies, and receive impression from the outside through the mediums of the senses. Great men have by great thoughts developed a finer quality of brain than others; this leads people to think that the great mind was the outgrowth of the fine brain, when if they will look upon the brain as any other organ of the perishable body they will see that it is but the organ through which the mind finds expression.

All attainments come in their regular order, as orderly as the movements of the sun and planets; first we desire, second we believe, third we try the belief, fourth we have knowledge.

We entertain a belief, and the belief comes into our minds and controls us. A man in the throes of poverty can throw off the shackles, if he can add to his belief.

A suggestion, to be a controlling influence, must be a positive suggestion left undisturbed; it must be regarded by the person entertaining it as a fixture in his life; not subject to change or modification.

Still another method of making an application of the principle of suggestion is described by Mr. J. R. Seaward, of Hamilton, Mont. He says:

"I am a man 36 years of age and have a family, and they rejoice with me that I am free from the use of tobacco. I chewed, or rather ate the weed for 15 years. Didn't mean to form the habit when I started in, but thought that it was conducive to my growth from youth to manhood. After the habit had grown on me for several years unresisted, I discovered that I was in the grip of a slowly but surely growing octopus that had me freely within its embrace, and I was helpless to release myself.

I had followed carpenter and shop woodwork for trade, and all woodworkers know there is something about lumber that makes a man want to use tobacco. When I got so that I had to chew all the time and the strongest I could get and then was not satisfied, I began to wonder where I was headed for. Slowly the idea that I was a slave to the weed dawned on me and I began to think about cutting down on it, or out altogether.

I will now explain to you the way in which Friend Wife broke me of a vile habit and convinced us both of the marvelous power of Suggestion when properly applied.

At about the time that I struck bottom, there came to my notice some literature, telling of the power of directed thought, and I became interested in the study of that, and also in some inspirational literature which later came to my notice. I was rather skeptical at first, but as I read and thought and commenced to look for proof in the events of our daily lives and in our environment, the truth commenced to dawn upon me. I began to see and know that life manifestations were fed from within and grew from within, and if the within be in a state of decay, it invariably showed without. In fact, I know now that "The Man of Gallilee," said something when He said, "As a man thinketh in his heart, so is he." If he thinks himself a slave to tobacco or other obnoxious habits, so is he. He must think himself free to remain free.

But to think one's self away from a habit that clings as close as thought itself, is a hard matter unaided. At the time we tried suggestion for the elimination of my tobacco habit I slept in one bedroom with one of the children and wife slept in another bedroom with our then youngest boy, about eight months old. As often is the case she had to be up at times during the night to wait on the baby and it was at those times that she gave me mental treatments while I was asleep.

It isn't necessary to be in the same room, though it is all right if it happens to be the case. While I was sleeping she would visualize herself or mentally project herself as though she was standing or kneeling beside my bed and speaking to me. Her suggestions were of a constructive and positive nature rather than of negative. It went something like this: "You are now desiring freedom from the tobacco habit; you are free and desire and enjoy mastery more than indulgence; tomorrow you will want only about half the normal amount of tobacco and each day it will be less until you are free within a week and shall never have any more craving for tobacco. You are Master and free."

She made the above suggestion (in substance) to me each time that she was awake during the night and I do pledge on oath that within six days from the time she started treatment I had completely quit craving tobacco, and quit using it.

That has been several months ago, and today I am more master of my habits of thought and word and deed than ever before in my life. I have changed from an under-weight, nervous wreck to a full-weight, healthful, strong, energetic, and clear-thinking man, and everyone who knew me remarks how differently I look and act and seem. Since that time, I have followed the study and the practice of constructive and directed thinking."

You know that in wireless telegraphy or telephony they use an instrument called the tuning coil that vibrates in harmony with an electrical wave or vibration of a certain length. It is in tune with that particular tune of wave and consequently they are in harmony and allow the vibration to go on to the other receiving instrument unhindered. Yet there may be other wireless vibrations of a higher or lower "tune" or key passing at the same time, yet only those in harmony are registered by the receiver.

Now our minds are just about the same way only we regulate our "tuning" coil by our Willpower. We can tune our minds to low-vibration thoughts such as the animal impulses of nature, or we can "tune" them to thoughts of an educational or mental nature, or we can, after some qualifications are met, tune ourselves to receive purely spiritual thought vibrations. This power constitutes the Divine power that is given to man. Of course you will readily see that there never was a primitive hut or modern mansion built without the application of this principle of directed constructive thinking and visualization.

The backbone of salesmanship of all kinds if the understanding and skillful use of suggestion. When cleverly used it tends to relax one's conscious attention and warm up ad quicken the Desire, until a favorable response is gained. Window displays and counter displays as well as illustrated advertising all rely on the power to drive a suggestion into the very center of Desire, where it grows to the point of action if in harmony with the thought vibrations of the Desire. If the desire does not recognize or is not in harmony with the suggestion it is as "seed that has falled upon stony ground," and is without harvest of action.

Thought and action do produce material results as is easily verified in the builder and his plans—the dressmaker and her pattern, or the school and its product, all in harmony with the leading constructive thought. The quality of thought determines the measure of success in life.

PSYCHO-ANALYSIS

"Canst thou not minister to a mind diseased," asked Macbeth of the Doctor—but the passage is so strikingly fitting, so prophetically explanatory of psychoanalysis, that it must be given in full:

Macbeth: Canst thou not minister to a mind diseased.
Pluck from the memory a rooted sorrow.
Raze out the written troubles of the brain.
And with some sweet oblivious antidote
Cleanse the stuff'd bossom of that perilous stuff
Which weight upon the heart?
Doctor: Therein the patient must minister to himself.

There is hardly a person today exempt from some form of phobia, or fear, whose origin may date so far back as to be lost among the shadows of childhood; hardly a person is free from some aversion, or "complex," whose effects are a matter of daily occurrence, despite the will of the victim. In a sense, the subconsciousness has never forgotten the incident, and still harbours the unpleasant memory of it; the consciousness, however, in an attempt to protect our dignity, or vanity, whichever you prefer, may evolve some apparent, better reason than the original one.

Thus complexes are formed. Brontephobia, or fear of thunder, was brought about in the case of one patient by hearing a cannon go off very near her when she was a child; a fact which had been "forgotten" for years; to confess to such a fear, even to one's self, would have been childish—and fear to the somewhat more dignified cause of thunder. Needless to say, it is such disguises of the memories which make difficult the labor of the psychoanalyst to pluck from the memory a rooted sorrow, to raze out the written troubles of the brain, its "traumas" or the original shocks. And when we remember that Psyche in Greek means not only the mind, but the soul, we can better understand Shakespeare's amazing grasp of psychology when he speaks not only of the "mind diseased," but of "that perilous stuff which weighs upon the heart."

We all have these complexes, in forms ranging from the mild to the severe; sitophobia, the aversion to certain foods; claustrophobia, the fear of locked doors—to which the fear of open spaces forms a striking contrast; stage-fright; touching wood and other superstitions—a thorough list would indeed be a very long one.

For the greater part, the patient must minister to himself—with the help of the skilled psychoanalyst. In some cases elaborate processes are needed, and the use of psychometers and other delicate registering devices enlisted; but usually, the procedure is a simple one. The subject of investigation is made comfortable physically, and put in a quiet mood;

he is then told to utter whatever may come into his mind in connection with his complex—with occasional promptings and questions from the psychoanalyst. Sooner or later the association of ideas will bring to the surface the original, cause or experience, which had become "rooted," submerged; very often the mere explanation will suffice to eradicate the obsession.

But there is another group of disorders, hysteria, which may partake both of the physical and the psychical, or where either state may induce the other. Richard Ingalese in his "History and Power of Mind," has summed up the matter very clearly: "Disease may be divided into two classes, the imaginary and the real. Imaginary disease is a picture held firmly by the objective mind, which causes more or less physical correspondence. This kind of disease is often created in total disregard of the laws governing anatomy or physiology; and is the hardest to cure, because persons possessed of it hold to it so persistently that an entire revision of their mode of thought must be made before it can be cured. It is not at all infrequent to have a patient complain of kidney disease, locating the pain and the organs several inches below the waist line. The spleen is often supposed to be in the right side of the body, and phantom tumors appear and disappear. But all these mental pictures, if held long enough, create matrices or vortices, and draw into them the elements that will bring finally the actual disease that was at first purely imaginary."

Psycho-analysis proceeds upon the assumption that a very large number of cases of disease are caused by repression of normal desires, or by disturbances that have occurred in the past life of the individual. In such cases the root of the disease is so concealed, sometimes through years and years, that it must be searched for.

The Psycho-Analyst is enabled to locate such difficulties, through dreams, or rather through the interpretation of dreams, or by questioning the patient concerning his past life. The well trained analyst must of necessity secure the friendly confidence of the patient to such an extent that the latter will not hesitate to reveal any experience, no matter how intimate.

As soon, as the patient has been led to remember a particular experience, he is encouraged to talk about it in detail and thus it is brought up from the subconsciousness. The analyst then shows him what has been causing the difficulty and when the cause is eradicated it can do no more harm.

It is exactly parallel to a foreign substance in the flesh; there is a horrible swelling, with inflammation, pain, and suffering; the surgeon is called, removes the difficulty, and natures does the rest. The psychological law follows the same procedure. If there has been any abnormal activity, any festering sore in the subconscious mind, going on for years and years, if it can be located by a process of mental analysis and put out of the mental complex and shown to the patient, the catharsis is complete.

Dr. Hugh T. Patrick, clinical professor of nerves and mental disease in Northwestern University Medical School, mentions several interesting cases.

"In many cases of functional nervous disorders the factor of fear is quite obvious. But in many cases, though equally important, it is not at once apparent. Of the latter there are numerous varieties which may be divided into groups. One group embraces patients known to have physical courage. A few years ago there was referred to me one of the most noted as well as fearless men in the ring, a man who was peculiarly carefree, if not careless. He was suffering with what were considered rather vague and baffling nervous symptoms, principally insomnia, lack of interest, and moodiness. A careful analysis soon revealed that some trifling symptoms, due to high living and domestic friction, had served to put the idea into his head that he was losing his mind. This phobia was sickness, and the fear so possessed his soul that he was good for nothing until he got rid of it. Needless to say, the patient himself was quite unconscious of the nature of his trouble, and his physician had overlooked it.

So they could not cure the trouble from a physical standpoint. The situation had to be mentally analyzed, and the cause of the fear dragged out from subconsciousness and exposed to the man. When he had a look at it, why, it had exactly the same effect as pulling an eyelash out from an inflamed eye and letting you see it. Your troubles are all over right away, because you are very sure the disturbing cause has been removed, and you forget about it then.

"A sheep rancher of Wyoming complained of insomnia, loss of appetite, abdominal distress, general nervousness and inability to look after his ranch. What really was the matter with him was fear of cancer of the stomach. This phobia completely unnerved him and cause him to enormously magnify every bodily sensation. But was he a nerveless coward? Decidedly not.

There was a time when the cattlemen of the Far West made sheep raising a hazardous occupation. Through these dangerous years he lived without a tremor, though he never went to sleep without a rifle by his side. Once he was informed that three cattlemen had started out to 'get him,' and the information was correct. He mounted his horse and properly armed, rode out to meet them. As he expressed it, he 'talked them out of it,' and the three would-be assassins turned and rode away. In this encounter he was not in the least apprehensive or uncomfortable, and I learned of the incident only in a conversation about his business."

He had plenty of physical courage, but when something in the inner organism seemed to be wrong, he was scared. As soon as this doctor discovered what the fear was, he probably produced an X-ray or something of that nature to show the patient that there was nothing the matter. Then drawing the patient's attention to the groundless fear, the doctor was able to convince the patient of the groundlessness of his fears.

A policeman, 49 years old, suffered from intractable insomnia, head pressure, general nervousness and loss of weight. He was not a man to suspect of fear. For many years he had been in active service in one of the worst precincts of Chicago, and on account of his familiarity with criminals was frequently sent after the worst types. He had been in numerous 'gun' fights. Once a notorious 'gunman' standing beside him fired point blank at his head. All this disturbed his equanimity not a whit. And yet his illness was the result of fear pure and simple. It came about in this way; a malicious person had preferred against him charges of misconduct, and he was cited to appear before the trial board.

This worried him greatly. Innocent he keenly felt the disgrace of the accusation and feared that he might be suspended or even discharged. He trembled for his well-earned good name and for his home, on which there was a mortgage. Naturally he began to sleep poorly, to have queer feelings in his head, and then to feel uncertain of himself. at this juncture some friends sympathetically told him that one could go insane from worry. These were the steps: Fear of disgrace, fear of financial collapse, fear of insanity. But did the patient know all this? Not he. He knew only that he was nervous, and that he suffered, that he did not feel sure of himself."

When that was dragged out of his consciousness and shown to him as a root of his trouble, and a physician was able to assure him that fear was all in the world that was the matter with him, he made up his mind that he had better give that up. Then he was healed.

The subconscious mentality is sick in a chronic way; it has been made sick by some kind of mental experience—usually of many years standing—and the sickness is a result of its continuing to cherish that experience and keeping it before itself. This constitutes what is technically called a "running sore" in the subconsciousness—that is, mentally not physically.

A woman had suffered from general debility for a number of years, and had been unable to secure relief; the psychologist began to probe, to see what the trouble was. He began to pronounce words—just anything that came into his thoughts: "desk, book, rug, Chinaman." When he pronounced the word "Chinaman" the woman appeared startled, and he asked her what the word "Chinaman" suggested to her and why it startled her. The woman said that when she was a little girl, she with a playmate, used to play around a Chinese laundry, that they used to plague the Chinaman by throwing pebbles at him through the open door; that one day the Chinaman chased them with a big knife, and that they were nearly scared to death. "Yes," said the psychologist, "that is one of the things that I wanted to know." Then he began to pronounce more words, presently the word "water," and again the woman was startled. It developed then that one time when she was a very little girl, she and her brother were playing on the wharf and that accidentally she pushed him into the water and he was drowned. She said it was many years ago, when she was a mere child. He said: "Do you think of these things very often?" She said: "No, I do not know that I have thought of them before in fifteen or twenty years."

"Well," he said, "I will tell you what I want you to do." (She was at that time in a sanitarium, under the care of a nurse.) "I want you to tell the nurse every day that experience about the Chinaman and also the experience about your brother, and I want you to keep telling it until you have told it so many times that you do not feel bad about it any more; then, see me again in two or three weeks." She did as he directed, and at the end of sixty days she was well. The effect of telling it so often was its becoming commonplace to the conscious mentality, without touching the feelings. So the suggestion then went down to the subconsciousness that it did not feel badly about the incident any more, and the conditions of fear which had persisted for twenty or twenty-five years were erased, and the complex in the subconsciousness was no longer in evidence.

The subconscious mind has perfect memory and is fully equipped at birth. Every child inherits certain characteristics from its ancestors. These are carried in the subconscious mind and brought into play when the life or health of the individual requires them.

It is natural to be born without pain, to develop without pain, to live without pain, and to die without pain. This is as natural as it is for a tree to blossom and bear fruit, which at the proper times drops off without distress. The subconscious will take care of every situation; even when it is interfered with it has a remedy available for every situation. Again, you forget something, but the subconscious mind has not forgotten; as soon as the conscious mind dismisses the matter, it comes to us.

Every engineer knows what it is to sleep over a problem; while he is asleep the subconscious is working it out;; or he may lose an article, get excited and anxious about it, and not be able to find it; yet as soon as the conscious mind gives it up and lets go, the sense of where it is comes without effort.

Again there is a difficult situation in your affairs, if you can only persuade your conscious mind to let go, to cease its anxiety, dismiss its fear, give up the tenseness and struggle, the subconscious will ordinarily bring about prosperity. The tendency of the subconscious is always toward health and harmonious conditions. To illustrate, you are in the water over your depth, you cannot swim, you are sinking. If the moment the life guard approaches you, you grab him around the neck and impede the action of his arms and limbs, he may be unable to do anything with you, but if you will simply trust yourself in his hands, he will get you out. And so it is absolutely certain that subconscious will be present in every difficult situation and that it will tend to play life guard in your favor, if you can but persuade your consciousness to cease its anxiety, to dismiss its fears, to give up the tenseness of the struggle.

Suppose the conscious mind suffers itself to become angry over every trifle. Every time it gets angry the impulse is transferred to the subconscious. The impulse is repeated again and again, each time it is stirred up. The second record of anger is added to the first, the third to the second, and the fourth to the third. Soon the subconscious has acquired the habit, and before long it will be difficult to stop. When this situation develops the conscious mind will be subject to the irritating influence from without and the habitual impulse from within. There will be action and reaction. It will be easier to be angry and more difficult to prevent it. Yet every time the conscious mind gets angry an additional impulse will be given to the subconscious, and that impulse will be an additional incentive to get angry again.

Now the, anger is an abnormal condition, and any abnormal condition contains within itself the penalty, ad this penalty will be promptly reflected in that part of the body which has the least resistance. For instance, if the person has a weak stomach, there will be acute attacks of indigestion, and eventually these will become chronic. In other persons, Bright's Disease may develop; in other, rheumatism; and so on.

It is evident therefore, that these conditions are effects, but if the cause be removed the effect will vanish. If the individual knows that thoughts are causes, and conditions are effects, he will promptly decide to control his thoughts. This will tend to erase anger and other bad mental habits; and as the light of truth gradually becomes clear and perfect, the habit and everything connected with it will be erased, and the accumulated distress destroyed.

What is true of anger, is true of jealousy, of fear, of lust, of greed, of dishonesty, each of these may become subconscious and each of them eventually result in some diseased condition of the body, and the nature of the disease indicates to the trained analyst the nature of the cause which was responsible for the condition.

Frederic Pierce tells us in "Our Unconscious Mind":

"It is a matter of common observation that everything is in greater or less degree suggestible. The reaction to suggestion may be either positive or negative, either an acceptance or heightened resistance. In this we see a censorship. An epidemic of a certain type of crime shows, on the part of the perpetrators, imitative response to suggestion implanted both by the elaborate descriptive accounts in the newspapers, and by the great amount of discussion of the outrages, heard on all sides.

Primitive effects of great intensity are aroused; they break through the primary cultural censorship (which is weak in the criminally disposed person), accumulate energy be being dwelt on in consciousness, and finally become sufficiently strong to surmount all fear of punishment and to control the conduct.

The remainder of the social group, having a higher cultural censorship, reacts to the same suggestion negatively, and discharges the energy of whatever primitive effects have been aroused, in the form of wrath and the desire for punishment of the criminals.

In this connection, it is interesting to note that one often hears the desire for vengeance expressed in terms of much greater primitive violence than the crime itself actually showed. Psycho-analysts hold that this is a method by which the individual is reinforcing his own none too strong censorship of his Unconscious.

Mind in itself is believe to be a subtle form of static energy, from which rises the activities called "thought," which is the dynamic phase of mind. Mind is static energy, thought is dynamic energy—the two phases of the same thing.—Walker.

Tradition whispers that in the sky is a bird, as blue as the sky itself, which brings to its finders happiness. But everyone cannot see it; for mortal eyes are prone to be blinded by the glitter of wealth, fame, and position, and deceived by the mocking Will-o-the-Wisp of empty honors.

But for the fortunate ones who seek with open eyes and hearts, with the artlessness, simplicity and faith, which are richest in childhood, there is an undying promise; and to them the Blue Bird lives and carols, a rejoicing symbol of Happiness and Contentment unto the end.

PSYCHOLOGY

The observation and analysis, knowledge and classification of the activities of the personal consciousness, consisting of the science of psychology, has been studied in colleges and universities for many years, but this personal or conscious, self-conscious mind does not by any means constitute the whole of the mind.

There are some very highly complex, and very orderly activities going on within the body of a baby. The body of the baby, as such, cannot induce or carry on those activities, and the conscious mind of the baby does not know enough to even plan them or be aware of them. Probably also in most cases there is no one around the baby who even remotely understands what is going on in this highly complex process of physical life; and yet all those activities manifest intelligence, and intelligence of a very complex and high order.

From the examination of what goes on in the human body, from all the complex processes, the beating of heart and digestion of the foods, the secretion and excretion of the glands, it is apparent, that there is in control an order of mentality which has a high degree of intelligence, but it is the mentality which is operating in the millions of cells which constitute the body, and so operate below the surface of what we term consciousness. It is therefore, subconscious.

The subconscious mind, again assumes two phases. Connected with each human person there is a subconsciousness which may in some sense be regarded as the subconsciousness of that person, but which merges at a still deeper level into what may be termed Universal subconsciousness, or into cosmic consciousness. That may be illustrated in this way: If you will think of the waves on the surface of Lake Michigan, insofar as they are above the level of the troughs, as standing for so many personal mentalities; and then, if you will think of a small body of water not rising above the surface, but in some degree running along with each wave and merging indistinctly at the bottom into the great unmoved mass below, which may be thought of as the deepest level, then those three levels of the water in the lake may illustrate to you personal consciousness or self-consciousness, personal subconsciousness, and universal subconsciousness or cosmic consciousness. Now, out of cosmic consciousness springs personal subconsciousness, and out of that in turn, or in connection with it, rises personal consciousness.

At the beginning of the experience of the child, its government is almost wholly from subconsciousness, but as it goes on, it becomes aware maybe unconsciously, but still in a degree aware of the presence of laws of consciousness which manifest as justice, truthfulness, honesty, purity, liberty, loving-kindness, and so on, and begins to relate itself to them and to be governed by them more and more.

The first thing to note is that, while this mental action is going on continuously, we are normally quite unconscious of it. For this reason it is known as the subconscious department of the mind to distinguish it from that part which functions through the senses of which we are conscious, and which we call the self-conscious. The existence in the body of two distinct nervous systems, the cerebro-spinal and the sympathetic, each with its own field of operation and its special functions, prepared us for these two mental departments.

The cerebro-spinal system is used by the self-conscious and the sympathetic by the subconscious. And just as we find in the body that, while the functions and activities of the two nervous systems are different, provision has been made for very close inter-action between the two, so we will find that, while the functions and activities of the two mental departments are different, there is a very definite line of activity between them.

The main business of the subconscious mind is to preserve the life and health of the individual. Consequently it supervises all the automatic functions, such as the circulation of the blood, the digestion, all automatic muscular action and so on. It transforms food into suitable material for body building, returning it to conscious man in the form of energy.

Conscious man makes use of this energy in mental and physical work, and in the process uses up what has been provided for him by his subconscious intelligence.

The action of the subconscious is cumulative and may be illustrated in the following manner. Suppose you take a tub of water and begin to stir it with a small piece of wood from right to left, with a circular motion. At first you will start only a ripple around the wood, but if you keep the wood in motion with the circular movement, the water will gradually accumulate the strength which you are putting into the wood, and presently you will have the whole tub of water in a whirl. If you were then to drop the piece of wood, the water would carry along the instrument that originally set it in motion, and if you were suddenly to stop the wood while it is still projecting in the water, there would be a strong tendency to not only carry the wood forward, but to take your hand along with it. Now, suppose that after you have the water whirling, you decide that you do not want it to whirl, or think that you would prefer to have it whirl in the other direction, and so try to set it going the other way, you will find that there is great resistance, and you will find that it will take a long while to bring the water to a standstill, and a still longer time before you get it going the other way.

This will illustrate that whatever the conscious mind does repeatedly the subconscious will accumulate as a habit, any experience which the subconscious receives is stirred up and if you give it another one of the same kind it will add that to the former one and so keep on accumulating them indefinitely, the tendency being to accumulate activity along any definite line in increasing measure, and this holds true concerning any phase of activity that comes within range of human consciousness. This is true whether the experiences are for our benefit or otherwise, whether the experiences are good or evil. The subconscious is a spiritual activity and spirit is creative, the subconscious therefore creates the habits, condition and environment which the conscious mind continues to entertain.

If we consciously entertain thoughts associated with art, music and the aesthetic realm, if we consciously entertain thoughts associated with the good, the true and the beautiful, we shall find these thoughts taking root in the subconsciousness and our experiences and environment will be a reflection of the thought which the conscious mind has entertained. If, however, we entertain thoughts of hatred, jealousy, envy, hypocrisy, disease, lack or limitation of any kind, we shall find our experience and environment will reflect the conditions in accordance with these thoughts: "As we sow, so shall we reap," the law is no respecter of persons; we may think what we will, but the result of our thoughts is governed by an immutable law. "There is nothing either good or evil, but thinking makes it so." We cannot plant seed of one kind and reap fruit of another.

Consciousness consists in the power to think, to know, to will and to choose, self consciousness is the power to be aware of the self as a thinking, knowing, willing and choosing individual. The brain is the organ of the conscious mind and the cerebro-spinal nervous system is the system of nerves by which it is connected with all parts of the body.

The process of growth is a subconscious process, we do not carry on the vital processes of nature consciously, all the complex processes of nature, the beating of the heart, the digestion of food, the secretion of the glands require a high degree of mentality and intelligence. The personal consciousness or mind would not be capable of handling these intricate problems, they are therefore, controlled by the Universal Mind, which in the individual we call the subconscious.

The Universal Mind is sometimes referred to as the Super-Conscious, and sometimes the Divine Mind. The subconscious is sometimes called the subjective and the conscious the objective mind, but remember that words are simply the vessels in which thought is carried. If you get the thought you will not be concerned about the terms.

Mind is a spiritual activity and spirit is creative, hence the subconscious mind not only controls all the vital functions and processes of growth, but is the seat of memory and habit.

The sympathetic nervous system is the instrument by which the subconscious keeps in touch with the feeling or emotions, thus the subconscious reacts to the emotions, never to the reason, as the emotions are much stronger than the reason or intellect; the individual will therefore frequently act in exactly the opposite manner from what the reason and intellect would dictate.

It is axiomatic that two things cannot occupy the same space at the same time. What is true of things is true of thoughts. If, therefore, any thought seeks entrance to the mental realm which is destructive in its nature, it should be quickly displaced by a thought which has a constructive tendency. Herein lies the value of a ready made affirmation, such as the Coue affirmation, "Day by day, in every way, I am growing better and better," or the Andrews' affirmation, "I am whole, perfect, strong, powerful, loving, harmonious and happy."

These or similar affirmations may be committed to memory and repeated until they become automatic or subconscious. As physical conditions are but the outward manifestations of mental conditions, it will readily be seen that by constantly holding the thought expressed in the affirmation in the mind, that it will be but a comparatively short time until conditions and environment begin to change so as to be in accordance with the new method of thinking.

This same principle can be brought into operation in a negative way, through the process of denial. Many make use of this with excellent results.

The conscious and subconscious are but two phases of action in connection with the mind. The relation of the subconscious to the conscious is quite analogous to that existing between a weather vane and the atmosphere. Just as the least pressure of the atmosphere causes an action on the part of the weather vane, so does the least thought entertained by the conscious mind produce within the subconscious mind, action in exact proportion to the depth of felling characterizing the thought and the intensity with which the thought is indulged.

It follows that if you deny unsatisfactory conditions, you are withdrawing the creative power of your thought from these conditions. You are cutting them away at the root. You are sapping their vitality.

The law of growth necessarily governs every manifestation in the objective, so that a denial of unsatisfactory conditions will not bring about instant change. A plant will remain visible for some time after its roots have been cut, but it will gradually fade away and eventually disappear, sot he withdrawal of your thought from the contemplation of unsatisfactory conditions will gradually but surely terminate these conditions.

This is exactly an opposite course from the one which we would naturally be inclined to adopt. It will therefore have an exactly opposite effect to the one usually secured. Most persons concentrate upon unsatisfactory conditions, thereby giving the condition that measure of energy and vitality which is necessary in order to supply a vigorous growth.

METAPHYSICS

Creation consists in the art of combining forces which have an affinity for each other, in the proper proportion, thus oxygen and hydrogen combined in the proper proportions produce water. Oxygen and hydrogen are both invisible gases but water is visible.

Germs, however, have life; they must therefore be the product of something which has life or intelligence. Spirit is the only Creative Principle in the Universe, and Thought is the only activity which spirit possesses. Therefore, germs must be the result of a mental process.

A thought goes forth from the thinker, it meets other thoughts for which it has an affinity, they coalesce and form a nucleus for other similar thoughts; this nucleus sends out calls into the formless energy, wherein all thoughts and all things are held in solution, and soon the thought is clothed in a form in accordance with the character given to it by the thinker.

A million men in the agony of death and torture on the battlefield send out thoughts of hatred and distress; soon another million men die from the effect of a microbe called "the influenza germ." None but the experienced metaphysician knows when and how the deadly germ came into existence.

As there are an infinite variety of thoughts, so there are an infinite variety of germs, constructive as well as destructive, but neither the constructive nor the destructive germ will germinate and flourish until it finds congenial soil in which to take root.

All thoughts and all things are held in solution in the Universal Mind. The individual may open his mental gates and thereby become receptive to thoughts of any kind or description. If he thinks that there are magicians, witches or wizards who are desirous of injuring him, he is thereby opening the door for the entrance of such thoughts, and he will be able to say with Job, "The things I feared have come upon me." If, on the contrary, he thinks that there are those who are desirous of helping him, he thereby opens the door for such help, and he will find that "as thy faith is, so be it unto thee" is as true today, as it was two thousand years ago.

Tolstoi said: "Ever more and more clearly does the voice of reason become audible to man. Formerly men said: 'Do not think, but believe. Reason will deceive you; faith alone will open to you the true happiness of life.' And man tried to believe, but his relations with other people soon showed him that other men believed in something entirely different, so that soon it became inevitable that he must decide which faith out of many he would believe, reason alone can decide this."

Attempts in our day to instill spiritual matters into man by faith, while ignoring his reason, are precisely the same as attempts to feed a man and ignore his mouth. Men's common nature has proven to them that they all have a common knowledge, and men will never more return to their former errors.

The voice of the people is the voice of God. It is impossible to drown that voice, because that voice is not the single voice of any one person, but the voice of all rational consciousness of mankind, which is expressed in every separate man.

Reason tells man that the Universe is a Cosmos, and is therefore governed by law, so that when we see that some persons secure extraordinary results by mental or spiritual methods, reason tells us that we can all do exactly the same thing, because the law is no respecter of persons, and that this is being done every day all the time, everywhere, is apparent to everyone who has taken the trouble to ascertain the facts.

All manifestations are governed by principles which we recognize as universal laws, and in the manifestation of those laws we recognize system, order and harmony.

If the Infinite is omnipresent it must encompass and interfiltrate all that seems to be matter and be one with it and inseparable from it.

Science teaches that so-called matter exists in a diversity of grades from its crudest visible form to the most refined and invisible state in an inseparable relationship with spirit, from which it can never be disassociated.

The latent, or electric, power in the gaseous condition of the elements acts through vibration upon all matter in the combinations lower than the gases by induction, raising them also to a fluidic or gaseous condition and enabling them to form new combinations on a higher plane.

By the same principle is the mineral raised to the sphere of electricity, magnetism, or light, which of themselves are nothing more than ether in different velocities of vibration.

Radio activity consists in setting in motion certain electric vibrations, which after passing through the ether, record themselves on a distant receiver. The whole system depends on the intangible substance known as ether. It is a substance invisible, colorless, odorless, inconceivably rarefied, which fills all space. It fills the space between the earth and the sun and the stars, and it also fills the minute space between the atoms of the densest substance, such as steel. Even when electricity passes through a wire it is merely a vibration of the ether which circulates between the atoms composing the copper wire.

In turn we have abundant proof of the subjugation of Ethereal Matter by the still more rarefied sphere of force which we recognize as Psychic Force or Mind Force.

Matter thus refined becomes the plastic associate of the mind for the transmission of its forces in the manifestation of its power.

That mind does transmit its forces through, or by, its vibrations, we have proof of in the expression of its power of mind over mind, as in the manifestation of the mind of the hypnotist over his subject through mental suggestion, by which he is enabled to control the entire organism of his subject to such an extent as to suspend the functions of the organs of the body at will.

Thus we see that the subtle or refined elements of matter at the disposal of the mind are subject to his control. Matter in itself has no consciousness or feeling, and is active only when controlled by spirit or mind in accordance with the laws that govern its action, and when active gives forth the manifestation and power of the spirit, mind or intelligence behind it, and acting upon it; and in its varied manifestations symbolizes the wisdom or intelligence of the mind of man, or of the Infinite Mind itself.

As the Infinite Mind rules and governs the Universe, so it is ordained for man to rule and govern his living Universe which he has created or evolved, known as "The Temple of the Living God," an abridgment or Microcosm of the Universe of the Infinite.

Wisdom is the proper use of Knowledge to bring about harmony, happiness, ease and health. Ignorance is the darkness which the light of truth disperses, which light alone can enable us to understand the priority of mind in the control of matter.

The office of Metaphysics is to bring man into a true comprehension of his relationship with the world, in which he lives, moves, and has his being, and an understanding of how to gain dominion over all which is his rightful heritage.

The Metaphysician gives the patient nothing which he can see, nothing which he can hear, nothing which he can taste, nothing which he can smell and nothing which he can feel. It is therefore, absolutely impossible for the practitioner to reach the objective brain of the patient in any way whatever.

It will be said that he may give a mental suggestion; he may send him a thought. This might be possible if it were not for the fact that we do not consciously receive the thoughts of others except through the medium of the senses.

Again, admitting that it might be possible to reach the conscious mind without the aid of any material agency, the conscious or objective mind would not receive it because the objective mind is the mind with which we reason, plan, decide, will, and act. The practitioner invariably suggests perfection, and such a thought would be instantly dismissed by the objective mind as contrary to reason and therefore unacceptable, so that no result would be accomplished.

The Mind which the metaphysician calls into action is the Universal, not the individual. Their formula is: "Divine Mind always has met and always will meet every human need." This Divine Mind is the creative principle of the Universe. It is the "Father" which the Nazarene had in mind when he said: "It is not I that doeth the work, but the Father that dwelleth within me. He doeth the work."

It will at once become apparent that this power which the metaphysician utilizes is spiritual, not material; subjective not objective. For this reason it becomes necessary to reach the subconscious mind instead of the conscious mind. Here then is the secret of the efficacy of the method. The sympathetic nervous system is the organ of the subconscious mind. This system of nerves governs all of the vital processes of the body—the circulation of the blood, the digestion of food, the building of tissues, the manufacture and distribution of the various secretions; in fact the sympathetic nervous system reaches every part of the body. All vital processes are carried on subconsciously. They seem to have been purposely taken out of the realm of the conscious and placed under the control of a power which would be subject to no change or caprice.

The subject mind, the subconscious mind, the Divine Mind, are therefore simply different terms of indicating the "One mind in which we live and move and have our being." We contact this mind by will or intention. Mind is Omnipresent, we may therefore contact it anywhere and everywhere, neither time or space require consideration.

As spirit is the Creative Principle of the Universe, a subjective realization of this spiritual nature of man, and his consequent perfection, is taken up by the Divine Mind and eventually manifested in the life and experiences of the patient.

Some will say that this ideal state of perfection is never realized. To be sure, the Great Teacher anticipated this criticism for did He not say: "In my father's house are many mansions?"—indicating that there are many degrees of perfection; that although the law operates with immutable precision, the operator may be uninformed or inexperienced. The ability to throw the thought up and beyond the evidence of the senses into the realm of the uncreate, where all that ever was or ever will be, is waiting to be brought forth, to be organized, developed, and crystalized into tangible form, is not the work of the enthusiast who has just come into the knowledge of his spiritual inheritance. It is rather the work on one who has become responsive to the most subtle vibrations, he who can hear the Voice of the Silence, he who has come into the terrible realization that the oasis he saw as he passed over the desert was but a mirage, and as he approached, it receded; he who is no longer astonished or amazed to find that after all, real power is impersonal, that it may make a super-beast of one and a super-man of another.

A great many do not understand the Principle of Metaphysics and the method of applying it so as to work intelligently in their own behalf. Under such conditions they can only expect to rely on some one else, and when that is done continually or at frequent intervals, it tends to weaken rather than strengthen the spiritual factor in consciousness.

It is, therefore, desirable and necessary to secure an understanding of the nature of Truth. Most persons who have become interested in metaphysics have had some wonderful experience or they know of some one who has had such an experience.

It has been declared by philosophers, religionists, and scientists, again and again, that no proof of the existence of the absolute Truth is possible, in other words that the only way in which a man can be convinced of the creative power of Truth is by demonstration, or by assuming that Truth is all powerful and then on the basis of this assumption make the demonstration. This is proof, this is freedom, this is why it has been said: "Ye shall know the truth and the truth shall make you free."

Observation of the characteristic manifestations of anything and deductions based upon such observation, constitute knowledge of that thing; it will readily be seen, therefore, that, if you have observed and have become aware of the fact of certain characteristic manifestations of Truth, you will have knowledge. If it should come to pass that you had observed and carefully noted all the characteristic manifestations of Truth, and then in addition perceived the uniformities that run through those manifestations, especially if they are complex, and see the laws or system upon which their characteristics are based, then your knowledge of Truth would be complete.

Through the mental and spiritual awakening of a century ago, which was responsible for modern progressive thought, certain higher forces and principles were discovered in the mind of man; and in the same way new realms of thought and spiritual reality were opened to consciousness—revelations, literally, that give life a changed and marvelous meaning, and that caused the cosmos to extend into infinity, seemingly, in every direction. And therefore a two-fold purpose appeared at the very beginning of this movement—to know the Real Man, and to know the Real Cosmos; an ancient desire, but which was reborn at this time, and with so much life and virility that it has become today a soul passion in the minds of millions.

What then are the characteristics of Truth? All agree that in the philosophical sense Truth is that which is absolute and changeless. Truth must then be a fact; what then is a fact? Well, three times three equals nine. That is a fact, always was a fact, always will be a fact; there can be no evasion, no argument, no equivocation. It is truth in the United States, in China, in Japan, it is true everywhere; all the time. A fact exists in the nature of things without beginning, without end, without limitation, it governs our actions and our commercial operations. Those who would undertake to disregard it, would do so at their peril. It is, however, a fact which you cannot see, you cannot hear, you cannot taste, nor can you smell or feel it, it is inapprehensible to any of the physical senses; is it therefore, any less a fact? It is without color, size or form; is it for this reason any less true? It is without years; is it for that reason not the same yesterday, today, and forever?

You may use this fact as long as you live, millions of other persons may use it as often as they like, that will not destroy it. Use does not change it; from everlasting to everlasting—three times three equals nine. This is therefore a fact or the Truth.

Truth is the only possible knowledge which man can possess, because knowledge which is not based upon truth would be false, and would therefore, not be knowledge at all.

Counterfeit money is not true money, it is false, however much it may pass for true. The Truth is therefore, all that any one can know, for what is not true does not exist, therefore we cannot know it. We all think we know much that is not so, but what is not so, does not exist, therefore we cannot know it.

Therefore, the Truth or absolute knowledge is the only possible knowledge and any other use of the word is not scientific or exact.

The metaphysicians of the East will not give out spiritual knowledge miscellaneously. They will not give it to children or young people except under conditions when they have them directly under control and directly under instruction as definitely as we have our children under instruction, in the intellectual life in our schools.

In India when a young man is to be initiated into things spiritual, a definite seven year's course is provided for him under a master, and he is given first the things that he first bout to know along those lines. He is forewarned with regard to dangers that may arise, and the whole course of his journey is guarded by his master with the greatest care, so as to prevent his stumbling during the early stages.

If spiritual metaphysics becomes popular in our Western world, the same thing will develop here. People will not take up the most advanced work, before becoming acquainted with the simpler forms of knowledge. Attainment amplifies obligation, if you are somewhere up the ladder of culture, if you have entered the school of understanding, if you have seen the light of spiritual Truth, you are supposed by that very fact to know more than the one who has not yet arrived. Your nervous system will automatically organize itself on a higher plane, and because of this you must live closer to the law of your being or experience suffering more quickly; there are no exceptions to the law.

The resurrection from the dead is not a process of getting corpses out of the grave, it is the elevation of mentalities from the plane of the material to the plane of the spiritual, it is crossing the river Jordan and entering the "Promised Land." It is not until one becomes acquainted with the laws governing in the spiritual world that he really begins to "live," consequently those who are still functioning in the material world are "dead," they have not yet been resurrected. "Eyes have they but they see not, ears have they but they hear not."

Those who have been raised to the spiritual plane, find that there are many practices which they must drop, in most cases these practices leave the individual without difficulty, they drop away of their own accord, but when the individual persists in functioning in the old world, he usually finds that: "A house divided against itself will not stand," and frequently must suffer severely before he learns that he cannot violate spiritual laws with impunity.

PHILOSOPHY

Physical Science has resolved matter into molecules, molecules into atoms, atoms into energy, and it has remained for Mr. J. A. Fleming, in an address before the Royal Institution, to resolve this energy into mind. He says: "In its ultimate essence, energy may be incomprehensible by us except as an exhibition of the direct operation of that which we call Mind or Will."

We find, therefore, that science and religion are not in conflict, but are in perfect agreement. Mr. Leland makes this quite plain, in an article on "world Making." He says: "First, there is wisdom that has planned, and so adjusted all the parts of the universe in such a perfect balance that there is no friction. And as the universe in infinite, the wisdom that has planned it must be infinite, too.

"Secondly, there is a will that has fixed and ordained the activities and forces of the universe, and bound them by laws inflexible and eternal. And everywhere this Omnipotent Will has established the limitations and directions of the energies and processes, and has fixed their everlasting stability and uniformity.

"And as the universe is Infinite this Will must be Infinite.

"And thirdly, there is a power that sustains and moves, a power that never wearies, a power which controls all forces; and, as the universe if Infinite, the Power must be Infinite, too. What shall we name this Infinity trinity, Wisdom, Will and Power? Science knows no simpler name for it than God. This name is all embracing."

We can conceive something of its meaning, though we cannot comprehend its significance. and this Being is the indwelling ultimate. He is imminent in matter as in spirit; and to Him all Law, Life, Force, must be referred. He is the sustaining, energizing, all-pervading Spirit of the universe.

Every living thing must be sustained by the Omnipotent Intelligence, and we find the difference in individual lives to be largely measured by the degree of this intelligence which they manifest. It is a greater intelligence that places the animal in a higher scale of being than the plant, the man higher than the animal; and we find this increased intelligence is again indicated by the power of the individual to control modes of action and thus to consciously adjust himself to his environment. It is this adjustment that occupies the attention of the greatest minds and this adjustment consists in nothing else than the recognition of an existing order in the Universal Mind, for it is well known that this mind will obey us precisely in proportion as we first obey it.

As we increase in experience and development, there is a corresponding increase in the exercise of the intellect, in the range and power of feeling, in the ability to choose, in the power to will, in all executive action, in all self consciousness. That would mean that self-consciousness is increasing, expanding, growing, developing, and enlarging; it increases and develops because it is a spiritual activity; we multiply our possession of spiritual things in proportion to our use of them. All material things are consumed in the using. There is a diametrically opposite law governing the use of the spiritual and the material.

Life is that quality or principle of the Universal energy which manifests in so-called organic objects as growth and voluntary activity, and which is usually coexistent in some degree, with some manifestation of that same Universal Energy as the quality or principle termed intelligence. There is only one Supreme Principle, evading all comprehension of its essential nature. it is the Absolute. man can think only in terms of the relative. Therefore, he sometimes defines it as the Universal Intelligence, the Universal substance, as Ether, Life, Mind, spirit, Energy, Truth, Love, etc. His particular definition at any moment is governed by the particular relationship of the phenomena of Being in which he thinks of this Principle at that moment.

Mind is present in the lowest forms of life, in the protoplasm, or cell. The protoplasm, or cell, perceives it environment, initiates motion and chooses its food. All these are evidences of mind. As an organism develops and becomes more complex, the cells begin to specialize, some doing one thing and some another, but all of them showing intelligence. By association their mind powers increase.

Whereas in the beginning each function of life and each action is the result of conscious thought, the habitual actions become automatic or subconscious, in order that the self-conscious mind may attend to other things. The new actions will, however, in their turn, become habitual, then automatic, then subconscious in order that the mind again may be freed from this detail and advance to still other activities.

Until very recently, it was said that matter, in its ultimate nature was eternal, though all the forms thereof change. We were told that a building destroyed by fire with nothing but a few ashes left had gone up in smoke and gas, and that only the form of the manifestation had changed; that the essential substances were still in existence in different chemical formations.

We were told that all forms of matter exist in the form of molecules, that these molecules are resolvable into certain smaller elements called atoms. Until recently the atom was supposed to be the ultimate particle of matter, so until recently scientists supposed that matter could be resolved into atoms and that was final.

But with the discovery of radium, it was found that the atom is made up of a large number of smaller particles called electrons or ions, and these electrons vary according to the kind of atom, that is under consideration. A hydrogen atom contains a different number of electrons than an oxygen atom, and so on.

The atoms within the molecule are separated from each other by very great distances as compared with their diameter, the electrons in turn are separated from each other by distances as compared to the diameter, as are the planets in the solar system. When we remember that the molecule which is the larger of the group is so small that it cannot be discovered by the most powerful microscope, so small that you could place many millions of them into an ordinary thimble, you can conceive how infinitesimal is the ultimate particle of matter called the electron or ion.

It has been discovered that the atoms of radium are constantly radiating their ions into space, producing what is called radio activity, that these particles are apparently lost, they simply vanish.

Finally it has been discovered that other forms of matter besides radium are throwing off their ions into space, and that these seem to be absolutely lost in the process, thus the atoms of matter are constantly wasting away, so that the modern physicist no longer claims that matter is indestructible; it is in a constant state of flux, it is forever changing in form.

What then is the director which controls the action of the ion, which indicates the form which it is to take? Mind is the director, and this direction is the process called creation.

It will therefore readily be seen that the basis upon which matter rests is mind or spirit. The spirit of a thing is therefore, the thing itself, it is the spirit of a thing which attracts to itself the necessary electrons for its development from the ether, and which are gradually assembled by the law of growth; it is evident therefore, that the saying of St. Paul is true: "The things which are seen are temporal, but the things which are not seen are eternal."

Many years ago, John Bovee Dods, wrote:

"We have mounted from lead up to electricity, and though as we rose, we found each successive substance more easily moved than the one below it, still we have not as yet found a single material that possesses inherent motion as its attribute. Lead, rock, earth, and water are moved by impulse. Air is moved by rarefaction and electricity is moved by the positive and negative forces. True we have mounted up, as before remarked, to electricity, but even this cannot move, unless it is thrown out of balance in relation to quantity as to its positive and negative forces.

Electricity is a fluid most inconceivable subtle, rarefied and fine. It is computed to require four million particles of our air to make a speck as large as the smallest visible grain of sand, and yet electricity is more than seven hundred thousand times finer than air! It is almost unparticled matter, and is not only invisible, but so far as we can judge, it is imponderable.

It cannot be seen—it cannot be weighed! A thousand empty Leyden jars, capable of containing a gallon each, may be placed upon the nicest scale, and most accurately weighed. Then let these be filled with electricity, and, so far as human sagacity can determine they will weigh no more. Hence to our perception a thousand gallons weigh nothing.

As electricity, in regard to motion, stands upon the poise, being completely balanced by the positive and negative forces, that equalize each other, so it is easily perceived, that if we mount one step higher, we must come to that substance whose nature is to move, and the result of that motion is thought and power. It is *mind*. Hence it will be distinctly perceived, in view of the argument now offered, that we cannot, as philosophers, stop short of motion in the highest and most sublime substance in being. This conclusion, as the result of argument, is absolutely and positively irresistible, and challenges refutation.

When we mount up in our contemplations through the various grades of matter, and see it continually brightening—as we press onward in our delightful career of rapture, until we arrive at that sublimated substance which can neither be seen or weighed; which moves with a velocity of twelve million miles per minute, and can travel around this globe in the eighth part of a second,—we are struck with astonishment and awe! But as this is not the last link in the immeasurable chain, we are forced to proceed onward till we arrive at the finest, most sublime, and brilliant substance in being—a substance that possesses the attributes of inherent or self-motion and living power, and from which all other motion and power through out the immeasurable universe are derived. This is the Infinite Mind, and possesses embodied form. it is a living being. This Infinite Mind comes in contact with electricity, gives to it motion, arms it with power, and through this mighty unseen agent, moves the universe, and carries on all the multifarious operations of nature.

Hence, there is not a motion that transpires amidst the immensity of His works, from rolling globes to the falling leaf, but what originates in the Eternal Mind, and by Him is performed, through electricity as His agent. mind is, therefore, the absolute perfection of all substances in being; and as it possesses self-motion as its grand attribute, so it is, in this respect, exactly the reverse of all other substances, which are, of themselves, motionless. Mind, or spirit, is above all, and absolutely disposes and controls all. Hence, Mind is imponderable—invisible, and eternal."

RELIGION

Destiny is determined, for nations and for individuals, by factors and forces that are really fundamental—such as men's attitude toward one another. Ideals and motives are more potent than events in shaping History. What people think about the abiding concerns of life means more than any contemporary agitation or upheaval.

A few centuries ago it was thought that we must choose between the Bible and Galilco. Fifty years ago it was thought that we must choose between the Bible and Darwin, but as Dean W. R. Inge, of St. Paul's Cathedral, London, says: "Every educated man knows that the main facts of organic evolution are firmly established, and that they are quite different from the legends borrowed by the ancient Hebrews from the Babylonians. We are not required to do violence to our reason by rejecting the assured results of modern research. Traditional Christianity must be simplified and spiritualized. It is at present encumbered by bad science and caricatured by bad economics and the more convinced we are of this, the less disposed we shall be to stake the existence of our faith on superstitions which are the religion of the irreligious and the science of the unscientific.

Modern discontent and unsatisfactory conditions are the symptoms of a deep-seated and destructive disease. Remedies applied to these symptoms in the form of legislation and suppression, may relieve the symptoms, but they do not cure the disease which will manifest in other and worse symptoms. Patches applied to an old decaying and obsolete garment in no way improve the garment. Constructive measures must be applied to the foundations of our civilization and that is our thought.

A Philosophy of life having as its basis blind optimism, a religion that won't work seven days a week, or a proposition that isn't practical appeals to the intelligent not at all. It is results that we want and to all such the acid test is: Will it work?

The apparent impossibilities are the very things that help us to realize the possible. We must go over the unbeaten trail of thought, cross the desert of ignorance, wade through the "Swamp of Superstition" and scale the mountains of rites and ceremonies if we ever expect to come into the "promised land of revelation." Intelligence rules! Thought intelligently directed is a creative force which automatically causes its object to manifest on a material plane. Let him that hath an ear to hear, hear!

One of the characteristic signs of a general awakening is the optimism shining through the midst of doubt and unrest. This optimism is taking the form of illumination, and as the illumination becomes general, fear, anger, doubt, selfishness and greed pass away. We are anticipating a more general realization of the Truth which is to make men free. That there may be one man or one woman who shall first realize this Truth in the new era is barely possible, but the preponderance of evidence is for a more general awakening to the light of illumination.

Everything which we hold in our consciousness for any length of time becomes impressed upon our subconsciousness and so becomes a pattern which the creative energy will wave into our life and environment. This is the secret of the power of prayer.

The operation of this law has been known to a few in all ages, but nothing was more improbable than the unauthorized revelation of this information by any student of the great esoteric schools of philosophy. This was true because those in authority were afraid than an unprepared public mind might not be ready to make the proper use of the extraordinary power which the application of these principles disclosed.

We know that the universe is governed by law; that for every effect there must be a cause, and that the same cause, under the same conditions, will invariably produce the same effect. Consequently, if prayer has ever been answered, it will always be answered, if the proper conditions are complied with. This must necessarily be true; otherwise the universe would be a chaos instead of a cosmos. The answer to prayer is therefore subject to law, and this law is definite, exact and scientific, just as are the laws governing gravitation and electricity. An understanding oft his law takes the foundation of Christianity out of the realm of superstition and credulity and places it upon the firm rock of scientific understanding.

The Creative Principle of the Universe makes no exception, nor does it act through caprice or from anger, jealousy or wrath; neither can it be cajoled, flattered or moved by sympathy or petition; but when we understand our unity with this Universal Principle, we shall appear to be favored because we shall have found the source of wisdom and power.

It must be conceded by every thinking person that the answer to prayer furnishes the evidence of an all pervasive, omnipotent intelligence which is imminent in all things and all person. We have heretofore personalized this every present intelligence and called it God, but the idea of personality has become associated with form and form is a product of matter. The ever-present intelligence or mind must be the Creator of all form, the director of all energy, the source of all wisdom.

In order to secure the best thought of the world on the value of prayer, "The Walker Trust," recently offered a prize of $100.00 for the best essay on "Prayer." The meaning, the reality and the power of prayer, its place and value to the individual, to the church and the state, in the every day affairs of life, in the healing of disease, in times of distress and national danger, and in relation to national ideals and to world progress."

In response to the invitation 1667 essays were received, they came from every quarter of the globe, they were written in nineteen different languages, the prize of $100.00 was awarded to the Rev. Samuel McComb, D.D., of Baltimore, Md. A comparative study of these essays is published by the MacMillan Company of New York. In giving his impressions Mr. David Russell of the Walker Trust says: "To practically all the contributors prayer is something real and of inestimable value, but unfortunately there is little information given as to the method by which the law is placed in operation."

Mr. Russell, himself, agrees that the answer to prayer must be the operation of a Natural Law, he says: "We know, that to make use of a Natural Law, the intelligence must be able to comprehend its conditions and to direct or control its sequences. Can we doubt that to an intelligence great enough to encompass the spirit, there would be revealed a realm of spiritual law." It seems that we are rapidly coming into an understanding of this law and understanding is control.

The value of Prayer depends upon the law of spiritual activity. Spirit is the Creative Principle of the Universe and is Omnipotent, Omniscient and Omnipresent. Thinking is a spiritual activity, and consists of the reaction of the Individual against the Universal Mind. "I think, therefore I am," when "I cease to think, I cease to exist." Thinking is the only activity which spirit possesses. Spirit is creative, thinking therefore is a creative process, but as the larger part of our thinking processes are subjective rather than objective, most of our creative work is carried on the subjectively. But because this work is spiritual work it is none the less real, we know that all the great eternal forces of Nature are invisible rather than visible, spiritual rather than material, subjective rather than objective.

But exactly because thinking is a creative process, most of us are creating destructive conditions, we are thinking death rather than life, we are thinking lack rather than abundance, we are thinking disease rather than health, we are thinking in harmony rather than harmony, and our experiences and the experiences of our loved ones eventually reflect the attitude of Mind which we habitually entertain, for be it known that if we can pray for those we love, we can also injure them by entertaining and harboring destructive thoughts concerning them. We are free moral agents and may freely choose what we think, but the result of our thought is governed by an immutable law; this is the modern scientific phraseology for the Scriptural statement: "Be not deceived for God is not mocked, whatsoever a man soweth, that shall he also reap."

Prayer is thought in the form of a petition, and an affirmation is a statement of Truth, and when reinforced by Faith, another powerful form of thought, they become invincible, because "Faith is the substance of things hoped for, the evidence of things not seen," this substance is spiritual substance which contains within itself the Creator and the Created, the germ, the Elohim, that which enters in, goes forth and becomes one with its object.

But prayers and affirmations are not the only forms of creative thought. The architect when he plans to erect a wonderful new building, seeks the quiet of his studio, calls on his imagination for new or novel features embodying additional comforts or utilities and is seldom disappointed in the results.

The engineer who designs to span a chasm or river, visualizes the entire structure before making any attempt to embody it in form, this visualization is the mental image which precedes and predetermines the character of the structure which will eventually take form in the objective world.

The chemist seeks the quiet of his laboratory and then becomes receptive to the ideas from which the world will eventually profit by some new comfort or luxury.

The financier retires to his office or counting room and concentrates on some problem in organization or finance and soon the world learns of another co-ordination of industry requiring millions of additional capital.

Imagination, Visualization, Concentration are all spiritual faculties, and are all creative, because spirit is the one Creative Principle of the Universe, and he who has found the secret of the creative power of thought has found the secret of the ages. The law stated in scientific terms is, that thought will correlate with its object, but unfortunately the large majority are allowing their thoughts to dwell upon lack, limitation, poverty and every other form of destructive thought,. As this law is no respecter of persons their things become objectified in their environment.

Finally, there is love, which is also a form of thought. Love is nothing material and yet no one will deny that it is something very real. St. John tells us that "God is Love;" again he says: "Now are we all sons of God?" which means that Love is the Creative Principle of the Universe and St. Paul tells us "In Him we live and move and have our being."

Love is a product of the emotions, the emotions are governed by the Solar Plexus and the sympathetic nervous system. It is therefore a subconscious activity and is entirely under the control of the involuntary system of nerves. For this reason it is frequently actuated by motives which are neither dictated by reason or intellect. Every political demagogue and religious revivalist takes advantage of this principle, they know that if they can arouse the emotions, the result is assured, so that the demagogue always appeals to the passions and prejudices of his audience never to the reason. The revivalist always appeals to the emotions through the love nature and never to the intellect, they both known that when the emotions are aroused intellect and reason are stilled.

Here we find the same result obtained through opposite polarities, one appealing to hatred, revenge, class prejudices and jealousy; the other appealing to love, service, hope and joy, but the principle is the same. One attracts, the other repels; one is constructive, the other destructive; one is positive, the other negative; the same power is being placed in operation in the same way, but for different purposes. Love and hatred are simply the opposite polarities of the same force, just as Electricity or any other force may be used for destructive purposes just as readily as it may be used for constructive purposes.

Some will say that if God is Spirit and is Omnipotent and Omnipresent, how can He be responsible for destructive conditions; He cannot bring about disaster, want, disease and death. Certainly not, but we can bring these things upon ourselves by a non-compliance with the spiritual laws. If we do not know that thought is creative, we may entertain thoughts of in harmony, lack and disease, which will eventually result in the condition of which these thoughts are the seed forms, but by an understanding of the law we can reverse the process and thereby bring about a different result.

Good and evil are thereby seen to be but relative terms indicating the result of our thoughts and actions. If we entertain constructive thoughts only, the result will benefit ourselves or others, this benefit we call good, if on the other hand we entertain destructive thought, this will result in in harmony for ourselves and others, this in harmony we call evil, but the power is the same in either event. There is but one source of power and we can use the power for good or for evil, just as we can make use of electricity for light, heat or power by an understanding of the laws governing electricity, but if we are careless or ignorant of the laws governing electricity, the result may be disastrous. The power is not good in one case and evil in the other; the good or evil depend upon our understanding of the law.

Many will ask, "how does this thought agree with the scripture?" Many millions of Bibles are sold annually, and every discovery in chemistry, science or philosophy must be in agreement with the vital Truth of religious thought.

What then was the thought of the Master concerning the Creator? It will be remembered that the question was put to him by a lawyer: "Master what shall I do to inherit eternal life?" Did He evade the question? Did He quote some ancient authority? Did He recommend some creed or theological dogma? He did not. His answer was direct and to the point: "Thou shalt love the Lord thy God with all thy heart, will all thy soul, with all thy mind and with all thy strength, and they neighbor as thyself."

Where is this God which the lawyer is told to love? Jesus refers to Him as the Father and when asked concerning Him says: "He that hath seen me hath seen the Father," again "The Father and I are one," again, "It is not I that doeth the work, but the Father that dwelleth in me, He doeth the work," again He taught His disciples to pray: "Our Father who are in Heaven," and when asked concerning the location of Heaven, He said: "Men shall not say Lo her or Lo there, for behold the Kingdom of Heaven is within you." Here then is authority as to the immanence of the Creator, the Father from the Master Physician himself. Thus, we find that Science and Religion are not in conflict and that within the Church and without there is a setting aside of traditional creeds and a return to the things which the Great Teacher taught and the things for which He stood.

The Old Testament has much to say concerning the God of Jacob and of Moses, but this conception of an Anthropomorphic God is principally interesting as indicating the thought of a people who believed that the world was flat, that the sun moved, when science was but magic and religion the dogma of the scholastics.

This was the result of the deductive method of reasoning which originated with certain statements of fact which were universal and absolute, and which were incapable of verification, all other facts must be arrived at by a process of deduction from these original axioms. If facts were observed which seemed to contradict the deductions from which these original axioms were formulated, so much the worse for the facts, they could not be facts. Facts are nothing compared with "statements of Truth" as given by the scholastics. If there were those who persisted in seeing these unwelcome facts, there was the hemlock, or the stake or the cross.

But in the New Testament all of this is reversed, the doctrine of the immanence of God is taught, an objective God is converted into a subjective God, we are told that, "In Him we live and move and have our Being," we are told that "The Kingdom of Heaven is within you," and we are led to infer that God is always in the "Kingdom."

In this connection it is interesting to note that the miscellaneous collection of manuscripts which have finally been put together and called the Bible were written by many different men, of many different locations, and at widely different times. At first these manuscripts were circulated separately, later they were collected into a single volume and for a long time there were serious disputes among the ancient Jews and the early Church Ecclesiastics as to what manuscripts should have a place in the sacred book. In fact until quite recently there were many of these manuscripts included which are not now to be found in the Bible as recognized by the Protestant Church of today.

The manuscripts comprising the old testament were written originally in Hebrew, those of the new testament in Greek, and not a single original manuscript of any book either of the old or the new testament is in existence today, nor have they been in existence for hundreds of years. We have then only copies of copies of copies many times removed from the original.

When we remember that those who undertook to translate these manuscripts into the English language for the purpose of giving them to the people met with violent opposition, frequently being driven from the country and excommunicated from the church, we see that there was little uniformity in the various translations of these manuscripts which are now called the Bible or the "Word of God."

The King James edition which finally became popular with the people was the work of fifty-four churchmen who agreed with each other that all differences of opinion should be settled at special meetings to be held from time to time and that all marginal notes concerning the Greek or Hebrew text should be eliminated. The fact that this edition had the sanction of the King was probably the determining factor in favor of its general adoption, but aside from this the work came to be held in high esteem by the scholastics because of the smoothness and beauty of the diction, the churchmen who had the revision in charge evidently sacrificing accuracy for euphony and rhetoric.

And now we have a strictly "American" Bible, the word of the American Revision Committee in which the famous definition of Faith by St. Paul, "Now Faith is the substance of things hoped for, the evidence of things not seen" is changing to "Now Faith is the assurance of things hoped for, a conviction of things not seen," from which it would appear that Paul did not begin to have the insight, the vision, the intuition with which he has been credited, the latter translation completely nullifying and destroying what has heretofore been the most wonderful definition of faith ever given to the world.

It will readily be seen that the Nazarene completely reversed the process of thought in vogue at that time, instead of using the deductive method of thinking he used the inductive. He accepted no authority, no dogma, no creed, instead of reasoning from the seen to the unseen, the visible to the invisible, from things temporal to things eternal, He reversed this process completely and as the idea of this immanent God took hold of man, as they began to understand that, "Closer is he than breathing, nearer than hands or feet," then gradually came an awakening, which marks the birth of a splendor such as had never before been known.

If the inductive method of reasoning obtained in religion, we should find all religions co-operating for the purpose of bringing about "Peace on Earth and good will toward men." We should find every school of theology co-operating with every other school for the purpose of spreading the "glad tidings of great joy," telling of a Redeemer who has come "That we might have life and have it more abundantly," and that this abundant life may be had by looking within instead of without.

That objective peace is the result of subjective peace, that harmony without is the natural consequence which follows harmony within, that "men do not gather figs from thistles, or grapes from thorns," and that a man's character is the evidence of the value of his religion: "For by their fruits shall they be known," such a religion satisfies the brain as well as the heart, religion is to love justice, to long for the right, to love mercy, to forget wrongs and remember benefits, to love the truth, to be sincere, to love liberty, to cultivate the mind, to be familiar with the mighty thoughts that genius has expressed, the noble deeds of all the world, to cultivate courage and cheerfulness. To make others happy, to receive new truths with gladness, to cultivate hope, to see the calm beyond the storm, the dawn beyond the night. This is the religion of reason, the creed of science.

"For we know in part and we prophecy in part. But when that which is perfect is come, then that which is in part shall be done away."

Lightning Source UK Ltd.
Milton Keynes UK
UKHW051905051221
395142UK00010B/104